# The Films of
# MAKHMALBAF
## Cinema, Politics & Culture in Iran

*by*

## ERIC EGAN

MAGE PUBLISHERS
WASHINGTON, DC
2005

Copyright © Eric Egan 2005

Library of Congress Cataloging-in-Publication Data forthcoming

**The Films of Makhmalbaf:**
**Cinema, Politics & Culture in Iran**

Hardcover ISBN 0-934211-94-9

Paperback ISBN 0-934211-95-7

Mage books are available at bookstores or directly from the publisher.
Visit Mage online at www.mage.com. Call 202-342-1642 or email
info@mage.com

# CONTENTS

# FOREWORD

The history of filmmaking in Iran is almost a hundred years old, but, unfortunately, there have been only a handful of studies in the field of Iranian cinema. Among the English-language works, M. Ali Issari's *Cinema in Iran, 1900–1979*, published in 1989, is the only source that has examined, in detail, the development and progress of the Iranian motion-picture industry from its birth to its almost total collapse in conjunction with the Iranian revolution in 1979. Issari carefully examined the struggle of locally produced Iranian feature films from a personal, historical and industrial perspective, and sought to detail the development of commercial cinema, as well as the emergence of an artistic form of cinema, in response to changing social and cultural attitudes. However, his study ends at the point when the country was convulsed by revolution, and before Iranian society and cultural norms were radically redefined by the Islamic Republic. The political upheavals and the social revisions engendered by the revolution resulted in the near-disintegration of the film industry, followed by its complete centralization and ideological restructuring under the new regime.

Bahman Maghsoudlou's book *Iranian Cinema* (1987) was one of the first to cover the films of the early years of the Islamic Republic, as well as providing a short history of the development of cinema in Iran. But, despite the fact that the first Iranian feature film was made in 1930, and despite the welcome addition of a number of recent works on the subject, there still remains something of a gap with regard to serious academic and popular research in English on Iranian cinema, though it has achieved international fame and critical acclaim in recent years. A few distinguished scholars—Hamid Naficy and Hamid Dabashi chief among them—and recent works like *The New Iranian Cinema* edited by Richard Tapper (2001) and *Life and Art: The New Iranian Cinema* edited by Rose Issa and Sheila Whitaker (1999), have set about addressing this shortfall, by analyzing and attesting to the complexity of recent Iranian cinema, from its filmmakers in exile and internationally acclaimed auteurs, to the new generation of young filmmakers and emerging and excellent female directors. What seems to be missing now, and in serious need of redress, is to place these various developments—the whole motion of Iranian cinema, from inception to revolution and beyond—within their social, political and cultural contexts, both before and after the 1979 revolution, in order to highlight Iranian film's origins and influences and to explain the complicated conditions in which cinema, and art in general, operates and is produced in Iran.

This is Eric Egan's undertaking in the present book, which attempts to examine Iranian cinema by considering it within the conflux of the larger social and political developments that have occurred since Iran's Islamic revolution. Taking as his example the avatar of post-revolutionary filmmaking—Mohsen Makhmalbaf—and his imaginative, provocative and often controversial work, Egan looks at a cinema made in response the Iranian revolution and the ideological and social changes that it created. After all, who better represents Iranian cinema as it is now and has been for the last two decades than the man whose life and career have been shaped so fully, in some ways made possible, by the revolution and the greater historical circumstances beyond it?

It is crucial, though, to note that Egan has gone beyond the limits of case study and textual analysis to bear witness to Makhmalbaf's work, and Iranian cinema as a whole, as simultaneously a product and a form of critique of the current ruling system. In this respect it can be said of Iranian cinema that is both a document and documenter of the changes that have obtained in Iran over the past twenty-five years, concluding with the increasing frustration and disillusionment among the people with the slow pace of change under the current Khatami administration. In the Islamic Republic film, officially at least, has acted to legitimate and consolidate those in power. Conversely, in the absence the typical outlets of public protest in a civil society, film has also provided a means of questioning the ideological manipulation of the Islamic regime.

The figure of Mohsen Makhmalbaf is of particular interest in illuminating this duality. A product of the Islamic regime, Makhmalbaf's cinema charts the development of the citizen and revolutionary society over the past two decades, from zealous advocate, to a questioning of beliefs, to frustration with the powers that be. In this detailed account of Makhmalbaf's work, Egan has also explored and highlighted the limitation of visual arts and the incredible challenges that Iranian filmmakers face in having to operate within the strictures of an officially decreed Islamicized culture, which operates through the arbitrary implementation of a set of rules that have shown themselves to be changeable to the dictates of political expediency. These are crucial elements to consider when approaching any serious analysis of Iranian cinema, particularly now, given its increasingly high profile in international film festivals, awards ceremonies, and as a staple element on the screens of Western art cinemas.

This work on Makhmalbaf and Iranian cinema, will be, I think, an important starting point for serious research into this complex of themes and issues, and stands not only as an impressive contribution to the developing field of Iranian cinema studies but to world cinema as a whole. In this way I hope that this book will act as a springboard for other cinema students to follow his method in engaging with the social, political and cultural complexities that lie behind cultural production in Iran.

Ali Mohammadi
Nottingham Trent University
2004

# ACKNOWLEDGMENTS

I would like to thank the staff at Nottingham Trent University, particularly Professor John Tomlinson, Viv Chadder, Dr. Ben Taylor and Dr. Steve Jones, for their help and support during my time at the university. I would also like to thank the staff at the British Library, the British Film Institute and the Library of Iranian Studies in London. Further thanks goes to Hugh MacDonald and Mage Publishers for their belief in this project. My deepest gratitude goes to Professor Ali Mohammadi for his support, encouragement and friendship, without whose knowledge and guidance this work would not have been possible. Finally, I would like to thank my parents, Paul and Pearl, and my family, Paula and Rory, whose understanding, encouragement, and good humor made the completion of this book possible.

# INTRODUCTION

Cinema as a mode of cultural expression acts as both a product and document of a society. As such it derives its immediate existence and relevance from a localized context of social institutions, events, and upheavals, and most particularly, a culture that is reflected in the lives and aspirations of all people living within a society. Film situates itself within this cultural milieu as an art form that "reflects, directly or indirectly, both the components and the historical process of society.[1] The starting point for a critical engagement with cinema in Iran must begin with an interrogation of the processes involved in the formulation, and use, of cultural images as elements of differing ideological struggles.

This book sets out to examine the development of cinema in Iran since the 1979 revolution as a reflection of the social, political and cultural development of the Islamic Republic, as illustrated through a critical case study of the work of Mohsen Makhmalbaf. To understand Iranian cinema is to understand the complex society from which it comes, the unique cultural elements from which it is derived, and the particular ideological circumstances in which it operates. To understand the cinema of the most controversial film director to emerge under the Islamic regime is, to stand in the eye of a storm where all these elements collide in a body of work that is provocative, committed, and challenging, and which stands as a cultural document and testimony to one man's attempt to make sense of his society, his art and himself.

## Mohsen Makhmalbaf: The Anxious Eye of the Revolution

In attempting to document and critically evaluate the Islamic Republic of Iran and its cinema from the 1979 revolution to the present day, one figure stands out as a living embodiment of the social, cultural and political contradictions and upheavals that have taken place in the country over the past twenty-five years. Since his feature-film debut in 1982, Mohsen Makhmalbaf has continuously produced work that stirs controversy, provokes debate, and is critically acclaimed both inside Iran and around the world.

Makhmalbaf was born in Tehran in 1957 to a staunchly religious family and was raised by his grandmother after his parents divorced and his father left to begin another family. Growing up in the politically charged atmosphere of the 1960s and 1970s he became a supporter of the militant religious and political ideology of Ayatollah Khomeini, and began to agitate against the shah's regime. In 1972 he formed his own urban guerrilla group and was jailed two years later for attacking a policeman. He remained in jail until 1978 when he was released during the revolutionary fervor that toppled the shah. Following his release he began to turn his attention from armed action to cultural activities in support of the new Islamic regime and joined the Islamic Propagation Organization, a semi-governmental center for the promotion of artistic projects, described as "an outfit of avowed militancy."[2] It was here that he began his cinematic career, directing his first film, a poorly made piece of Islamic sloganeering and regime propaganda entitled *Tobeh Nasuh* (*Nasuh's Repentance*), in 1982. However, since this inauspicious beginning his work has matured and taken on a chameleon-like quality in dealing with a host of complex and controversial themes such as poverty, disillusionment with revolutionary ideals, forbidden love, and the role of the artist in society. It is this desire to constantly stretch himself as an artist and explore difficult and often highly contentious issues in his work that has made Makhmalbaf's films exhilarating and incendiary.

Indeed, it is the constant self-examination implicit in Makhmalbaf's art that has helped it to evolve toward maturity through a series of different stages governed by similarities of theme, a preoccupation with certain issues, and a particular aesthetic approach.* The first such phase may be referred to as the "Islamic" period, 1982-85, and covers his first four films. These were propagandist in nature, reflecting the idealism and faith in the Islamic utopia promised by the revolution and its leaders. The unifying theme is one of looking to God, a belief in the miraculous, and the simplistic division of the world into good and evil. His second period forms a trilogy of films—*Dastforush* (*The Peddler*, 1987), *Bicycleran* (*The Cyclist*, 1989), and *Arusi-e Khuban* (*Marriage of the Blessed*, 1989)—that were impassioned social and political commentaries. These works were concerned with documenting the state of the nation and the course and development of the revolution in its first decade. The subject matter is still dark and religiously inflected but God and religion are portrayed as more forgiving, understanding and less pedantic, yet still firmly located within the mores of Shia Islamic doctrine. Indeed, in explaining *Dastforush* (*The Peddler*, 1987) Makhmalbaf has said that the film intended to convey the message that God is the light and therefore the source of all life. Furthermore, death is seen as an eventual return to the light, with

---

*These periodic divisions arose during the course of an interview I conducted with the film producer and critic Bahman Maghsoudlou in New York, 14 October 1999.

a person's actions during the course of his life acting as the main factor in determining the quality of one's life after death.[3] In these films he is trying to distance himself from intolerance and focus instead on the human aspects of everyday life and humankind's relationship with God.

The third period, beginning with *Nobat-e Ashegi* (*Time of Love*, 1991) and ending with *Nun-o Goldun* (*A Moment of Innocence*, 1996), is one of doubt. Here, Makhmalbaf moves toward a more reflective, philosophical and tranquil cinema. A time of prolific if problematic output, he also set out during this period to examine and question, in films such as *Nassereddin Shah, Actor-e Cinema* (*Once Upon a Time, Cinema*, 1992), and *Salaam Cinema* (1995), the very basis of film as a form of representation, its power of persuasion and perversion, as well as the responsibilities of the artist to his art and to society. Finally, his current phase of development is a more personal poetics of culture, the position of the individual in society, and a preoccupation with form, revealed in the films *Gabbeh* (1996) and *Sokut* (*The Silence*, 1998). Certain critics have decried this change in Makhmalbaf's work, seeing it as the somewhat empty predominance "of the aesthetic over the political, an escape into the obsession of beautiful images."[4] However, such sentiments are somewhat disingenuous in that they deny Makhmalbaf (and Iranian cinema as a whole) the opportunity to develop outside the narrow and didactic notion of "political art," as well as ignoring the sociocultural context in which such artistic developments take place. It also highlights the fact that foreign critics seek elements and signs that ratify their subjective images and preconceived notions of different cultures and as a consequence "do not expect to like a film by a Third World filmmaker, for example, on the crisis in the relationship of a couple, unless this relationship derives from a social or political background."[5]

The concept of the political is a much broader and complex phenomenon in Iranian cinema, and arises from a study of the human condition and an interrogation of cinematic form. Makhmalbaf's cinema has at different times and to varying degrees been an attempt to save humanity, to save his country and to save himself by attempting to present the simplicity, joy, beauty and poetry of everyday life. In this

---

*The Bolivian filmmaker Jorge Sanjines has attempted to intervene critically and directly in the tumultuous history of his country through an activist and interrogative form of cinema that is intimately linked to immediate and indigenous social and political developments. Beginning his career during a time when Bolivia was experiencing a period of unprecedented democratic rule (the 1952-1964 social experiment of the Nationalist Revolutionary Movement) his early short films celebrated the new indigenous revolutionary movement. However, the years 1966-1971 saw a period of coup and counter-coup, in which the government was increasingly at the mercy of the military, and of failed revolutionary ideals. Sanjines documented these changes by focusing on the problems of the ordinary people and social issues like poverty and infant mortality. It was this committed and critical approach for which his work banned and resulted in Sanjines being exiled. It is this belief in revolution followed by disillusionment and the suffering portrayed in his work, as a category of struggle and search, at the hands of the authorities that bear similarities with Makhmalbaf's own career trajectory.

respect, his work is very close to Jorge Sanjines' broad categorization of "revolutionary art."* According to Sanjines revolutionary art "will always be distinguished by what it shows of a people's way of being, and of the spirit of popular cultures which embraces whole communities of people with their own particular ways of thinking, of conceiving reality and of loving life."[6] This is very much in keeping with the general ideological thrust of Makhmalbaf's work and indeed of much of the Iranian cinema to appear since the revolution. This kind of undertaking has given rise to the emergence of one of the worlds most exciting and engaging cinematic movements, in which Iranian filmmakers are constantly striving to combine their own interests and aspirations with a popular discontent while at the same time questioning film's ability to express these desires. However, such an endeavor is by no means unique to recent Iranian cinema. Indeed, in adopting this attitude Iranian filmmakers have placed themselves firmly within a developmental and experimental Persian cultural tradition, one that "has shown the slow but steady rise of a rebellious stance framed by such seemingly discordant ideals as the vision of an egalitarian future, a greater artistic freedom and an undertone of nostalgia all clad in an esoteric language at odds with objective reality."[7]

### Cinema in the Islamic Republic

The media, and more particularly cinema, has been the central cultural element in adopting a rebellious stance to the "objectively" created realities of the nation and the new society that emerged after the 1979 revolution. In many respects cinema, like the country itself, returned to year zero, being remolded to fit and reflect the changed ideological requirements of the new regime and to serve the needs of a "hierocratic state."* The cinema came to play a vital role, arising from what was essentially a media-influenced cultural revolution, in operating under a system of government in the Islamic Republic that has shown itself high on rhetoric and more interested in "changing cultural and educational institutions than in overthrowing the modes of production and distribution" that existed under the shah.[8] As such, cinema has at times found itself used as an ideological weapon in the struggle to maintain power in response to shifting sociopolitical contexts. The result has been the operation of what might be termed a dual revolutionary cinema. The first is defined as that employed by the government, serving to the goals of the revolution and acting as a form of Islamic propaganda. This was a vaguely defined desire by the

---

*Asghar Schirazi, *The Constitution of Iran: Politics and State in the Islamic Republic*, 3. In essence this term refers to the rule of a particular class, in this case the clergy, and in contrast to the officially presented image of rule, enacts a situation where real religious issues recede into the background and serve merely as a means of legitimizing political power.

present regime to establish the idea of an "Islamic cinema." According to Mohsen Tabatabai, director of the government department for Islamic film production, "The best definition of Islamic cinema is that the cinema must play its role in propagating Islam, just like the mosque."[9] In contrast, and as a type of reaction to this format, there has emerged a socially committed cinema comprised of "non-believing" directors who act as the "anxious eyes of the revolution,"* creating a cinema that politically and philosophically reflect the complexities of Iran and its society. In this regard it is inevitable that cinema has become a key element in highlighting and intervening in these problems, which as Makhmalbaf has noted, have "their roots in history and were of a cultural rather than a political nature."[10] And Makhmalbaf's films are perhaps unique in the sense that they have been examples of a revolutionary cinema both for and against the rhetoric of official ideology, having been at one time a zealous supporter of the Islamic regime before becoming one of its most vocal critics.

This use of cinema in articulating contrasting ideological positions sees Iranian cinema in one sense being defined as a cinema of reaction. The Islamic Republic has sought to react against the "prostitution cinema" of the shah's era by redefining it for its own ends as an "Islamic cinema." Likewise, the uneasy development toward a "quality cinema" (with the re-emergence of a number of pre-revolutionary and so-called non-believing directors) could be read as a reaction against the failure of a superficially Islamic cinema and an attempt by artists to regain and maintain control of the cultural landscape. Defining it as such allows for an explanation of the oft-cited simplicity of Iranian cinema as it has constantly had to remake itself to present a cultural form that, due to institutional pressures, has had to, in appearance at least, erase all forms of ambiguity. In the case of many Iranian directors this led to a superficially simple form and narrative style to which layers have been constantly added in order to achieve as much density as possible. This helps to explain the universal significance of a cinema located in and addressed to the local. The importance of the national is emphasized within Iranian cinema as it attempts to question the complex nature of Iran, its people and their problems, while simultaneously engaged in an exploration of the vicissitudes of the project of cinema, itself.

**Cinema Reborn**

The 1979 revolution, the ensuing struggle for power in the country, and the clerics' subsequent attempts to Islamicize all aspects of life had a devastating effect on the film industry in Iran. Associated with the ills of

---

*This is a phrase that I have taken from Makhmalbaf's film *The Marriage of the Blessed* (1989) where it is used to describe the main character, Haji, who tries to use his position as a photojournalist to document the ills of the country through the lens of his camera.

the former regime and seen as a symbol of Western modernization cinema became a prime target of revolutionary zeal. Indeed, the spiritual leader of the revolution and Islamic state, Ayatollah Khomeini, decreed in a rather obscure statement that "We are not against cinema, we are against prostitution,"[11] the interpretation of which Iran's film industry has been trying to establish ever since.[12] By the time the Islamic government was installed in power in the early 1980s, the industry was in ruins, production had become nonexistent, some 180 cinemas nationwide had been destroyed and an atmosphere of fear and uncertainty pervaded as to what was permissible in the changed ideological system. The situation was made even worse by the exile and departure of many of those who had worked in the industry during the time of the shah. It seemed at one point that the cinema would not be part of the cultural landscape of the new regime when the Ministry of Art announced the closure of all the country's cinemas in 1980.[14] However, once the clerics had gained power their task was to set about consolidating their position. Political consolidation meant cultural consolidation and as a result, the role of cinema changed. It soon became one of the most important elements in promoting the revolutionary Islamic ideology of the new regime. As a result, the medium was brought under the control of central government and placed under a restrictive set of regulations designed to create a cinematic form in the service of Islam and the revolution.

This situation has succeeded in creating a complex, fractious and uncertain relationship between the state and cinema. In the highly centralized and ideologically governed system of the Islamic Republic all institutions are designed to be at the service of consolidating and reproducing the clerical interpretation of Islamic ideology. Under such restrictive circumstances cultural norms are seen to have a greater and more direct influence on peoples' daily lives and how they evaluate their social world. In this sense culture and political development have a large influence on one another and are sensitive to and defined by the changes that occur in both fields. The ideologues in the Islamic Republic have attempted to control all aspects of Iranian society in order to create a Shia-influenced political culture, infused with, when deemed necessary, elements of nationalism, revolutionary populism and concepts of social justice. As a key element in such an undertaking the cinema has served as both the legitimator of those in power as well as the voice of criticism in attempting to open a critical space whereby it can articulate the social realities of the country.

### Cinema, Culture and Conflict

Once the Islamic regime had succeeded in eliminating its enemies, silencing internal dissent, and monopolizing the reigns of power, attention quickly turned to cultural matters. Buoyed up by the belief of the revolution as a unifying cause, the charisma and stature of Khomeini as a leader and the possibility of a utopian society, cinema began to emerge in its new Islamic format. The desire to construct a visual art form based on and in the service of Islamic revolutionary ideology led to the appearance of three new genres of mass cinema in Iran. These can be broadly summarized as the miraculous, which attempts, through depictions of piety and divine intervention, to justify an Islamic philosophical outlook on life; the "crime does not pay category"; and finally the war genre.[15] The latter genre was also known as "Cinema for the Scared Defense" and played a key role as part of the 1980-1988 war with Iraq. Jingoistic and propagandist in nature these films were forged out of the political dedication and fervor of that conflict. They were intended to promote action rather than contemplation, to convince the populace of the righteousness of the war and to promulgate the ideology of the Islamic Republic. This was by no means unique to cinema and was very much a defining feature of much Iranian art during this period. The literature of the time showed similar tendencies, and was seen as "mechanical in flow and metallic in flavor...too propagandistic—i.e. chanting, revolutionary slogans etc.—to contain any engaging intellectual reflections on the meaning of the revolution."[16]

Thematically much of this work was enacted in the language and symbols of the Shia themes of sacrifice, dispossession and mourning, and portrayed in the simplistic division between good and evil, oppressed versus the oppressors. Mohsen Makhmalbaf has commented on his own work during this period, stating that on reflection the Manichean division between good and evil was too simplistic and superficial and that ideological positions are much too complex to defend in blind faith.[17] However, it was not until the war had ended, and the leader of the revolution Ayatollah Khomeini had died, that filmmakers began to question and analyze the complexity of the conflict and the first decade of the revolution and its effects on the populace. In films like Makhmalbaf's *Marriage of the Blessed* (1989) and Ebrahim Hatamikia's *From Karkheh to Rhine* (1993), a more critical, personal and humanistic form of filmmaking began to emerge. It was this humanist message that was a key characteristic of much of the "new" Iranian cinema that appeared on the international stage after 1989. Indeed, the rise to world prominence of Iranian cinema has been quite remarkable and unprecedented. Its presence in international film festivals mushroomed from eighty-eight films in 1989 to 744 in 1995, with a concomitant rise in the number of awards won, eleven in 1989 to forty-one in 1995.[18] However, these figures should not be considered in isolation, and were the result of a number of different factors.

Despite the lack of artistry in many of the films made during the first decade of Islamic rule this period did succeed in establishing an industrial and economic base capable of supporting and sustaining a production capacity that rose from seventeen features in 1981 to a high of sixty-six in 1992 and that currently averages around fifty productions per year.* Of equal importance was the emergence of an atmosphere of increased artistic freedom, which obtained as part of a larger drive to create a more liberal society following the war, allowing artists to explore a greater range of sensitive, controversial, and hitherto taboo subjects. Furthermore, the desire of the regime to open up to the outside world and to present a more humane façade saw the cinema function, through the film festival and art cinema circuits of the West, as a means of counteracting negative stereotypical images of mad mullahs, terrorists and revolutionary zealots. However, given the multitude of meanings that a film generates and the friction that arises from a government intent on strictly controlling the medium—against the filmmakers' desire to surmount these restrictions in an attempt to meaningfully engage with their art form—such developments only serve to highlight the fact that in Iran cinema is a cultural form that is at the vanguard of Iran's unique social, political and cultural milieu. In this regard one of the main unifying themes of the films made in Iran since the revolution have been their restless journey of constant discovery, curiosity and search intimately connected to the immediate world around itself.

## The Basis of a New Wave?

This notion of search is a prevalent preoccupation of much of Iranian cinema, and it illustrates films' ardent social engagement. The first decade under the new regime could be seen as a belief in and a search for the utopia promised by the revolution, followed in turn by disillusionment, a reappraisal of its broken promises and failures and another search for a better social and economic life. This search continues following the post-1989 changes and is focused more on political issues—calls for a more liberal and tolerant society, a desire to open up to the outside world and an attempt to understand the role and position of the individual within a changing society. Following the election of President Khatami in 1997 began a new phase where culture, and cinema in particular, has formed the main factor in the search for greater freedom, liberalism and the establishment of a civil society. The notion of search is a crucial aspect of Iranian cinema's active intervention in social and cultural discussions for it allows the possibility of opening up a space of engaged debate that acts as a "guide to action rather than a specific or easily achieved solution."[13] Instructive in attempting to

---

*The figures for the years up to 1999 were as follows: 1993–50; 1994–45; 1995–62; 1996–63; 1997–54; 1998–64; and 1999–46. *Film International* 7, nos. 2 and 3 (Autumn/Winter 1999/2000).

articulate such a space and standing as a manifestation, both person-
ally and artistically, of the development of the Islamic state is Mohsen
Makhmalbaf. He more than anyone has embraced this notion of search
in attempting to find himself and Iran through cinema.

## Structure of the Book

This book devotes a chapter to each of the different stages of Makhmalbaf's cinematic development. Each of these chapters begins with an
examination of the social and political situation in Iran at that particular time, followed by its effect and influence on the cinema industry
as a whole, before situating and analyzing a number of Makhmalbaf's
films within these developments. Chapters 1 and 2 establish a work-
able theoretical framework for critically analyzing, and understanding,
the development of cinema in the Islamic Republic. The former seeks
to understand it from within a reconstituted Third Cinema frame of
reference as well as within the history of indigenous cinematic development. The latter examines the cultural and ideological foundations of
the new Islamic state showing that its founding principles comprised a
number of competing intellectual traditions. Chapter 3 examines the
claims for the establishment of a new form of cinema as the new regime
sought to create an "Islamic cinema" that reflected the changed ideological circumstances. This new cultural form is evaluated by placing
it within the historical development of Islamic art as a whole and the
clergy's attempts to instigate a form of cultural revolution by Islamiciz-
ing all aspects of society. It will also assess the efficacy of this process
and the truth claims of a new and unique cinematic form. In Chapter 4
I look at the development of this new cinema through a decade of war
and revolution and the debate between culture as an official propagandist tool and the beginnings of more socially engaged cultural forms.
Chapter 5 evaluates the development of a "quality" cinema in the era
of reconstruction when Iranian films began to emerge in large numbers and gain recognition on the international stage. The final chapter
looks at the current development of cinema in Iran as part of the power
struggle that is attempting to introduce reforms and elements of civil
society into the Islamic system.

Throughout its twenty-five year history the Islamic Republic has
constantly sought to create a society (based on the teachings of the
Qur'an and the writings of its spiritual leader, Ayatollah Khomeini, as
enshrined in its constitution) devoted to the service of Islam and the
perpetuation of the revolution. Under such ideological conditions culture has become the main sphere of social transformation as the clerical
rulers have sought to Islamicize all aspects of society. In such a context,
culture, and in particular the media, have become the main method
and means of disseminating the new regime's message to the populace

and instructing them of their expected role in the new society. Such an undertaking, which sees the Islamic state defined on the basis of a universal religious allegiance, has in effect abolished the mediation of culture. Under this highly centralized and repressive system culture and politics are intimately linked in a volatile and unstable relationship, holding a mirror up to official discourse. In this respect, the development of the Islamic state in Iran over the past two decades has been reflected in, documented by and developed in tandem with cultural modes of representation, which have, intentionally or not, functioned in the realm of the political. Because the new regime has sought to remove all traces of political opposition and abolish the notion of a civil society by enforcing its own all-pervasive notion of a religious society they have paradoxically succeeded in creating a situation where, having attempted to control or abolish all forms of oppositional discourses, have merely succeeded in creating a situation where every field of cultural production has become "a potential site for the expression of dissent."[19] Nowhere is this more relevant than in the cinema, given its popularity and universal appeal, and nowhere has its volatility and dissent been more evident than in the work of Mohsen Makhmalbaf.

From ardently advocating the Islamic system to casting a critical eye on the shortcomings and failures of the revolution, from an exploration of controversial social issues to an examination of the cinematic medium itself, Makhmalbaf's films are indicative of, and serve as commentaries on, the historical progression of the Iranian state and its people. Placed within the social and political developments of the past twenty-five years, Makhmalbaf's films provides cultural documents with which to understand, evaluate and critically assess the development of the Islamic Republic and the significance of Iranian cinema.

---

*Manucher Sanadjian, "The World Cup and Iranians' 'Home-coming': A Global Game in an Islamicized Context," in *Islam Encountering Globalization*, ed. Ali Mohammadi.

# 1 | FROM NEW WAY
## TO NEW WAVE

A critical examination of Iranian cinema after 1979 requires a historical background of Iranian film in general. A timeline of Iran's cinematic history is essential in providing a means of understanding the social, cultural and historical conditions that have informed the films that emerged after the revolution. To locate Makhmalbaf's work within that context calls for a look at a complex cinematic and social history—a sense of political relationship in which cinema is the reflection of the social milieu from which it emerges, and a cultural specificity that is characterized by an intimacy and familiarity with indigenous cultural forms as a site of struggle and contested meanings. A number of issues are crucial in drawing points of comparison between the cinema produced in Iran before and after the revolution: the import of linking theory and practice; the awareness of a social and cultural historiography; and seeing film as an art form that exhibits a cultural specificity that is derived from and speaks to the local, and that is capable of articulating universal themes and concerns.

From these perspectives a composite and identifiable picture of pre-revolution Iranian cinema comes into view. This critical perspective is also part of a process that seeks to understand the particularities and nuances of Iranian society, politically and culturally, and also the diverse nature of its cinematic history, which ranges from the commercial Film Farsi to public-relations documentaries funded by the state, to international award-winning films such as *Gav* (*The Cow*, 1969). Iranian cinema since its inception has operated within the conflux of Persian, Western and Islamic influences, each exhibiting a stronger influence depending on the ideological context of the time. Whether a monarchical dictatorship or Islamic theocracy, culture, art and communications—in the absence of autonomous democratic political activity—has been used by those in power to propagate their vision of Iranian society, enforce nationalist or religious sentiment and legitimate their right to rule.

## Cinema in Iran, 1900-1979

The history and development of cinema in Iran prior to the Iranian
Revolution in 1979 provides the first step in approaching the current
wave of films. It also allows for an assessment of the similarities, differences and interrelationships of a national cinema operating under two
ideologically different regimes. This pre-revolutionary history highlights
ways to combine the theoretical and practical historical development of
what is often seen as a distinct cultural movement.

Throughout Iranian history, from the conquests of Alexander of
Macedonia (334 BCE) through to the Qajar dynasty (1779-1925), when
Iran was first introduced to cinema, Iranians have accepted, synthesized
and transformed different and varied cultural influences to suit their
own needs and sensibilities. As early as the fifth century BCE, the Greek
historian Herodotus remarked that, "There is no nation which so readily adopts foreign customs as the Persians. As soon as they hear of any
luxury they instantly make it their own."[1] This process of overcoming
conquerors by assimilation has led to the survival and transformation of
traditional cultural codes that have come to find expression in unique
forms.* It is therefore to be expected that a rich Persian history and
particular cultural nuances were manifested in, and influenced, the
cultivation of foreign art forms according to the uniquely original and
specific cultural needs and sensibilities of the people adopting them.
Indeed, one of the defining aspects of Iranian cinema has been this
ability to assimilate, imitate and replicate established cinematic codes
and fashion them into new forms. Unlike the progression of cinema in
the West, from vaudeville fairground attraction to bourgeois respectability, cinema in Iran followed a different path. Initially brought to Iran
by the fifth shah of the Qajar dynasty, Mozaffer al-Din Shah, after his
visit to the International Exhibition in Paris in 1900, cinema was strictly
the preserve of the Iranian elite and in the service of the royal court
before becoming in later years a popular form of mass entertainment.[2]
This was the first incidence in Iranian film of state sponsorship, as the
court or government, due primarily to its centralized and autocratic
structure, commissioned filmmakers to make documentaries or newsreels promoting the activities of the royal family or recording occasions
such as state visits and official ceremonies. This form of state sponsorship set a precedent for the relationship between the government and
film in Iran that has persisted up to the present day. However, once
cinema moved from the court into the public arena as a form of mass

---

*Perhaps the most telling example is the way in which Iranians accepted Islam. While adopting the new
religion they simultaneously rejected Arab culture and set about adapting Islam to their pre-Islamic Persian culture. The wedding of these seemingly contradictory elements led to the Shia sect of Islam, which
appealed to Iranians' emotive and aesthetic nationalism, and was responsible for heralding the beginning of
a golden age of Islam. This issue will be dealt with in more detail in Chapter Three

entertainment it proved a troublesome newcomer to what was still a deeply traditional society.*

Before the advent of cinema in Iran passion plays (*rowzeh* and *tazieh*) coffeehouses provided the most popular forms of mass entertainment, and their influence on cinema, both on a practical and sociopolitical level, is seen in their rapid assimilation into (rather than replacement by) the cinematic art form. The *naqqal*, or storyteller, of the coffeehouses moved into the cinema to narrate silent movies and was extremely popular with audiences until the inception of sound films and dubbing. Of more importance was the influence of the tazieh, a play within Shia tradition that recalls and enacts the death of Hossein at the battle of Karbala in 680.† Aesthetically tazieh had an overarching influence on the bulk of early commercial Iranian films. The *tazieh* uses little scenery and few props, relying instead on an audience's imagination, placing importance on the actors, dramatic delivery and theatrical atmosphere. These features carried over into early film productions, which were at the time necessarily primitive. But the tazieh also served a sociopolitical function, and this was a fact not lost on Reza Shah, who introduced a royal decree in 1932 banning it. The shah's desire to weaken the power of the conservative clerics over the masses of people, and to facilitate his modernization programs, resulted in a policy of secularization that privileged Western-style progress at the expense of archaic religious custom.‡ Thus, as soon as film was made available to a large audience, it became the nexus of the struggle between tradition and modernity in Iran. Aesthetically and formally linked to the religious ritual of tazieh, cinema

---

*Although the first commercial cinema in Iran was opened by Ebrahim Khan Sahhafbashi-e Tehrani in 1905 it was not until the Pahlavi dynasty (1925-1979) that cinema emerged as the main form of mass entertainment. Until then most films were locally-produced newsreels. However, with the rise to power of Reza Shah (1925-1941), the instigation of his modernization projects, and during WWII when Iran was occupied by foreign troops, and his son Mohammad Reza Shah (1941-1979) took to the throne, foreign films flooded onto Iranian screens and cinema became the main source of entertainment for the majority of the population. It was only following the end of the war (1948 with the production of *Toofan-e Zendegi* (*The Storm of Life*), the first Persian sound feature to be made in Iran) that an indigenous industry began to produce films for the local market.

†The death of Hossein at the Battle of Karbala is an event of huge significance for Shia Muslims. At its heart lies the question of succession after the death of the Prophet Mohammad. Shiites believe that the Prophet entrusted succession to his cousin and son-in-law Ali, who was assassinated by rival Sunni tribe leaders. Ali's son Hossein was then decreed his successor, but he was killed in the battle of Karbala in an attempt by his enemies to end the bloodline to the prophet. The Battle of Karbala has imbued the rituals and mythology of the Shia sect with the themes of oppression, rebellion, the true lost tribe, the search for justice, and martyrdom. In the battle, Hossein led an army of seventy-two against an opposing force of thousands. All were killed including Hossein's infant child, struck down by an arrow through the throat. At the end of the battle, Hossein, standing alone and mortally wounded, was finished off by Shemr, a figure of evil to which Ayatollah Khomeini would later compare the Shah.

‡Toward this end the shah also instituted a ban on women wearing the *chador*, or veil, and changes to the judicial law that led, much to the consternation of the clergy, to clashes with Qur'anic law. In an effort to reduce the power of the clergy and to remove the influence and traces of Islam on life in Iran the Pahlavi regime sought simultaneously to emphasize the Persian (non-Islamic) aspects of Iranian culture and the need for progress on Western terms.

also seemed the essence of progress, both scientific and cultural. This debate between tradition and modernity structured the terms of much Iranian intellectual thought up to and through the revolution of 1979.

Cinema as a form of mass entertainment proved a troublesome newcomer as the clergy, along with a number of intellectuals, grew concerned with what they perceived to be the detrimental effects of film on the population, and lobbied the government to censor what they considered morally unsuitable films. Consequently film censorship commenced in Iran in 1936 with regulations drawn up by the Ministry of Justice, which were updated in 1950 and again in 1968. Despite the fact that these laws forbade a whole host of activities, such as attacking Islam, inciting revolt, and portraying immoral activity, the reality was that they were implemented in a haphazard manner and were, for the most part, not stringently adhered to. Indeed, it is hard to imagine the survival of the pre-revolutionary commercial sector, with its high quotient of risqué content and violence, if films had been subjected to the letter of law. However, that these laws existed and could potentially be invoked did make producers cautious; once they found a formula that worked they tended to stick to it in what amounted to a form of self-censorship. The only aspects of the censorship laws that were strictly obeyed were codes restricting criticism of the ruling elite. This was a situation that is now strongly echoed in the implementation of censorship laws under the current Islamic regime: among the multitude of topics forbidden, only those criticizing Islam (and therefore the legitimacy of the regime) and by extension issues of morality, are carefully avoided.

During the Qajar era, in the late 1800s, Iran first came under the influence of European colonial powers, which played a significant role in the development of cinema in Iran as foreign films flooded onto Iranian screens. It was not until 1931 that the first indigenous feature film, *Abi va Rabi*,* a copy of a popular Dutch comedy series *Double Patte Patchon*, was made. One of the lasting legacies of foreign influence came with the USIS/Syracuse documentary and newsreel productions of the 1950s, which marked a turning point both technically and aesthetically for future indigenous film production.† The USIS project arose from the desire of the US embassy in Tehran to expand their

---

*This film was directed by Ovanes Ohanian, a veritable one-man cinema industry, who was also responsible for setting up the Cinema Artist School in 1930, to train those wishing to enter the industry.

†The United States Information Services (USIS) was an independent organization that developed from the Information Services of the US Embassy in Tehran. Initially involved in showing US films in villages around the country through their network of mobile cinema units, they signed a contract with Syracuse University in 1951 with a view to making a series of indigenous educational films focusing on specific Iranian needs and problems. Working in conjunction with the Fine Arts Administration of the Ministry of Culture and employing film technicians and specialists from a number of American universities such as St. Louis University, University of Michigan, University of Minnesota, they produced a series of travelogues, films on agricultural and sanitation subjects and educational films. The contract between the USIS and Syracuse ended in 1959 and

information services in the immediate post-war era, 1945-1950, as a counterweight to the activities of a number of other foreign embassies, (particularly Britain, the Soviet Union) who were using film as means for education and diffusing propaganda.

This period, which saw the production of educational documentaries and a weekly newsreel that was shown in local cinemas, was to leave its mark on the local film industry.* By the time the Syracuse team left in 1959 Iran had the most up-to-date audio-visual center in the Middle East with well-trained and technically proficient filmmakers about to emerge. This laid the infrastructural basis for an unprecedented artistic flourishing of cinematic talent in the 1960s and 1970s. Known as *Cinema-ye Azad Iran* (Iranian New Wave) it was a loose grouping of exceptionally talented filmmakers who produced a body of work that was to change the face of cinema in Iran and influence all that came in its wake.

## The New Way

For a country that had produced its first indigenous sound feature film in 1948 progress was rapid. By the end of 1965 some 336 films had been produced in seventy-three local studios and shown in 264 cinemas across the country. The majority of these films were low-quality melodramas and comedies made for commercial gain. However, a newly emerging documentary and alternative cinema tradition started to bring fame and recognition to Iranian cinema in the international arena. This enhanced artistic and intellectual creativity was a cultural byproduct of the government's modernization program, otherwise known as the 1963 Revolution of Shah and People, or the White Revolution.† This period of creativity was significant because it signaled the end of an intellectual moratorium that had been ushered in with the fall of Mossadegh's nationalist government following a CIA- and MI6-backed coup in 1953.‡

---

another one was signed between Syracuse and the International Co-operation Administration (the film division of USIS) which continued the work already undertaken and in addition assisted the Iranian government in developing an audio-visual program that included the training of Iranian technicians and the establishment of an audio-visual center. For a more detailed and personal account of this project see M. Ali Issari, *Cinema in Iran 1900-1979.*

*Between 1956 and 1964, when the project was finished, some 402 such newsreel films had been made. Issari, *Cinema in Iran*, 193.

†This was the cornerstone of the shah's modernization program. It consisted of major land reform, workers' rights and women's suffrage. Many of the reforms did not develop as envisioned due to poor planning. However, this period saw Iran's infrastructure, public health and educational institutions expand as the country experienced rapid economic growth and increased prosperity. The shah's desire to modernize and "catch up" with the West extended to the cultural realm where increased financial support was aimed at producing an official culture, Pahlavism, reflecting the rich culture of the pre-Islamic past and in the process promoting the picture of a vibrant, tolerant and artistically sophisticated nation.

‡During the years 1951–1953 the Iranian parliament, under the leadership of Dr. Mossadegh, passed a law nationalizing Iranian oil, wresting it from British control. The British, enraged by the threat to their oil concessions, froze all of Iran's Sterling assets and took the case to the International Court of Justice, which promptly ruled in Iran's favor. The ensuing debacle caused the shah to flee the country and the British, backed by the American CIA, used the pretext of a communist takeover to instigate a coup, which toppled Mossadegh and placed the British-compliant shah back in power.

Until the demise of the Pahlavi regime in 1979, Iran, politically and culturally,* entered the American sphere of influence, which acted as the
main pillar of support to an increasingly autocratic shah, who sought
to crush all forms of political opposition and voices critical of his rule.
Furthermore, the reforms of the White Revolution had created new
social structures and class differences that resulted in increasing social
tension. Given the lack of a genuine form of political opposition capable
of expressing grievances or articulating the changed social conditions
it was perhaps inevitable, or at least desirable, that artists would come
to occupy a socially active role, attempting to fill the political vacuum
left after the Mossadegh affair. Dariush Mehrjui, the director of *Gav*, has
commented on the traditional role of the artist in Iran. "Because of dic-
tatorships, suppressions and lack of freedoms…people expected artistic
works to express their feelings. Even if the artist did not want this the
circumstances necessitated such a commitment."[3] Mehrjui's comments
highlight the importance of the artist in a country like Iran, where,
"When the central authority is at its weakest, a dynamic political public sphere emerges…. When central authority is strong, an atmosphere
of repression exists, with central control over activity and expression."[4]
Since his reinstatement to power following the 1953 coup the shah had
sought to consolidate his authority. His modernization programs were a
central tenet of this undertaking, and yet they also served as a means of
allowing certain dissenting voices to emerge. Such an apparent paradox
arose as a result of the new structures and social relations created by
the rapid changes and the desire to give the appearance of a liberal and
progressive society to the outside world.† Artists sought, and in a sense
were able, to reconcile these two conflicting notions. In the absence of
political opposition they were provided with the opportunity for a limited form of dissent, given the regime's investment in the arts.

With that investment in culture in mind the Pahlavi government
established the National Film Board, under the direction of the Ministry
of Culture and Arts, which was responsible for administering the film
production activities of the entire country. The Ministry also controlled
National Iranian Radio and Television, which in addition to developing
the country's visual media culture also provided regular jobs and training
in television for those working in the cinema industry. The commit-

---

*A prime example was the development of the first television station in Iran. Established by Harvard gradu-
ate Iraj Sabet (whose family were agents for RCA and Pepsi-Cola in Iran) with the assistance and planning
of American firms, the station was privately run and commercially driven. "RCA technicians trained the
station's staff and U.S. advertising agencies imported its programmes, the bulk of which consisted of MGM
films and NBC TV series. Naficy in *Life and Art: the New Iranian Cinema*, 16.

†The Kennedy administration had been pressing the shah since 1960 to instigate socioeconomic
reforms and relax political repression as the price of their continued financial, military and moral support for
the regime. This pressure was one of the key factors in influencing the shah to begin the White Revolution.
See A. Saikal, *The Rise and Fall of the Shah*.

ment to developing a sustainable infrastructure capable of a high level of quality cinematic output was enhanced with the establishment (again through the Ministry of Culture and Arts) of the College of Dramatic Arts in 1963, which offered students comprehensive training in filmmaking. This governmental framework gave birth to the socially, politically and artistically committed cinema that became known as the Iranian New Wave. Directors such as Dariush Mehrjui, Amir Naderi, Sohrab Shahid-Saless, Parviz Kimiavi, Abbas Kiarostami, Bahman Farmanara, Naser Taghvai, and Bahram Bayzai, created a body of between forty and fifty films in the years 1969–1974 that elevated Iranian cinema to a socially engaged cultural endeavor that won international recognition and awards. But the environment fostered by the new governmental agencies was not always a kind one for filmmakers. These programs were part of the shah's dual policy of creating the appearance of a liberal and vibrant cultural environment through investment in what was considered to be serious art while at the same time restricting access, through censorship and state controls, to this often critical cinema and "leading the private sector cinema toward vulgarity by keeping the doors open to commercial films from abroad."[5] This contradictory policy was also evident in the regime's provision of inexhaustible funds in launching a massive building and development program for both movie studios and theatres, most of which never exhibited the films that the burgeoning auteurs made.[6] These socially engaged, abstract art films had little resonance in Iran because, despite winning awards and critical acclaim abroad, they were ignored at home by the majority of filmgoers, primarily as a result of official censorship, and can therefore be also seen as an exercise by the regime in repressive tolerance and self-promotion. This does not, however, detract from the influence of these films, which far exceeded the numbers produced or exhibited.

The shah's cultural investment program reflected his centralized and autocratic rule, which essentially sought to introduce modernization, industrial and economic growth, without modernity, liberalism, the presence of political opposition and debate, freedom of speech and protest. The shah's support, and particularly that of his wife, Empress Farah, through her patronage of the Institute for the Intellectual Development of Children and Young Adults and its Department of Cinema can be seen as an official attempt to channel a limited form of protest.* Thus, the regime was able through its control of the cinematic medium to promote selectively films that were of a critical bent, by showing them

---

*Set up in 1974 under the auspices of the Ministry of Culture and Arts the institute allowed the youth of the country the opportunity to experiment with the medium as well as to make films that would educate and better inform them of art and culture. It was a breeding ground for some of the most famous and creative directors of the era: Abbas Kiarostami, Dariush Mehrjui and Bahram Bayzai. It is one of the few institutions to have survived the revolution.

to an international audience at prestigious gatherings like the Tehran International Film Festival* or allowing them to be shown as examples of high cultural development in film festivals abroad, and then bury the films by banning them at home.† Ironically, this is the policy that officials in the Islamic Republic have adopted in response to the development of a socially critical cinema—they like the fact that it is popular abroad but are wary of its power at home.

### The Legacy and Influence of the New Wave

The art films of the New Wave were a contrast to the escapism of the bulk of films shown on Iranian movie screens at the time. The former generally pursued an avant-garde, experimental and realist agenda that engaged critically with the cinematic medium and the surrounding world. Following the departure of the Syracuse team, local productions came under the control of the Ministry of Culture and Art. These films boasted a high technical standard and began to receive prestige and awards in the West. One of the first such films, *Dawn of Capricorn*, won two awards at the Cannes Film Festival in 1964.‡ Similarly, films like *Siavash at Persepolis* (1964) and *Gav* (1969) were well received at Western festivals yet failed to receive a commercial release or experienced censorship problems at home. In light of current Iranian film productions this situation seems relevant and all too familiar: certain directors are forced to live in exile or are lauded in the West but have difficulties releasing their films in Iran. But, despite their restricted availability on the domestic market these films were important in the sense that they challenged the formulaic and indulgent escapism of the Iranian commercial cinema, increased the profile of Iranian cinema abroad, and sought to develop new and experimental forms in seeking to critically engage with and explore the social, political and cultural realities of the Iranian past and present.

One of the most startling examples of this new artistic undertaking was the film *Siavash at Persepolis* (1964). Directed by the poet Fereydoun Rahnema, the film was influenced by Persian folklore and legend (it is based on Ferdowsi's *Shahnameh*) and employed theatrical, stylistic forms and a complex series of cultural and filmic codes that expertly juxta-

---

*The Tehran International Film Festival was established by the Ministry of Culture and Arts in 1972 as show-case gala event aimed at promoting Iranian cinema, and the regime itself, by recognizing the best films on an international stage in front of the world's leading cinema personalities. The event regularly attracted the cream of the movie world with actors of the caliber of Gregory Peck attending.

†See Peter Cowie's article on Dariush Mehrjui's film *Mina Cycle* in *Sight and Sound*, Spring 1975.

‡Directed by Ahmad Faroughi this was a picaresque thirty-five-minute short following a young boy and girl through a series of encounters with various people—a drunken undertaker, a travelling salesman and a mullah—during a day wandering around the city of Isfahan. In its focus on the everyday, having young children as the main protagonists and combining the real with the surreal, the film is an antecedent to the current type of Iranian film to be screened and win awards at foreign festivals.

posed the past and the present.* The film posits a symbiotic relationship and inextricable link between history and culture, past and present, made evident through the non-chronological but seamless mixing of scenes of present-day foreign tourists visiting the ruins of Persepolis, while the ancient tragedy of Siavash takes place around them. Here the past and present become inextricably linked, but are not merely reflections of one another. Modern art and ancient history fuse in shedding light on the historical imagination, which is crucial to the understanding of a people and their sense of identity. This interrogation of the past encourages a critical evaluation of national and personal character and forces the viewer to distinguish between transformations that are inevitable and irreversible and those that are not. The film also postulates a complex contradiction whereby the past, while appearing to be irrevocably lost, continues to resonate in the present and infuse it with new forms of meaning.† In this sense history is presented as a cultural construct carrying an infinite set of meanings that societies formulate according to present contexts. In other words a complex combination of historical elements underlies cultural form.

*Siavash at Persepolis* revealed an entirely new approach to film-making in which time and place are irrelevant phenomena, and past, present and future are interwoven through an intertextuality of forms that was unique to Iranian cinema at the time. In their self-reflexivity and mixing of historical and cultural forms *Siavash at Persepolis* (1964) and other films like *Mogolha* (*The Mongols*, 1973)‡ and *Shahzdeh Ehtejab* (*Prince Ehtejab*, 1974)§ attempted to engage with Iranian society by looking to the past in creating a symbiotic relationship with the present through a rigorous interrogation of the filmic form. In this respect they were attempting to highlight and engage with the phenomenon of different layers of social time coexisting and emerging in different forms in the present.[7] Furthermore, they articulated a form of social

---

*The film is based on a story from Ferdowsi's epic *Shahnameh*. Set in ancient Iran it tells the tragic story of crown prince Siavash who, after a falling-out with his father and stepmother (who has tried unsuccessfully to seduce Siavash), leaves Iran and settles in Turan, or modern-day Turkey. There he marries the daughter of King Afrasyab. However, Siavash is eventually killed by the king's scheming and jealous brother. This initiates a war between Iran and Turkey.

†The lament for the past, particularly the glories of ancient Persia, has been a constant theme of much Iranian art, from Ferdowsi's epic *Shahnameh*, to the poetry of Omar Khayyam and Hafez and into the modern era in the works of writers such as a Sadeq Hedayat and Gholam-Hossein Sa'edi. Indeed, such is the weight of the past that, in a different context, the ideologues of the Islamic Republic have also turned to history, revering the glories of Iran's Islamic heritage and the society and times of the Prophet.

‡Directed by Parviz Kimiavi, this film takes a highly stylized Godardian approach in comparing the coming of television in Iran to the Mongol invasion, making oblique reference to the Western cultural invasion that was occurring at the time as a result of the shah's modernization program.

§Based on Houshang Golshiri's eponymous masterpiece novel, the first feature film of the acclaimed filmmaker Bahman Farmanara tells the story of a dying prince recalling the extravagances, cruelty and ruthlessness of his and his ancestors' rule. A searing indictment on the abuse of power it drew heavy parallels with the shah's regime at the time.

commitment based on self-realization and a belief that the creative process can provide "a quasi-utopian space in which more ideal social relations may develop,"[8]

This process called into question the monolithic pervasiveness of official ideology and opened a space for debate. A cultural conflict lies within the interpretation of specific cultural and historical facts, which form part of the entire cultural composition of the Iranian nation, especially the way in which these facts are employed to represent a manufactured example of the whole of Iranian culture—for example the Pahlavis' exclusive emphasis on Iran's pre-Islamic history and the glory of the ancient Persian kings.* *Siavash at Persepolis,* through its fractured presentation of history as a contested site and its constant dialogue of interpretation, is an affront to the official portrayal of history as a twenty-five-hundred-year-old unbroken monarchical narrative. The film's method calls into question the use of cultural and historical forms by those in power as a tool of the political system, a tool that has provided a stamp of authority and moral rectitude to those who wield power. And it is the conflict between the Persian and Islamic aspects of Iranian culture, the desire to posit an isolated and singular aspect to represent the whole, that has framed all aspects of the cultural debate in Iran. As a result Iranian cinema has been informed by, indeed been a part of, the struggle to articulate the myriad facets of a contested Iranian culture. This has seen the development of a cinema attuned to the dangers of didacticism and blind faith in grand ideological themes. Films in this vein take as their starting point individual dilemmas, derived from a specific cultural context, and project them onto the plane of universal values and the search for truth or meaning. The Iranian New Wave cinema, and its legacy, attempted to give voice to a plurality of lives, of those who struggle in order "to highlight the ambivalent unities...and emergent and oppositional discourses that cohabit the national space, thereby setting in motion a de-totalizing dialectic.[9]

### Case Study: *Gav (The Cow)*

Perhaps the defining moment of this new artistic flourishing occurred with the release of Dariush Mehrjui's celebrated film *Gav (The Cow)* in 1969.† This film serves as a template with which to examine the complex problems plaguing the cinematic art form in Iran, the sociopolitical elements that impinge on its development and the resonances and influ-

*Known as Pahlavism, this was attempt of the shah to legitimate his rule ideologically and culturally by laying claim to the glories of the ancient kings of the Persian empire. In doing so he sidelined the Islamic aspect (a traditional voice of opposition to his rule) of Iranian culture by taking the emotive force of secular Iranian nationalism and turning it into a cult of monarchy.

†This is believed to be the only film that Ayatollah Khomeini watched during his life and one to which he is said to have voiced his approval.

ences that it bears on current developments in post-revolutionary cinema. Financed by the Ministry of Culture and Arts, *Gav* told the story of the relationship between a farmer and his cow. Following the death of the cow the farmer, so distraught by his loss, begins to take on the cow's characteristics. *Gav* was based on a short story by the celebrated playwright and novelist Gholam-Hossein Sa'edi.* The incidence of collaborative adaptation is one of the distinct attributes of the New Wave cinema. This contrasts sharply with the experience of the commercial cinema at the time, which produced films based on loose treatments rather than full scripts, with very little time spent in the pre-production stage. Many non-commercial post-revolutionary films, which in many ways, not least in certain formal respects, bear testimony to the legacy of the New Wave, are from scripts and scenarios written by the directors themselves, or like Abbas Kiarostami's, *The Wind Will Carry Us* (1999) and Makhmalbaf's *The Silence* (1998) are attuned to the nuances of Persian poetry.[10] This can be attributed to the revolution's targeting of writers and intellectuals. Many were imprisoned or exiled or had their work banned, particularly during the cultural revolution that occurred during the early 1980s, in a bid to ensure conformity to the new Islamic ideology. As a result literature, along with most of the social sciences, was in a worse state than cinema by the beginning of the 1980s. The intellectual lacuna caused by these purges is one from which Iran has never fully recovered.

However, what has remained a constant under both the Pahlavi and Islamic regimes is the position of the artist and intellectual as the voice of frustration in a society that lacks the means of political opposition and civil dissent. In the case of Iranian cinema this has type of political expression continues to be its most ardent task, as it attempts to articulate "a space where conflicting elements coexist without coming to a neat synthesis."[11] In this respect Iranian films have opened up the possibility of an open-ended and potential struggle against the certainties of an officially enforced ideological program.

The release of *Gav* highlights the interaction of literature, cinema and government, and the complex relationship between artists and officials in depicting the "reality" of a society. The government, familiar with Sa'edi's story, approved the film adaptation, thinking it would be a psychological exploration of one man's obsessive love for his cow. However, the film turned out to be a savage social satire on poverty and how the loss of a cow affected the entire life of a village. It also painted a grim picture of Iran—which was supposedly in the midst of the shah's modernization program—as a nation centuries behind the modern world. So infuriated was the government that it banned the film, only relenting

---

*Sa'edi also provided the story for another of the critically and artistically important New Wave films at the time, Naser Taghavi's *Tranquility in the Presence of Others* (1973).

two years later when, having been secretly smuggled out of the country, the film won an award at the 1970 Venice Film Festival. Despite this success it was only shown on condition that a disclaimer was added at the start explaining that the events of the film took place prior to the shah's rule.[12] The close relationship of the government to the cinematic art form is evident in many forms, and raises the question of patronage, which is necessary for artistic survival under an autocratic regime, where all roads, financial and social, inevitably lead to the government. In Iran this is a highly fraught alliance where, for the most part, final decisions rest in the hands of the government. The revolution has not seen the end of the close relationship between government and film and there has persisted a seemingly contradictory policy that oscillates between regressive and progressive policy measures enacted according to political expediency. For example, the Pahlavi regime introduced a policy of high taxes on the importation of film equipment while at the same time appearing to encourage the development of the industry through measures such as the 1958 tax exemption for the building of new cinemas. The Islamic authorities for their part have also shown themselves adept at pursuing such seemingly discordant policy objectives through the introduction of strict censorship laws, operating through the councils in the Ministry of Culture and Islamic Guidance, and implementing investment programs for the promotion of Iranian cinema abroad and instigating a building program to offset the shortage of cinema theaters in the country. For these reasons there is considerable complexity, if not confusion between the state and filmmakers in Iran, where filmmaking, for the most part, operates under a system of state finance and patronage, and is subject to strict governmental control from start to finish.

Both cinema and government are inextricably linked by mutual interest, but an explanation of their relationship is much more complicated than the simple assertion that state funded cinema simply equals government propaganda. The story of *Gav* reveals the fundamental problems of government interference, the nature and potential of cinema for indirect and ambiguous communication, and the importance of film festivals and foreign markets, that Iranian cinema has historically faced. However, rather than distant fragments of the past, these issues, despite the change in regime, are still very much the conditions under which Iranian cinema continues to operate. Indeed they are perhaps more pertinent given the higher profile and unparalleled success of current Iranian films in the international arena in festivals abroad.*

---

*Abbas Kiarostami's film *The Taste of Cherry* was banned from Iranian screens before being allowed a limited domestic release after it had won the Palme d'Or at Cannes in 1997. The question of subjective interpretation and ambiguity of meaning within changed ideological, social and political circumstances can be seen in Ayatollah Khomeini's approval of *Gav* (the only film it is believed he ever saw) extolling it as an example of the potential for cinema to educate rather than corrupt. See *Islam and Revolution: Writings and Declarations*, 258.

On an artistic level *Gav* introduced the mode of realism to Iranian cinema, a formal trait that has been the defining characteristic of many post-revolutionary films. The impact of *Gav*'s realism should not be understated, because "for the first time since feature film production began in Iran in 1930, a Persian film was not packed with singing and dancing and trite comedies.... The film was an honest exercise in realism."[13] And a realist cinema was crucial in developing a critical and socially engaged form of filmmaking in Iran.

Foremost, realism advocates a cinema that seeks to show the world as it is, to discover its visual texture and to understand the place of the individual within it. Realism is a political endeavor because of its epistemic engagement with the world. Political agendas are pursued or promoted based on a particular conception of social reality, which sees rulers privileging their version of reality to the detriment of others that they deem to be false. It is no surprise, then, that given the contested nature of reality in Iran, as rulers have sought to intervene at all levels of society and impose their vision of ideological conformity (be it the pre-Islamic Persian past of or the neo-Shi'ism of the Islamic Republic) that, in the absence of political and civil forms of protest, filmmakers would see realism as the starting point for challenging the notion of social and political conformity its official reality. While attempting to articulate a particular reality, realism can refute an all-encompassing conception of the world. Realism "denounces, criticizes, and deconstructs...because it shows matters as they irrefutably are and not as we would like them to be, or as, in good or bad faith, others would like to make us believe them to be." However, despite its claim or appearance, a representation of reality[15] is never neutral. Realism arises from a conflict between a filmic and phenomenal reality. It does not exist in a pristine state, ready to be empirically discovered, but is created, a representation of reality that is shaped and brought into being by the filmmaker and his circumstances and attitudes. In the example of *Gav* the depiction of the lives of the poor and underprivileged was an attempt to show a reality that lay behind the official rhetoric of the Revolution of Shah and People. In this way it created a counter-narrative to the claims of those in power. The emergence of a realist cinema was also important on a functional level due to its low productions costs and easy accessibility. The result has been a cinema that uses non-actors, shoots mostly outdoors, and utilizes long takes in order to convey an authentic sense of the rhythms and daily dramas of everyday life.

There are no reproductions of absolute truth—only representations or different versions of reality. However, in portraying a particular marginalized community and the details of its everyday life, certain contingent and qualified factual claims emerge, such as the suffering and poverty many rural peasants experienced under the Mohammad Reza

Shah's modernization campaign. The unifying aspect of the New Wave and its legacy was the way it took different forms of realism—the poetic realism of Sohrab Shahid Saless,* Rahnema's self-reflexive blend of legend and realism, and the combining of the real and metaphoric in Kimiavi's *Mongols*—in approaching social problems or issues that the official version carefully ignored. The cinematic language that articulated these social concerns originated in a more personal politics, embedded in local context. Indeed, "filming everyday life as it is lived and experienced by the masses, by using their language and cultural forms...is already a defeat for cultural colonialism"[14]—or in the case of Iran the internal cultural tyranny of official state ideology. In this respect realism is less a question of fidelity to some preexisting truth or reality than it is an intervention in or orchestration of certain ideological discourses.

Because of the premature demise of the Iranian New Wave and the subsequent stifled film production of the post-revolution period, it is perhaps not surprising to see the emergence of a realist strand in current films. The post-revolutionary Iranian cinema has taken on the influence of the past and adapted it to the present, once again attempting to engage with the contested nature of reality in Iran. In this reincarnation of the New Wave films are confronting and questioning the very notion of an objective, transparent and neutral rendering of reality by constantly exploring the constructed nature of that purporting to be "real" and to disturb the artifice of representation. Aware of the contrived construction of reality these films have, much like *Siavash at Persepolis*, collapsed the distinction between reality and fiction. And while the ideology of the regime may have changed the task of the filmmaker remains the rendering of a problematic reality. The New Wave's legacy of commitment to issues of social and political concern has focused on flexible structures of representation that originate in and recognize the complexity and diversity of national and indigenous cultural experiences. However, while the New Wave and its heirs have been integral to the landscape of Iranian cinema, they form but one part of a much wider picture, in which the commercial sector represents the majority of productions.

**The Commercial Film Industry**

Historically, the typical Iranian commercial film of the Pahlavi era was generally of a low technical quality, bore the influence of Egyptian and

---

*Saless (1944-1998) is one of the most influential Iranian filmmakers of the late twentieth century. His reputation stems primarily from the two feature films, *Yek Etefagh-e Sadeh* (*A Simple Event*, 1973) and *Tabiat-e Bijan* (*Still Life*, 1974), which he made before his work encountered political problems; he left Iran for Germany in 1975. There he made another fourteen features before moving to the US in 1995, where he died in 1998. *A Simple Event* and *Still Life* were realist films with a sparse, slow and naturalistic style, depicting real locations, local people, their culture, social conditions and daily struggle. Adopting a documentary style and abandoning conventional narrative structure in favor of capturing the routine and rhythm of daily lives as they are lived, his films have influenced the work of Kiarostami, Naderi and Abolfazl Jalili. See M. Saeed-Vafa, "Sohrab Shahid Saless: A Cinema of Exile" in *Life and Art: the New Iranian Cinema*.

Indian song and dance films and melodramatic American B movies and was referred to as Film Farsi.* This derogatory term was used to denote films in which more often than not "the heroine was raped or forced to take up a career dancing, and the hero, the only man in Tehran not to desire her, engages in several fights, usually committing a series of murders, in order to avenge her honor."[16] The Film Farsi, with its simple plot, singing, dancing, sex and violence, comprised the majority of pre-revolutionary film production in Iran. In comparison with the New Wave these commercial films were trite, formulaic and mediocre at best, featuring banal or melodramatic stories from superficial and poorly executed treatments. Several factors contributed to the evolution of the Film Farsi. Firstly, cinemas in Iran developed into two types: a small number of first-class cinemas catering to the elite and middle classes, and a large number of second- and third-class cinemas that served the lower and uneducated classes. This division was very pronounced and had a direct impact on local feature film production. Sophisticated Iranians rejected local films because of their poor technical quality and risible subject matter. Consequently these films were driven into the second- and third-rate cinemas where profit was small but audiences were content as long as the film was Iranian-made and the dialogue spoken in Persian. Consequently moviegoers did not challenge the local industry to make better films, and were content with formulaic escapism, a situation compounded by the fact that the local industry was in the hands of short-term profiteers who were satisfied with a small gain rather than long-term investment in the industry. Moreover, producers were beginning to learn that the prerequisites for box-office success lay in films that exhibited comedy, action and Persian singing and dancing, and that generally bore the hallmarks of popular Indian films. For example, of the 324 major feature films released between 1950-1965, 102 were specifically slapstick comedies with singing and dancing, and comical characters and some form of singing appeared in some form or other in the other staples, the melodramas and action films, of the commercial industry.[17]

What was the relevance and lasting significance of the Film Farsi within the history of Iranian cinema, and its influence on the films that emerged after the 1979 revolution? Critical reactions have usually been of a negative bent, but Film Farsi, despite their poor technical quality, were local productions conceived and made purely for consumption by local audiences, who generally were enthusiastically receptive. Indeed, if we locate these commercial films within the context of the social, his-

---

*These films were also referred to as "meat-stew films" or "meat-stew cinema" because the "camaraderie of the poor was often feasted with meat stews." See "Iran's Cinema History" by Massoud Mehrabi in *Cinema '96*. Other terms included *cinema lati*, in recognition of a type of felt hat usually worn by the hero/main protagonist of the film.

torical and political context of the changes taking place in the country at the time, an alternative picture of their cultural relevance begins to emerge. For example, in a country of high illiteracy and poor education, cinema emerged as the most important factor in the cultural life of the country—in 1930 there were thirty-three cinemas in the country but by 1965 this number had risen to 304. Furthermore, in a period of rapid modernization, first under Reza Shah (1925-1941) and then under his son Mohammad Reza Shah's White Revolution, many people felt dislocated and unable to keep up with the pace of change, which, buoyed up by the rise in oil prices in the 1970s and the resulting influx of petro-dollars into the economy,* saw Iran rapidly brought into the orbit of international capitalism and Western influence. The large number of films dealing with the themes of the simplicity of life and values in villages, contrasted with the perceived sinister complexity of large cities, can be seen on one level as an attempt to articulate (however simplistically) anxieties about the onslaught of rapid change. Also, amid the fist fights and posturing the Film Farsi was structured by strong moral codes of friendship, honor and community, and attempted in its own way to express the local and knowable concerns and desires of its audience.

The first Persian language sound feature *Dokhtar-e Lor* (*The Lor Girl*, 1933)† was a melodramatic love story that told the tale of a dancer in rural teahouses who through an independence of mind and a strong will resists the advances of the local chief to marry instead the man she loves. No less startling to audiences than hearing Persian spoken on the screen was to see a self-reliant woman taking control of her own fate. The film was made during a time when Iran was experiencing the first pangs of modernization under Reza Shah, as the traditional power structures of society (most particularly the clergy) were being challenged through the introduction of reforms like public education, the abolition of the veil and the opening of schools and the work force to women. Thus the Film Farsi cannot be simply dismissed as trite entertainment, because its reception by the majority of spectators was incomparably more lively and intimate than with their foreign counterparts, or with the sophisticated cinema of the New Wave. Significantly, for the revolutionaries of 1979 it was the Film Farsi that was seen as symptomatic of the corruption and decadence of the shah's rule and immoral Western influences. During the revolution this resentment resulted in a backlash against the cinema that saw some 185 cinemas

---

*Between 1972 and 1978 the Iranian GNP grew from $17.3 billion to an estimated $54.6 billion. Fred Halliday, *Iran Dictatorship and Development*, 138.

†*The Lor Girl* was made in India by the Iranian poet Abdolhossein Sepenta, who went on to produce a succession of films based on Iranian folktales and epics, none of which were as successful as *The Lor Girl*.

burned down throughout the country.* In Tehran alone, with 118 theaters, only seven remained intact by 1978.[18]

The desire to purge what was considered a morally corrupting and politically subjugating form of cinema, and to promote an Islamic culture, lay at the heart of these attacks on the cinema.[19] However, this desire to remove all traces of the former regime in the march toward an Islamic utopia has not led to the total disappearance of the Film Farsi. The ideological atmosphere may have changed but many of the commercial films produced in Iran under the present regime exhibit many of the formulaic traits once attributed to the Film Farsi. War and martyrdom as the ultimate expression of self-sacrifice (in the service of the state and Islam) have been a recurrent theme in these, what might be termed "Film Islami," and have replaced the singing and dancing. As one critic has noted, "The commercial aspects of sex and violence have now been replaced with violence. It is noticed in over-abundance and at a disgusting level in the present films."[20] The influence of the pre-revolutionary era continues to be relevant, proving that there is much structural continuity beneath changed ideological forms. The antecedents of film in Iran lie in the conflux of a deeply rooted culture and indigenous social and political contexts.

### Iranian Cinema on the Eve of the Revolution

Infrastructurally and artistically the early 1970s in Iran saw the cinematic medium at its strongest. Indigenous production continued to grow annually from eight feature films in 1952 to an all-time high of ninety in 1972. Six years later, though, the situation had dramatically changed, with the daily newspaper *Kayhan* declaring "Iranian Cinema's Death Throes." A number of reasons can be posited for this dramatic decline, such as competition from television, inflated costs of production, economic and social instability, and high government taxes. In the commercial sector box office receipts began to dwindle as audiences became bored with local productions that compared miserably with foreign films, the importation of which had risen to five hundred a year by 1974. Things were little better in the non-commercial sector as the government, increasingly aware of the growing discontent in Iranian society at large and increasingly sensitive to criticism from the cultural quarter, began a gradual withdrawal of financial support for these films.

---

*This uneasy and at times violent relationship between the clergy and cinema has existed since its inception in Iran as a form of mass entertainment. The first public cinema in Iran, established by Ebrahim Khan Sahafbashi in 1905, was ordered closed by the shah to appease the protests of the clergy See J. Akrami, "The Blighted Spring" in *Iranian Political Cinema in the 1970s*, 133. This was done amid the rising waves of protest emanating from the 1905 Constitutional Revolution (a popular uprising, which succeeded in 1907 in establishing a new order in which the monarch would reign rather than rule, although this order was constantly violated by the ruling shahs until the monarchy's demise in 1979). What this event does show is the intricate connection of politics, religion and culture that would arise at important junctures in Iranian history.

The figures for the number of films produced during this period show a steep decline from the all-time high of 1972 to just nineteen in 1978, the last rites being administered the following year with the coming of the Islamic Revolution.

Despite the sea change of the 1979 revolution, the legacy of the New Wave and Film Farsi nonetheless served as a template for the development of post-revolutionary cinema. There remain more than a few constants in Iranian film then and now: censorship, the uneasy relationship with the state, the fact that controversial films have been more popular abroad and used as an ideological tool by the regime to promote the illusion of a culturally vibrant and liberal society advocating free speech and freedom of expression, and formally through the emphasis on realism. Repressive official policies have stifled the terms of public debate, not just in relation to the media but in all areas of society, and perhaps most damagingly in the attempt to suppress the intellectual development of an entire generation. For the cinema this has meant the termination of the unbridled artistic expression of the pre-revolutionary era that manifested itself in politically engaged works that attempted, through the confluence and interaction of different artistic modes such as poetry, theatre, and literature, to transform and develop the medium and to act as critical commentary of society and the voices of those unable to speak. The New Wave's intellectual pre-occupations, the question of Iranian-ness, the position of Islam, the influence of artistic tradition and modes of expression, and the position of art as an instrument of change, came to an end with the revolution and the ideological atmosphere that swept in.

Sadly, the artistic development of the 1960s and 1970s was prevented from being a process of continual development. Thus, the filmmakers of that era have either been unable to produce films under the new system (Bahman Farmanara examines this issue in his film *Smell of Camphor, Fragrance of Jasmine* (2000), telling an old friend, "Don't cry for my death, cry for the seventeen years that I was prevented from making films."), or have seen their work banned and censored. For many filmmakers, the inability to adapt artistically to the new system has resulted in compromised, uncertain and prevaricated work (much of Dariush Mehrjui's post-revolutionary output has exhibited confusion and frustration in adapting to the strictures of the Islamic regime) or attempts to stick to principles, resulting in sporadic output that suffers at the hands of the censors (Bahram Bayzai, for example, has continued to make films on controversial subjects, namely with women occupying a central position in his narratives). However, the ghosts of the past linger and the present manifestation of the cinematic form owes much to the influence of the slow, meditative, contemplative, realist works of New

Wave directors like Sohrab Shahid Saless and Amir Naderi. Far from being fragments of a distant unfinished project, they remain relevant.

Cinema in Iran cannot avoid politicization. The successive ruling regimes makes it so, and cinema in Iran can only be properly understood by examination of the system that has created it. Iranian cinema, and some filmmakers' theoretical engagement with it, aim to intervene in history, in a process that emits myriad and conflicting voices. The contested nature and abuse of Iranian history and the ideological use of culture as a means of legitimating and consolidating political power makes understanding Iran's past, cinematic and otherwise, a prerequisite. This is the task that Iranian filmmakers are constantly aspiring toward, "a culture-changing process capable of assuming entirely new dimensions of self-realization," "moving beyond nativism," or moving toward "the full development of a new cultural hegemony."[21] Combining these elements with the consideration of Iranian cinema according to the needs of Iranian society offers the possibility for the reclamation, emancipation and interpretation of cultural and political historical narratives.

# 2 | THE IRANIAN REVOLUTION & A NEW SOCIETY

> "There is no such thing as public opinion in Iran, there is only public emotion. But public emotion, since Mossadegh, has been certified as an agency of social change."[1]

The 1979 revolution and its attending cataclysmic political events present a frame of reference necessary for understanding Iranian culture and film. The event of the revolution can be placed in the uniquely Iranian religious/political rubric of Shia Islam, and examining the unfolding of events reveal that the revolution not only took on the language but also the form of religious cultural ceremony. This chapter sets out to explain the cultural and ideological transformation that occurred following the emergence of the Islamic Republic.* This ideological and cultural changeover was grounded on the pillars of the Qur'an and the newly drafted Constitution of the Islamic Republic of Iran. These wholesale and monumental reforms built the structural basis of the cinema that emerged after the revolution.

---

*The Islamic Republic has attempted to define all aspects of life in Iran—politically, socially, culturally and economically—according to the dictates of Islam. In doing so those in power have sought to deny, ignore or ban references to Iran's Persian and pre-Islamic cultural heritage. This is almost a perverse mirror image of the deposed Shah's modernization programs of "reform," which along with his right to rule, were legitimized in the language of a Persian culture containing no trace of Islam. Thus Iranians have suffered from a type of cultural imbalance in which certain aspects of their culture are denied them or suppressed due to the political needs of those in power. In other words, whoever controls culture in Iran controls power and whoever controls power dictates culture, or a particular version of it. It is this desire to monopolize cultural production and its interpretation that leads to its politicization and, paradoxically, holds within it the means of resistance and counter-readings. Such an interpretation is derived from the work of the Marxist theorist Antonio Gramsci and his analysis on culture and ideology as sites of resistance and domination by which society constructs and circulates meanings and values. See *Marxism and Social Science*, edited by Andrew Gamble and others.

## The Iranian Revolution as Cultural Praxis*

The Iranian revolution was one of the most remarkable political and social events of the twentieth century. While the root causes may have lain, for the most part, in social and political grievances, it is perhaps more accurately defined as a media-influenced cultural revolution shaped and voiced by the language and ritual of Shia Islam. Indeed, the uniqueness of the Iranian revolution lies primarily in the role played by religion in orchestrating the disparate voices of discontent.[2] This discontent arose from the rapid and uneven development experienced by the majority of the Iranian population under the shah's modernization program, the monarchy's political weakness and lack of legitimacy, cultural dislocation, and the frustration experienced at the lack of political representation. These grievances succeeded in unifying a broad coalition of disparate groups—Marxists, the middle class, intellectuals, and the poor—under the intransigent and charismatic leadership of Ayatollah Khomeini and his populist form of militant Islam that combined progressive and traditional elements in appealing to the complaints of these diverse social strata.

The cultural unifier of Shia Islam proved capable of encompassing several political cultures—socialism, democracy, liberalism, radicalism—which appealed to and concentrated diverse groups into a single social movement. Furthermore, as a means of orchestrating dissent and converting structural conditions into revolutionary action, Shiism possessed traditional authority, represented the absolute antithesis of the shah's West-supported regime, and appealed to the Iranian cultural touchstones of nationalism, justice and sacrifice. If the Iranian revolution can be seen as a popular collective uprising against the evils of dictatorship it was also a cultural reaction against what was seen as the by-product of the shah's modernization push: cultural dependence on the West. In a country that has never been directly colonized but has experienced some of imperialism's effects indirectly, through the political machinations and meddling of foreign powers such as Britain, the Soviet Union and the U.S., the question of the harmful influence of Western cultural forms on indigenous ones has been a preoccupation of Iranian intellectual and religious thought. Jalal Al-e Ahmad, one of the most influential figures of twentieth-century Persian literature, spoke and wrote at length about the dangers of cultural alienation and the duality of Iranian identity: "Today we stand

---

*This definition and approach seeks to align culture and historical practice, in the Gramscian sense, in which the former is a means of attaining a higher awareness through which "one succeeds in understanding one's own historical value, one's own function in life, one's own rights and obligations," Antonio Gramsci, *Political Writings 1910-1920*, 10-11. This is a particularly instructive means by which to analyze the Iranian Revolution as it derived its historical value, and articulated the frustrations of the people, by recourse to deeply felt indigenous cultural forms, such as Shia Islam.

under the [Western] banner, a people alienated from ourselves...we try to find solutions to every problem like pseudo-Westerners."[3] Ali Shariati famously labeled the problem "Westoxification" and Ayatollah Khomeini referred to the corrupting power of media in foreign hands in a speech, declaring, "We are not against radio, we are against corruption. We are not against television, we are against that which is in the service of foreigners and is used to keep our youth backward and destroy our manpower. We are against that."[4] This national resentment, which had resulted in the radical rejection by Iranians "not only of foreigners but of everything that had constituted for years, for centuries, its political destiny,"[5] and enacted in the language of a religious movement that took a seventh-century model as its ideal society, would seem to suggest that the division between traditional and so-called modern cultural forms was clear cut. The reality was much more complex, as the recourse to deeply held cultural beliefs was presented not simply as antithetical forms of protest to alien influences but as an alternative ideological system in tune with and capable of treating the realities of the twentieth century.

If Shia Islam is considered the governing ideology of the revolution, and more particularly the state that followed, it must be recognized that it comprised oppositional and divergent voices. These ranged from the liberal Islam of Ayatollah Motahari* and the democratic Islamic modernism of Mehdi Bazargan† to Ali Shariati's‡ radical activist fusing of Islam with Marxist politics and social analysis, and Ayatollah Khomeini's militant traditionalism.[6] These figures emerged from a tradition of Iranian intellectualism that sought to counter the growing autocracy, despotism, and incursion of Western influence under Pahlavi rule. They actively affected Iranian society by staging a constructive debate that orchestrated or reacted to events as they unfolded.[7] Through an appeal to deep-seated cultural beliefs they articulated a form of critical dialogue that spoke to the social and political frustrations of Iranian society and

---

*A former student and close confidant of Khomeini's, as well as a highly respected academic, Motahari engaged in a wide range of educational and cultural activities designed to promote an Islam that was relevant to the contemporary world and capable of dealing with social, political and economic issues. He is credited with highlighting the need for the reform of the religious hierarchy and in attempting to make them more responsive to pressing social issues. A group called Forqan who claimed to be disciples of Ali Shariati assassinated him in May 1979.

†Appointed by Khomeini as prime minister of the provisional government following the revolution, Bazargan was one of the most important political leaders of the revolution. A veteran of Iranian oppositional politics under the shah he advocated a progressive form of Islam in accord with technical and scientific progress and the concepts of democracy, human rights and the rule of law.

‡Recognized, along with Khomeini, as the most important ideologue of the revolution Shariati sought the reclamation of Iranian cultural identity and the employment of an Islamic humanism allied to radical political action and a doctrine of social justice. Although he did not live to see the revolution (dying in England under mysterious circumstances in 1977) his writings and lectures radicalized students, the intelligentsia, lay intellectuals as well as members of the clergy. In his youth, Makhmalbaf came under Shariati's influence.

formed the cultural language of revolution and the ideological bedrock for the development of the Islamic Republic. However, a distinction must be drawn between the revolution and the ensuing state, which differ greatly from one another in outlook, orientation and development. Ideologically this difference arises between the revolutionary discourse of Shia Islam, as articulated in the struggle against the Pahlavi state, and Shia dogmatism, which became the official monolithic ideology of the Islamic Republic once the clergy had assumed full control of the reigns of power.[8] An examination of the various analyses offered by Motahari, Shariati, Bazargan—and their skillful employment by Khomeini—shows the complexity of the revolutionary discourse and the way it succeeded in balancing all styles of Shi'ism, from the popular religion of the poor to the scholars of the religious colleges, the mystical counterculture of Sufism and the ethical and liberal religion of the upper and educated classes.

### New Paradigms of Ideological Discourse

It could be said that Motahari and Shariati influenced the language of the revolution with Bazargan shaping the development of society in the revolution's immediate aftermath. Ayatollah Morteza Motahari proposed a humane and liberal interpretation of Islam. He grounded his system of analysis in the individual, reforming the traditional structure of Islam, and improving the organizational structure and quality of the clergy, in order to formulate and disseminate a form of Islamic ideology applicable to all sections of society. According to Motahari, the individual was the main force of social change, exemplified by the psychological transformation that leads man to God on the path of righteousness provided by Islam. Consensus is built and based on the Qur'anic notion that this transformation is all-inclusive and that pious believers can come from all classes: "Whoso makes God his friend, and his Messenger, and the believers—the party of God, they are victorious."[9] In other words society is divided between believers and non-believers and each individual has within himself the ability to effect change and become pious by resigning himself to the will of God. According to Motahari, then, the revolutionary psychological change in the individual is the starting point for wider social transformation, shaped by the faithful acting in accordance with the dictates of the Qur'an. This was the type of religious language needed at the beginning of the revolution to appeal to as wide an audience as possible.

Within the deeper cultural resonances of Iranian Shiism, and the formal language of the passion play that was the Iranian revolution, this appeal to egalitarianism and equality among believers, submission to the will of God and adherence to the sacred texts, echoed the message and actions of the great historical symbol of Iranian Shia faith,

Imam Ali.* These resonances were not lost on Motahari, who drew a comparison between what he saw as the Iranian people's struggle against the corrupt and despotic rule of the shah and Ali's own struggle against an elitist and unjust Islamic leadership: "The revolution of the Moslem people in those days was very similar to today's revolution in Iran, since both were popular revolutions comprising all the people."[10] However, Ali's historical significance transcends his ability to align diverse groups. For Shiites Ali is a paragon of virtue, a figure of righteousness engaged in a moral battle with the corrupting forces of elitism, wealth, power and corruption. To Iranians, he "fulfilled within Islam, the tradition of charismatic kingship...a perfect model of the noble virtue of justice which they believe has always been a central part of their cultural tradition." This idea of charismatic kingship highlights aspects of ancient pre-Islamic Persian culture and its manifestation within the unique Iranian adaptation of Islam. The ancient kings of Persia were seen as the embodiment of a divine will, a symbol of perfection dedicated to the eradication of evil and the stewardship of peace and justice. When Islam arrived in Iran these ideals did not disappear from the national cultural character; rather they were fused with the incoming religion. Iranians contributed to Shiism many of their deeply held cultural convictions, such as hereditary leadership and absolute monarchical rule. Furthermore, the concept of the Imam and the virtues for which Ali is extolled are seen to form part of the continuing narrative of the charismatic king uniting the people in the creation of the just society.

Ayatollah Khomeini, as both the leader and symbol of the revolution, was seen as the latest manifestation in this unfolding historical narrative of the righteous leader come to deliver the country from tyranny. His charismatic leadership, piety and unyielding opposition to Pahlavi rule placed him within this Persian-Islamic cultural tradition and drew parallels with the struggle and virtues of Ali and the Shia tradition

*In Shia Islam, the honorific title "Imam" denotes the twelve infallible, saint-like successors to the Prophet Mohammed, among whom Ali is the first. The Prophet had designated no successor before he died, and the Muslim community was split on the issue. Ali, as the Prophet's cousin and first convert (he was also married to the Prophet's daughter, Fatima) was seen as a logical choice. However, consensus, as opposed to bloodline, finally determined succession and Ali was passed over in favor of Abu Bakr, a close confidant of the Prophet. It was not until the anarchy that followed the death of the third caliph that Ali emerged as leader of the Muslims. However, his reign was short, 656 to 661, and beset by conflict and internal division. Ali preached piety, equality and unity in a moral battle against what was seen as the corruption and elitism of the Islamic establishment. These divisions and internecine battles were to cost him his life, and he was killed by an assassin one day while returning from prayers. Ali is seen by Shiites as the first of the Prophet's true successors. Furthermore, his governance left profound questions as to the nature of Islamic rule, the method of succession and the issue of equality among believers. For Iranians Ali is the personification of piety, righteousness and the upholder of justice; he is a central part of their cultural history and belief in the power of charismatic leadership. See Hugh Kennedy, *The Prophet and the Age of the Caliphates*.

of the return of the Twelfth Imam.* This recourse to religio-cultural forms provided theoretical and emotional force to the revolution, and it was to prove itself adaptable and sensitive to the changing course of events. As revolutionary fervor increased and as expediency demanded, the themes of unity, protest, and piety, of Ali, gave way to the language of martyrdom, sacrifice and suffering from oppression, as embodied by the reverential figure of Imam Hossein.†

## The Revolutionary Use of Shia Symbolism

Five distinct phases can be discerned in the progression of the Iranian revolution: non-violent mobilization, usually small demonstrations organized by the intelligentsia (June-December, 1977); mass demonstrations (August-September 1978); mass strikes (October-November 1978); and finally, dual sovereignty (December 1978–February 1979).[12] Significantly, the role of the clergy and the position of Islam remained relatively unpronounced until the organization of mass demonstrations and strikes. The progression of thought from Motahari‡ and his egalitarian interpretation of the figure of Ali to a more militant rhetoric emphasizing the role of the oppressed originated in the idea of the revolution as envisioned by Ayatollah Khomeini. The most significant turning point came during the Ashura§ marches on 10 and 11 December 1978, which signified ratification of Khomeini as the leader

---

*Shiites believe that the true lineage of successors to the Prophet consists of the twelve semi-divine imams, beginning with Ali and ending with the last of the direct male descendants, the messiah-like Mahdi. However, the Mahdi is believed to have gone into hiding a century after the martyrdom of Hossein at Karbala, to appear some time in the future, to prepare for the Judgement Day when the world is rife with decadence and corruption. When Khomeini returned to Iran from his exile in France, he cast himself as the Twelfth Imam—indeed he is still known and referred to casually as "the Imam" or "Imam Khomeini"—and though this was a heretical assumption, he made no attempt to disabuse his followers of the notion. Reza Aslan, "Are There Two Irans?" http://slate.com/id/2106317/entry/2106413/

†Following Ali's death the question of succession reemerged. Ali's eldest son Hassan relinquished his claim to the title of caliph and leadership of the Islamic community passed to the house of the Umayyads. However, Ali's second son Hossein refused to relinquish his claim and placed himself as head of an insurrection against what he saw as unjust Umayyad rule. The two forces met at the Battle of Karbala where Hossein led an army of seventy-two of his followers against an opposition of thousands. All were killed and at the end of the battle, Hossein, standing alone and mortally wounded, was finished off by the reviled Shemr, a figure of evil for Shiites to which Khomeini would compare the shah. The importance of the Battle of Karbala for Shiites is that it imbued their faith with its defining elements of oppression, rebellion, the search for justice, self-sacrifice and martyrdom in overcoming evil.

‡Khomeini saw Motahari as the most important theoretician of Islamic ideology and as a bulwark against alternative "un-Islamic" currents. This importance was reflected in his appointment, by Khomeini, as one of the key members of the Revolutionary Council. "The Council was responsible for the coordination and implementation of the anti-Shah activities of the Islamic opposition forces during the revolution and was given the responsibility of acting as the nation's legislative body after the revolution, until the time when a new constitution was adopted and a parliament convened." Ali Rahnema and Farhad Nomani, *The Secular Miracle Religion: Politics and Economic Policy in Iran*, 39.

§Ashura is the tenth day of the Shia holy month of Moharram when Hossein's death at the Battle of Karbala is commemorated and mourned.

of the revolution and elected Islam as its language of revolt.* Furthermore, the increasing prevalence of these protests, organized by the clergy around religious ceremonies such as Ramadan and Moharram imbued the revolution with a more visible Islamic character.† Cyclical mourning rituals, acted out in the language and symbolism of Shia martyrdom and taking place on the fortieth day of mourning, were orchestrated to celebrate those "martyred" during the course of protests and demonstrations, while at the same time building momentum and increasing the ferocity of anti-regime sentiment. One of the most infamous and tragic examples of this use of religious rituals in orchestrating and directing revolutionary discontent among the masses involved the cinema.

On 19 August 1978, two weeks into Ramadan and twenty-five years to the day since the restoration of the Pahlavi monarchy to the throne following the 1953 coup, arsonists torched the Rex cinema in Abadan, killing over four hundred people. The authorities blamed fanatical Islamic reactionaries opposed to people attending the cinema during the holy month of Ramadan. The revolutionaries for their part blamed the shah's secret police force SAVAK for perpetrating the act in a bid to discredit the revolutionary movement. To date no one has been found responsible for the atrocity but it must be noted that traditionally and historically cinema has experienced the wrath of religious zeal in Iran. Seen as a force of Western corruption, many cinemas were burned during the course of the revolution "as a reaction to modernization."[13] However, in this case doubt has been cast on the involvement of Islamic fanatics, given the fact the film being screened at the time was a local production, Masoud Kimiai's *Ghavaznha* (*The Deer*, 1975), which told the story of an urban guerrilla engaged in anti-regime activities, and not the foreign productions detested by Islamic militants. What is undeniable is that the cinema was a prime target of revolutionary zeal and that the burning of movie theaters across the country took a huge toll on Iran's cinema industry. Within a month after the burning of Cinema Rex all film presentation and production activities in Iran came to a halt.[14]

The Rex incident at Abadan was a turning point in the increase of support and pace of the revolution. The shah subsequently tried to introduce a series of reforms, such as a pledge to purge corruption from his administration, in order to placate the revolutionaries. But Khomeini remained intransigent, using the months of Ramadan (September 1978) and Moharram (December 1978) and the spectacle of martyrdom as the

---

*Between one and three million people are estimated to have taken part in these marches, during which a seventeen-point article was read and ratified declaring Ayatollah Khomeini as the leader of the revolution and emphasizing Islam as its dominant ideology.

†Moharram is the month of mourning for the death of Hossein and forms the ceremonial center of the Shia calendar. Recitations of his martyrdom, public processions, *tazieh* (passion plays), sermons and elegies are conducted in mourning and atoning for his death.

final push in the triumph of blood over the sword.[15] Massive demonstrations were organized, with many people wearing shrouds signifying their willingness to be martyred, as Hossein and Karbala became the point of reference in a more proactive phase of revolt.

## The Karbala Paradigm*

The increasing reliance on the symbolism of Karbala signified a shift in the revolution's ideological emphasis. Passive demonstration was superseded by active protest, through the themes of self-sacrifice, martyrdom and death, of which Hossein became the primary motif. Drawing a comparison between an age-old story of religious conflict and present circumstances, Khomeini argued that Hossein had died at Karbala trying to liberate the oppressed from the clutches of satanic despots in the same way that the Iranian people were now struggling against the tyranny of the shah.[16] The demonstrations throughout the month of Moharram, particularly on Ashura, were the largest and most vocal of the revolution. The demonstrators became more confident in the righteousness of their actions and expressed this through religious symbolism—lines of men dressed in white (the color of death shrouds) leading the crowds against the army's guns, with many protestors waving black flags (the color of mourning omnipresent during Moharram). Within the changed ideological and structural framework the language of protest began to take on a more militant tone in response to changing sociopolitical conditions. Moving beyond opposition to the perceived encroachment of Western cultural forms, the voice of opposition began to link religion to politics and portrayed Islam as a truly revolutionary and anti-imperialist ideology that offered the fulfillment of the Iranian people's historical desire for justice.

The ability of Shia ideology to appeal to a wide range of apparently discordant elements was clearly evident in Ali Shariati's activist, revolutionary brand of Shia Islam.† Ali Shariati was a Sorbonne-educated intellectual who appealed to modern doctrines like liberalism, capitalism and Marxism and its call for the liberation of the downtrodden, which found many adherents among intellectuals, students and left-leaning groups. It was through his work and in the response to the unfolding revolution that Hossein and the Karbala paradigm began to emerge as emblems of activist revolt. Shariati's writings derived from a Third-Worldist genealogy influenced by Marx and Fanon, and espoused

---

*The ritualistic mourning of Hossein's death at the battle of Karbala is an endemic feature of Iranian Shia culture and it exerts a strong influence on the Iranian psyche. Significantly, "The Karbala paradigm has been honed over the years into a device for heightening political consciousness of the moral failings of the government." Michael Fischer, *Iran from Religious Dispute to Revolution*.

†See Ali Mazuri, "Ideological Encounters of the Third World," *Third World Book Review* 7, no. 6 (1986): 10. For a comprehensive explanation in English of Shariati's life and work see Ali Rahnema's *An Islamic Utopia: A Political Biography of Ali Shariati*.

a socially active anti-imperialist, anti-Western, anti-capitalist stance manifested in the cultural language and symbols of Shia Islam. Shariati's thought differed from Motahari's in his belief that man's fate is determined by his own actions, rather than by the will of God. Privileging the material over the spiritual, Shariati's ideology rested heavily on themes of class struggle (the oppressors versus the oppressed) rather than on notions of social harmony among the faithful. He encouraged a view of society that apotheosized Hossein as the key figure in revolutionary struggle. His aim was to create an Islamic utopia through social revolution that would lead to a classless community of Muslims ruled by enlightened intellectual thinkers.[17] By emphasising the "Karbala paradigm" and its notions of martyrdom and sacrifice, Shariati was appealing to, and attempting to revitalize through its application in a modern theoretical framework, elements deeply ingrained in the Iranian psyche. For him revolutionary struggle would prove fruitless unless it was allied to a realization of true cultural identity, which for Iranians was inextricably tied to Shia Islam.

Whereas Ali's message was seen as political protest demanding equality, compassion and justice, that of Hossein was characterized by political action, martyrdom and sacrifice. Taking these theological and traditional touchstones, and giving them modern ethical and socially progressive interpretations, made Islam more palatable to the intelligentsia and middle classes. The militant and activist nature of the discourse lay in transforming the religious processions, holy days and mourning rituals into activist demonstrations and occasions for political protest, rather than quiet performances of superstitious rites. Shariati had popularized a saying, which Khomeini was to use with much frequency, and was to become a popular slogan of the revolution: "Every month of the year is Moharram, every day of the month Ashura and every piece of land Karbala."[18] The revolutionary call to sacrifice and action was a reflection of the words of Hossein, himself: "O people the Apostle of God said during his life, He who sees an oppressive ruler violating the sanctions of God, reviling the covenant of God...[If a man sees such a ruler] and does not show zeal against him in word or deed, God would surely cause him to enter his abode in fire."[19]

In order to build and solidify a power base that would legitimatize his authority, Khomeini adopted the language of Shariati to express his moral and spiritual support for the dispossessed. This marked a shift from the position of social unity and harmony espoused by Motahari ("All together" and "Advance together with a single voice and purpose")[20] to a partisan position championing the cause of the dispossessed and oppressed ("All heavenly ordinances which have descended have the deliverance of the oppressed as their objective. The *mostazafin* [downtrodden] of the world should unite, and expel the oppressors from the stage, since the world belongs to God and the *mostazafin* are His inheritors").[21] This change in emphasis was the result of a number of factors dictated by events and Khomeini's belief that the revolution served as the precursor to the establishment of an Islamic state ruled by the clergy. In implementing such a system Khomeini realized that it would be impossible to appeal to all social classes, since the implementation of an Islamic state would ultimately alienate the middle-class professionals, civil servants, the bourgeoisie and segments of the young students.[22] In approaching the dispossessed Khomeini was taking the essence of Shariati's themes of class division and using them to appeal to that section of society who most ardently supported the clergy.

However, Shariati's revolutionary discourse of radical, class-based protest was in direct contrast to Khomeini's view of an Islamic state ruled by the *ulama* (clergy) under the auspices of the *velayat-e faqih*.* Thus, Khomeini extracted the term mostazafin from the internal logic and meaning under which it operated in Shariati's discourse and used it as a form of rhetoric as political expediency dictated.† This change in emphasis reflected deeper concerns than a mere response to the quickening pulse of revolution. The clergy were now assuming the position and voice of leadership and in doing so were seeking to secure their own position through rallying the support of the downtrodden masses who would become the foot soldiers of the Islamic state. While for the majority of people who supported the revolution the goal was the removal of a despot, for the clergy it was the first stage in the establishment of an Islamic state in which they would rule supreme. One of the best examples of Khomeini's ability to integrate contradictory elements from different systems of thought can be seen in his declaration on the establishment of the Islamic Republic, in which he makes opposite references to both social solidarity and social division: "The rain of Compassion of the Qur'an and the Traditions falls upon everyone evenly"; "All are brothers and equal"; while later on in the speech he states that "The slum dwellers around cities…they are the group for human rights, not you and I. Come and do something for them. The

---

*Velayat-e Faqih*—literally, "rule of the jurist"—refers to the form of Islamic government based on rule by religious clergy as laid out by Khomeini in a series of lectures in early 1970 called *Velayat-e Faqih: Hokumat-e Islami* [Rule of the jurist: Islamic government]. According to velayat-e faqih, the faqih, or leading jurist (Khomeini) becomes an absolute ruler, in the absence of the Twelfth Imam. According to Asghar Shirazi (1998) the pervading spirit of this style of rule is one of absolute hierocracy with the ruling jurists exercising the function of legal guardian, protector and liberator. The people are not acting subjects of the state but the state's objects.

†Ervand Abrahamian, in *Khomeinism*, 47-54, notes how the term changed from 1982 onward, as the need to secure a broader base of support became a priority. No longer was it viewed as an economic category, but instead became a political category denoting the regime's supporters, including wealthy bazaar merchants, intellectuals and the middle class.

people and the government should do something for them."[23]

Indeed, the issue of class division enacted in the language of spiritual sacrifice and the historical narrative of the search for justice through suffering highlighted a unique feature of the revolution—its anti-materialist message. Echoed in Khomeini's oft-repeated phrase, "We did not make this revolution for cheaper watermelons," the rejection of materialism lay in the elevation of the struggle against an evil despot into a spiritual battle that gained its legitimacy from the Qur'an, the words of the Prophet, and the lives of the Imams. However, the composition of the various groups involved in the revolution, and the language used, exhibited a complexity, diversity and ambiguity that exhibited "both institutional and ideological elements"[24] in what might be termed the first modern revolution. The success of this combinational strategy lay in the pragmatism and adaptability of the clerical leadership in presenting traditional religious cultural forms, not as a search for a lost pure essence, but as a dynamic, universalistic force engaged in a form of "ideological retraditionalisation."[25] This manifested itself in a self-conscious, politicized defense of tradition against forces that were seen as attempting to weaken or displace it. In the Iranian context we have the reconstituted and politicized identity of Islam, deeply embedded in the psyche of the people, a part of their cultural heritage that had been denied them under the Pahlavi regime,* which came to be manipulated by the clergy for its own interests in an engagement with, rather than an estrangement from, the modern world.

The ideology of the Iranian revolution when viewed in detail "emerges less a monolithic clash between modernity and tradition than as an attempt to actualize a modernity accommodated to national, cultural and historical experiences."[26] The shah's drive to create a modern state exhibited the tendency of many Third-World states, in that economic modernization assumed a higher priority than democratization or the creation of a public sphere of political representation. Such a situation had created a vacuum where secular opposition was weakly rooted and ineffectual. The only viable opposition came in the form of an orchestrated politicized Islam that articulated a cultural or social discontent.

If the voice of revolution was a re-traditionalized Islam operating from within modernity—and indeed Khomeini claimed that the Iranian revolution had ushered in a society surpassing the utopia created by

---

*The Pahlavi dynasty, 1921-1979, of Mohammad Reza Shah and his father Reza Shah, had constantly sought throughout their rule to limit, suppress and ignore the Islamic component of Iranian culture in their bid to construct a centralized secular state. This was undertaken both institutionally, in the 1936 law banning the wearing of the *chador*, to limit the influence of the clergy, and ideologically, with the emphasis on Persian cultural elements, which served as legitimators of their power and right to rule. Indeed examples of the latter can be seen in the name the dynasty gave itself, Pahlavi, which was the language spoken in Iran in pre-Islamic times, and the lavish 1971 celebrations by the shah at the ancient ruins of Persepolis to signify 2,500 years of unbroken rule.

the Prophet in the seventh century*—then the mode of expression was the uneasy and contradictory relationship between the clergy and the media, or more particularly their skilful use of localized media operating in the private sphere. The most persuasive weapons of the Iranian revolution were not guns and bullets but cassettes, fax machines, photocopiers and graffiti. The media in Iran were seen as symptomatic of the shah's modernization program, emanating from and reflecting Western cultural influence and dependency. Despite the traditional historical opposition of the clergy to what they perceived as the evil and corrupting influence of the media, they succeeded in using "small media" in infiltrating the private sphere (homes, the network of mosques) in creating a public domain of political protest and action.[27]

The cassette tape played a very important role in the revolution not only in transmitting the Islamic ideology of the clergy but also acting as an effective weapon in countering the repressive apparatus and large-scale state propaganda of the shah's regime.[28] In conjunction with clandestinely printed materials, recordings of Khomeini's speeches and declarations were widely circulated throughout the country, a process that was relatively simple. Readings of Khomeini's declarations would be repeated over the phone from his exile base to individuals in Tehran who would be waiting with tape recorders.† They in turn telephoned other individuals who would repeat the process, thus circulating these messages throughout the country, which were then further reinforced and spread to a wider audience by inclusion in the Friday sermons at the mosque.

It was the infrastructural network of the mosques and the traditional Friday sermons, supplanted and enhanced by the use of modern media, that allowed the clergy to get their message across and position themselves as leaders of the revolution. In this way the language of Shiism, through the authority of Khomeini and its dissemination through media channels and the clerical network, succeeded in challenging the official state media by offering an alternative message and acting as a rhetorical means of building solidarity through indigenous cultural forms. Khomeini's exile in Paris made the transmission of his messages much easier as he was surrounded by unrestricted access to modern communications systems. Furthermore, it allowed him access to the world media and to broadcast the Iranian revolution onto the world stage as a counterweight and oppositional voice to the state stranglehold on the Iranian media apparatus. However, the importance of

---

*Khomeini made these remarks in a speech printed in the *Iran Times*, 4 Dec. 1982.

†Khomeini had been exiled from Iran since 1964 for leading a campaign against certain reforms (greater freedom for women, opening posts in local government to non-Muslims) of the White Revolution, changes he thought ran counter to Islam. Having first settled in Turkey he then moved to the holy Shiite city of Najaf in Iraq. There he remained until the shah, worried about the rising tide of revolution and Khomeini's exalted figure, asked the Iraqi President, Saddam Hussein, to expel him from the country. On 6 October 1978 Khomeini arrived in Paris where he was to remain until his return to Iran in February 1979.

the media should not be overstated. The revolution would have happened without tape recorders and television coverage. These were just quicker and modern methods that were skillfully employed in transmitting an age-old message. What is significant is the way in which these various media were employed and the blueprint that it laid down for its control and propagandist use when the clergy assumed power and set began laying out their vision of an Islamic state.

If the transmission of Shia ideology during the revolution through the use of small media was aimed at employing religious metaphors, symbols, and ceremonies in transforming social discontent into revolutionary action, then the post-revolutionary period and the clerical ascension to power can be seen as the assumption of control over state media apparatus, big media, in legitimating the Islamic Republic. The use of religious symbolism in elevating the revolution to a moral and spiritual battle against an infidel was to become in the new post-revolutionary state a battle to preserve and defend the universal interests of Islam, to Islamicize the country, and propagate and consolidate clerical rule.

## The Hope of a New Order

On 16 January 1979, Mohammed Reza Shah was finally forced from the throne, and he fled the country. February 1 saw the messianic return of Ayatollah Khomeini to Iran, accompanied by scenes of unbridled joy and mass celebration. However, this was not to be the culmination of some two years of protest and struggle but merely the beginning of a more violent period, stretching from mid-1979 to mid-1981, as the struggle for power pitted group against group in the right to define the culture and direction of the Iranian state. These months were characterized by the conflict of different ideological subsystems competing to define the future orientation of the state, as evidenced by the marked progression from the liberal democratic stance of the provisional government to the institutionalization of absolute clerical rule as laid down by the new constitution, to the militant rhetoric and repressive measures used to eliminate all those deemed opponents of the new theocracy. The immediate aftermath of the revolution revealed the need to unite all the disparate elements of protest. Under such circumstances Khomeini appointed Mehdi Bazargan, a religious-minded liberal and leader of the Iran Freedom Movement,* as the man to lead Iran through this difficult

---

*The Iran Freedom Party, established on 15 May 1961, was a direct descendent of Mohammad Mossadegh's National Front. The latter was a broad coalition of political parties formed in 1949 with the express purpose of forcing the shah to hold free democratic elections and restore press freedom in the country. Following the oil nationalization crisis (Bazargan was the first president of the then newly nationalized Iranian Oil Company) and the ensuing coup, which led to the downfall of the Mossadegh government and the reinstatement of the shah to power, the National Front was outlawed. However in 1954 it emerged under a new name, the National Resistance Movement, and continued to pursue the goals of Mossadegh's nationalist movement. In 1956 the movement was once again outlawed and its leaders arrested on the

transitional stage and the one to transform the broad-based popular support into institutionalized legal state power. Bazargan had tried to combine liberal democracy and Islam in the formation of a democratic Islamic state and it was his provisional government that was entrusted with drawing up the constitution of the future polity. In his first official public address as prime minister Bazargan emphasized the notions of tolerance, democracy and unity by laying out standards of governance that recognized and respected individual freedom and an Islamic form of government that respected the rule of law and was to be for all people regardless of class.[29] The Bazargan-led government tried to accommodate all sections of society by formulating a "lay-dominated religion that would be acceptable both to the anti-Shah clergy, especially to the junior clergy, and to the modern, educated middle class"[30] in an attempt to show that Islam was compatible and relevant to the contemporary world.* However, the provisional government was constantly thwarted in its attempts at reconstructing the post-revolutionary society as hostile competing political alliances and autonomous centers of political power emerged.† In essence the real struggle for power evolved between Bazargan's government, which was becoming increasingly isolated and ineffectual, and the traditional clergy, who saw themselves as the true vanguard of the revolution and who had formed the Islamic Republican Party with the express purpose of instituting their vision of an Islamic Republic. The conflict between these competing power blocs finally came to a head with the drafting of the new constitution, which established the form of government and the ideological orientation of the new state.

### Iran's Internal Revolution: Clerical Rule and Official Religious Discourse

Aside from making declarations on all aspects of life in Iran, the constitution acted as the legitimator, consolidator and raison d'être of the

---

grounds that they were undermining the constitutional monarchy. This pattern was to continue with the formation of the Iran Freedom Party (IFM), which was subsequently banned two years after coming into existence. Despite this it had managed to bring together a broad coalition of disparate forces all struggling against the shah's autocracy. The IFM was not to make a true comeback on the political scene until 1978 but its existence shows that despite the lack of willingness of those in power to allow representative political protest and opposition the will existed strongly among the people..

*For Bazargan the relationship between country and religion was defined by the maxim "serving Iran through Islam." This put him in direct conflict with the traditional clergy who believed that all aspects of social and cultural life were subordinate to the needs of Islam.

†Examples of these centers of power that began to act in the name of Ayatollah Khomeini and independently of the provisional government, thus undermining its effectiveness, included: the Revolutionary Council, komitehs, the Islamic Revolutionary Guards, and the Islamic courts. The most glaring example took place with the occupation of the U.S. Embassy in Tehran on 4 November 1979 when a group calling itself Students Following the Line of the Imam held fifty-two Americans hostage for 444 days. This was an action supported by Khomeini, and left Bazargan's position untenable. See Riaz Hassan, "Iran's Islamic Revolutionaries: Before and After the Revolution," *Third World Quarterly* 6, no. 3 (1984): 675-678.

clergy's authority, instigating the rule of the reverend religious jurists. The 175-clause document, far from being a religious fundamentalist text, is a complex interaction of Islamic legalist (emanating from the divine law of the Qur'an, known as *sharia*), secular and democratic elements. Its central structure has been likened to the constitution of the French Fifth Republic in that it divides the government into the executive branch, headed by the president, supervising a highly centralized state; the judiciary, with powers to appoint district judges and review their verdicts; and the national parliament, elected through universal adult suffrage.[31] However, it is with the introduction of unique Islamic elements, especially the concept of velayat-e faqih, that we see the usurping of, and conflict with, these universal democratic elements.

The Islamic Republic has been criticized as undemocratic, because it deems the interpretation and implementation of *shari'a* (Islamic law) to be "the exclusive domain of the *ulama* (jurists), the *mujtaheds* (senior high-ranking clergy and Islamic legal experts)."[32] As Ayatollah Khomeini explained, "Expression of agreement and disagreement with the precept of Islam is the exclusive right of our reverend jurists."[33] The absolute control of power by the clergy was guaranteed and consolidated by the establishment of the Council of Guardians and the concept of velayat-e faqih. It is in these two institutions, rather than the parliament, where the real power resides. The Council of Guardians is a twelve-member assembly whose members are *mujtaheds* and who decide whether resolutions and laws passed by the *Majles* (parliament) are in accordance with Islamic law. In this respect the Council occupies a dominant position in the legislature in that it has the power of veto: only through its approval can resolutions passed in parliament become law. However, the power of the Council of Guardians is itself subservient to the power of the velayat-e faqih, or the Supreme Jurisprudent.

Article 107 of the constitution affirmed Ayatollah Khomeini as the *vali-e amr*—"The exalted *marja-e taqlid* [literally, the source of emulation; here the term refers to a cleric of the highest rank] and leader of the Revolution"—and Article 110 defined the position's power to appoint senior clerics to the Council of Guardians, to ensure that all laws passed by the *Majles* conformed to the sacred law, dismiss the president, appoint military commanders, and declare war and peace.[34] In essence this placed supreme and ultimate authority of the state in the hands of whoever occupied the position of velayat-e faqih. This institutional framework not only succeeded in placing the clergy in positions of power, and defined the state in their own image, but also laid the foundations for a system of government based purely on ideology. This arose from the fact that the legitimacy of all government policies must be sought in the authenticity, argumentation and subjective ideological interpretation of the principles of Islam. It was for this reason that

one of the chief architects of the constitution, Ayatollah Mohammad
Beheshti, called for continual *ejtehad* (seminary study), "because in a
government based on ideology all questions to do with legislation,
arrangements for implementing regulations and establishing pro-
cedures must be determined by ideological considerations."[35] This
created a system of government not by the people for the people but
by the clergy for Islam. And having laid the foundations of a state based
on interpretative ideology it was inevitable that culture and its transmission through the media would assume a position of prime importance.

## Media in the Revolutionary Aftermath

Under a system in which religion and politics are inseparable, culture
is the means by which it is determined who in society wields power and
authority. The constitution refers to issues concerning the media, culture and freedom of expression. In its preamble the fate of the mass
media is delineated in somewhat vague terms that leave it open to the
subjective interpretation/manipulation of those in power: "It must
serve the diffusion of Islamic culture in pursuit of the progressive path
of the Islamic Revolution."[36] In relation to freedom of expression Article 24 reads: "Publications and the press have freedom of expression
except when it is detrimental to the fundamental principles of Islam
or the rights of the public."[37] Again the principles are vague but what
is clear is that in the Islamic Republic, all is subservient to the force
and interests of Islam. Freedom of expression is subject to the ideological interpretation of those in power and must therefore conform to the
government's notions of propriety. The notion of freedom of expression is subject to qualifications and checks and is conditional on the
government's interpretation of Islamic norms and what it deems to be
in the public interest and the interest of Islam.[38] In essence the integral element impeding freedom of expression lies in the conflict and
contradiction between what might be deemed the secular/democratic
and Islamic elements in the constitution; notions such as sovereignty of
the people and the powers of the parliament are subservient to Islam.
In this regard the Constitution of the Islamic Republic pays lip service
to democracy while ensuring the dominance of clerical rule. In other
words the sovereignty of the Islamic jurists takes priority over the sovereignty of the people, the Council of Guardians deprives the parliament
of effective legistlative power, Islamic rules and regulations limit the
rights of the people and the principle of velayat-e faqih puts all final
decisions in the hands of the Supreme Leader, thus repudiating the
existence of a republic.

The enforcement of these new Islamic rules and regulations, and
the imposition of limits on civil society and individual liberty, was clearly
seen in the authorities' swift curtailment of the short-lived period of

unprecedented freedom of expression that occurred in the immediate aftermath of the revolution. The year following the revolution saw the appearance of 444 newspapers and magazines covering all shades of public opinion.[39] However this newfound freedom was not to last very long as the Islamic state began to take hold and the institutional framework was erected by the clergy for the control and governance of all aspects of life. A few years after their appearance fewer than half of these publications remained in existence. In 1981 alone, 175 newspapers were shut down, and by March 1988 the total number of newspapers and periodicals published in Iran was no more than 121. Cinema was somewhat different. The following is a table indicating the number of Iranian films produced per year over a thirty-year span, from 1970 until 1999.

| YEAR | 1970 | 1971 | 1972 | 1973 | 1974 | 1975 | 1976 | 1977 | 1978 | 1979 |
|------|------|------|------|------|------|------|------|------|------|------|
| FILMS | 58 | 82 | 91 | 83 | 59 | 65 | 56 | 43 | 19 | 3 |
| YEAR | 1980 | 1981 | 1982 | 1983 | 1984 | 1985 | 1986 | 1987 | 1988 | 1989 |
| FILMS | 23 | 17 | 22 | 30 | 40 | 40 | 48 | 48 | 42 | 49 |
| YEAR | 1990 | 1991 | 1992 | 1993 | 1994 | 1995 | 1996 | 1997 | 1998 | 1999 |
| FILMS | 42 | 54 | 66 | 50 | 45 | 62 | 63 | 54 | 64 | 46 |

Source: Film International, Tehran: Autumn/Winter, 1999/2000, Vol. 7, No. 2-3, p.6.

The revolution had resulted in the almost total collapse of the Iranian film industry, both artistically and infrastructurally. Cinema was seen by many revolutionaries as representative of the evils of modernization and Western cultural influence implicit in the shah's rule. As mentioned previously it experienced the full wrath of revolutionary zeal, with many cinemas destroyed. Thus the freedom experienced by the press during the immediate post-revolutionary period did not extend to cinema, as financially and infrastructurally it lay in ruins. And such was the uncertainty and fear engendered by the backlash against the film industry that many actors, producers and directors fled the country. Those who remained were unsure as to what was permissible amid the upheavals of the post-revolutionary struggle for power. This is reflected in the themes of the paltry number of films released in the early years following the revolution, which for the most part revolved around stories related to the revolution or moral tales, usually set in a rural setting. Examples from the period 1979-1980 include:

*Faryad-e Mojahed* (*The Cry of a Mojahed*), dir. Mehdi Ma'danian; A religious activist fights against the shah's regime.

*Parvaz Be Su-ye Minu* (*Flight Toward Daisy*), dir. Taqi Keyan Salahshur; A domestic servant is fired for his political sympathies. He decides to become an activist, fighting the shah's regime by kidnapping a member of SAVAK and attacking Evin prison. He is captured and faces a martyr's death by firing squad.

*Samad Be Shahr Miravad* (*Samad Goes to Town*), dir. Parviz Sayyad; The adventures of a simple-minded farmer who goes to town.

*Khiabaniha* (*Street Wanderers*), dir. Mohammad Saffar; The adventures of a group of honest but poor men.*

These films show a certain caution as well as a desire, in certain instances, to celebrate the momentous historical events that had just taken place. But for the most part they were poorly made and propagandist in nature with the overriding principles being the castigation and criticism of the former regime in not unsubtle terms.[40] The result is that of the small number of films produced during this period none seem worthy of mention,[41] and three distinct categories can be discerned from those films produced in the first four years after the revolution: quasi-political movies dealing with the campaign against the shah's regime; films about drug traffickers and drug addiction, used as symbols highlighting the corruption of the former regime; and films with rural settings where peasants revolt against feudal tyranny.[42] These were the early days of an ideological change and self-censorship in a shattered industry, as well as an example of what Ahmad Karimi-Hakkak has called, in relation to post-revolutionary literature, an art form forged out of "political dedication rather than creative impulse" and combined with a "deep-seated ambivalence or uncertainty about what may lie beyond the political present."[43]

Due to the highly centralized nature of the new state the only way for the industry to rebuild was through the investment efforts of the government. This process not only involved infrastructural investment but also institutional and ideological changes, as the new government sought to introduce its specific interpretation of culture in the service of the Islamic state by using a state-controlled modern technological network of communication and entertainment. The first steps toward the institutionalization of cinema had begun as early as March 1980 with the introduction of a number of measures aimed at reviving the domestic film industry. These included the banning of films from Iraq, Pakistan, India and Turkey unless these countries bought Iranian films, and the introduction of a points system from one to four, which allowed Iranian producers to import an equivalent number of foreign films based on the grading that their films received.[44] Ideologically these developments sig-

---

*For a comprehensive list of the films of this period see Bahman Maghsoudlou, *Iranian Cinema*.

naled a desire by the new regime to create a cinema that would be the antithesis of what it considered the decadent pre-revolution cinema, and instead would promote the virtues of Islam and the new state. For the ruling clerics this meant transforming the medium into an Islamic cinema. This transformation became part of the overarching effort of the clergy to Islamicize all aspects of society, and the media was to perform the central task in this respect, for as Ayatollah Khomeini stated, "If radio and television are not Islamicized it means that Iran is not Islamicized."[45]

Toward this end the Islamic government instituted the Farabi Cinema Foundation in 1983 to "streamline and control the import and export of films and to encourage local production."[46] The foundation described its duty as simply being "to make good movies and enhance Iran's cinema industry." In practice, however, it works to project Islamic values and revolutionary ideals through its films. Farabi reflected the tendency within the new state to establish revolutionary foundations controlling various aspects of society in order to create grassroots support for an Islamic regime and to confront the radical opposition to the Islamic Republic. A stringent set of guidelines to control content and promote "Islamic values" was introduced, and the Ministry of Culture and Islamic Guidance was charged with their enforcement. These included: any criticism of Islam was strictly forbidden, women had to wear Islamic dress, males and females were not to be photographed in close proximity to one another in the same shot, and signs of physical affection were totally unacceptable. In this regard the Islamic revolution in film set as its primary concern the maintenance of moral codes. This was a reflection of the larger ideological undertakings by the devotees of Islam to restructure society according to religious mores and in doing so create "a highly puritanical social system where moral and religious imperatives are dictated to the people and direct all their choices."[48]

In the early days of the Islamic Republic there was no relief for non-devotees of the revolution. Dictates were decreed for the establishment of an Islamic society to which art was made to conform. It was placed in the service of the state reflecting and promoting changed ideological/cultural conditions as well as consolidating the position of those in power. The fate of all mass communication has been the same in Iran over the past fifteen years, "a short-lived initial freedom that gave way to long-term strangulation...[in which] the media are either directly censored or they censor themselves."[49] This is a point not lost on the filmmaker Dariush Mehrjui who has worked under both the shahs and the Islamic regime: "For years I have been censoring myself, and it makes you crazy."[50] The government saw cinema and the media in general at the service of those in power and, aware of its potential power, sought to control it with an iron grip. This increased militancy on the part of the government in the cultural arena was a reflection of broader changes occurring in the sociopolitical arena at the time. The clergy, having assumed the reigns of power and laid out their blueprint for the future society in the constitution, now set about consolidating their position by eliminating all forms of opposition and dissent and beginning the first stage of a cultural transformation that would seek to Islamicize all aspects of Iranian society.

## The New Political and Cultural Arena

The constitution had marked the first stage in the Islamic institutionalization of all aspects of society in Iran. Almost sixteen million voters approved of the new constitution giving it a 99.5 percent margin of acceptance.* This represented a major victory for the clerics over the nationalist, liberal-minded intelligentsia, and made the position of Bazargan and his provisional government untenable, resulting in his resignation.† Bazargan was replaced in January 1980 by Abol Hassan Bani Sadr, who was elected the first president of the Islamic Republic.‡ This marked the beginning of a violent phase of internal revolution in which the clergy eliminated all opposition groups and began the political and ideological process of Islamicization. Relying on populist appeal, widespread repression and the brutal force of state coercion, the clergy had, by the summer of 1981, succeeded in gaining absolute control of the country.

To cleanse society of anti-revolutionary currents, the regime developed a vision of the model individual: one who mechanically rejects all that is non-Islamic or un-Islamic through blind faith and total devotion to Islam and to the high-ranking clergy. To achieve a population well-stocked with such people required the purging of those elements and individuals who were deemed un-Islamic or who perpetrated counter-Islamic acts. The main militant opposition to the clergy came in the form of the Mojahedin-e Khalq,§ and they experienced the full wrath of the Islamic state with an unprecedented bout of blood-letting. This campaign of extermination saw the execution of between twenty to thirty thousand of the Mojahedin-e Khalq's members.[51] The new presi-

---

*This figure is somewhat misleading in that the electorate was simply given the option of voting "yes" or "no" to the constitution, meaning that they were either for or against the Islamic Republic with no alternatives being offered.

†Bazargan objected to the principle of velayat-e faqih and the clerical nature of the constitution as a whole and he believed that a document containing some 175 articles could not be put before the people in a referendum in which they were simply asked to vote either "yes" or "no."

‡Abol Hassan Bani Sadr had been one of Ayatollah Khomeini's most trusted advisors and supporters while the latter was exiled in France. He played a key role in the revolution and was the first and only layperson to occupy the presidency of the Islamic Republic. After being ousted from power he was forced to flee the country where he initially joined the exiled leadership of the Mojahedin-e Khalq in opposition to Khomeini's rule.

§The Mojahedin-e Khalq was an organization that evolved out of the religious wing of the National Front in the 1960s. They began a militant campaign against the shah's regime in order to achieve a classless society and to eliminate all forms of oppression, such as imperialism, capitalism, despotism and conservative

dent, Mohammed Ali Rajaee (he had replaced Bani Sadr in the summer of 1981 as the final piece in the clergy's full monopolization of power) reflected the militant environment: "If the realization of Islam and the goals of the Islamic revolution require the sacrifice of our lives then death will become our greatest hope and desire."[52] Ayatollah Khomeini declared that all aspects of life were subordinate to Islam and that this was evident in the establishment of the new state: "It is a Republic of Islam that can implement all purposes. It is a Republic of Islam whose progressive laws are higher than all laws."[53] Ever aware of the threats posed to the Islamic state and the power of the clergy, he saw the Mojahedin-e Khalq as the most dangerous threat to the new state, referring to them as "the *monafeqin* [hypocrites] who want to destroy Islam."[54] He also proclaimed that the "hypocritical and self-righteous members of the outlawed Mojahedin-e Khalq organization and their anti-State elements must be put on trial and suitably punished."[55] However, Khomeini's one-dimensional view of the world, the militancy and dogmatism of his religious beliefs and his intolerance of dissent and opposition paradoxically held within them an adaptability to unfolding sociopolitical events and the complexities of maintaining power. Indeed, far from his stern and unyielding demeanor Khomeini showed himself in power to be less of a dogmatist and more of a pragmatic, opportunistic populist whose behavior was determined "less by spiritual principles than by immediate political, social and economic needs."[56] His uncanny ability to react effectively to the immediate political and social climate is clearly seen in the attempts to implement the official Islamic system of belief.

Khomeini's primary goal was to monopolize power and to consolidate that power by eliminating all forms of opposition in order to instigate his system of clerical rule. Achieved by the use of brutal and repressive means, the imperative was also carried out with the manipulation of the dispossessed and marginalized segments of the population. The foot soldiers of the revolution became, in the post-revolutionary society, the foot soldiers of the clerical regime. They were elevated to positions of power (based on revolutionary credentials rather than suitability or qualifications), from where they acted as the clergy's support base and vengeful executive arm.

Although the Islamic government has shown its expediency and adaptability over the years, the ideological and institutional systems

---

clericalism. By 1976 they had suffered heavy losses against the state and had seemed a spent force. However, following the 1979 revolution, in which they played an active part, they regrouped and became a viable and influential social organization. Opposed to the establishment of a clerical state under a clerical constitution they began to carry out guerilla attacks on members of the Islamic government, killing several hundred of them. The government reacted with extreme severity crushing the movement, with many of its members killed or exiled abroad.

founded in the early and formative post-revolutionary years set the tone and prefigured developments in the decade to come. It was not until 1984 that the atmosphere in the country began to relax as "the revolution and its bloody aftermath were starting to recede in people's minds, and the fervor which had created it was fading fast."[57] But by then the clergy had firmly entrenched their power and established an institutionalized network of control over Iranian society. And once absolute political control had been established the regime's primary concern became the political and ideological Islamicization of the polity. This process attacked on three fronts, the institutional, the educational and through mass communication, in what might be described as Iran's second revolution, the cultural revolution, which would decide the role of cinema and the creation of an Islamic cinema.[58]

However, despite the clergy's monopoly of power they do not present a unified monolithic ideological point of governance, and their beliefs comprise a variety of opinions ranging from conservatism to radicalism and pragmatism. Indeed, these groups and their various ideological positions have defined politics, and therefore all aspects of life, in the Islamic Republic, often to the point of stalemate, crippling the proper functioning of the political system. The central division has emanated from the question on how far the state should involve itself in the economic and social life of the country, and in this latter respect the control of culture is of crucial importance. Khomeini himself acknowledged the existence of ideological conflict but stated that this was permissible as long as certain irrefutable truths were adhered to: "It is clear that if disagreements occur among those who are loyal to the revolution, their differences would be solely political, even though they may take on an ideological form. This is because they all share the same bases and principles and that is why I endorse them all. They are all loyal to Islam, the Qur'an and the revolution." These conflicting opinions, the pragmatic implementation of shifting ideological subsystems, the institutional weapons of the constitution and the concept of velayat-e faqih, create a confliction environment in which state-sponsored and state-approved art is made. The use of force, censorship and other means of state suppression, and the drive to Islamicize all aspects of society, form the critical framework in which Iranian cinema must be considered.

# 3 | A NEW CINEMA EMERGES

It has been an article of faith since the early days of the revolution that whoever controls Iranian culture controls Iranian politics. Khomeini's Iran, based solely on Islamic principles, is as distorted a creation as that which operated during the Pahlavi dynasty, which sought to define the nation mainly by its ancient Persian heritage. Indeed they are mirror images of each other and highlight the fact that Islam and Persia are not mutually exclusive, but are both essential components of Iranian culture. Just as the shah sought to ground his authority to rule in the glories of ancient Persia, the ruling clerics, having failed to deliver on most of the promises of the revolution, have sought to anchor their legitimacy in Islam and its manufactured social manifestations.

This chapter examines the reconstituted cultural forms that emerged under the changed political and ideological conditions of post-revolutionary Iran. For the cinema this included a reappraisal of the medium both formally and thematically, in the official drive to create an "Islamic cinema" that reflected and served the new regime. The historical development of Islamic art, and its unique Persian manifestations, provides the framework with which to interrogate the notion of Islamic cinema and to question it as a radical departure in Iranian cultural forms. It also helps to describe the wider Islamicization project, which the regime undertook in order to create a society obedient to Islam, and with the express purpose of consolidating and perpetuating clerical rule in Iran.

Within these developments we must place and evaluate the early work of Mohsen Makhmalbaf. An ardent advocate of the new Islamic form of cinema, his early work is replete with religious and revolutionary fervor and dedication. This nascent period of his career stretches from 1982 to 1985 and covers four films: *Tobeh Nasuh* (*Nasuh's Repentance*, 1982); *Do Chashme Bi Su* (*Two Sightless Eyes*, 1983); *Este'azeh* (*Fleeing from Evil to God*, 1984); and *Baykot* (*Boycott*, 1985). These early works were the developmental nursery of his cinematic career, for which he was declared the most trusted and respected filmmaker by the new regime. This quartet also offers a body of work that serves as the perfect commentary and trajectory of the progression of the artist, cinema, culture, and the country itself, in the early, formative years of the Islamic Republic.

## Toward an Islamic Cinema

Iranian culture contains a long tradition of spiritual and existential contemplation. Within this tradition "mysticism, the ambiguity of poetry, belief in the many-faced subtlety of evil and the never fully resolved choice between the roles of the selfless devotee have created the great interior spaces in which the Iranian soul has breathed and survived."[1] This is a tradition that has extended from the pre-Islamic belief system of Zoroastrianism* and its concept of light and dark, the preachings of the prophet Mani (274 CE) who proselytized that knowledge was a means of releasing the soul from the evils of the material world, to the Sufi poets like Hafez (1324-1389) and Sa'di (1027-1291), describing a mystical union with God as an individual act akin to intoxication and the coupling of lovers, or the love and hope, death, despair and world-weariness of Omar Khayyam's poetry (1047-1123). A constant element in Iranian art, it has continued up to the present as is seen in the work of such as eminent and celebrated contemporary writers as Sadeq Hedayat (1903-1951) in his wrestling with existential questions of life and death, hopelessness, fear and alienation, or the poetry of Forugh Farrokhzad (1934-1967), which expressed female sexual desire and the search for a personal identity denied by a patriarchal society. Similarly, these elements have manifested themselves in Iranian cinema with the desire of filmmakers to engage with their art form and the world around them in attempting to understand their society and themselves.

To understand the many-layered nature of Iranian culture, and by extension its cinema, means recognizing that it is based on a complex duality arising from a dialectical interaction between a millennia-old Persian culture and that culture's interaction with the heritage of Shia Islam. This is a situation that is further complicated by the role played by culture in legitimating political power and authority in Iran: those who are in power, be they king or cleric, have sought to create and control a vision of this culture in their own image, emphasizing one element to the detriment of the other, resulting in a type of split cultural inertia. With twentieth-century Iran witnessing growing state control over all aspects of civil society, the question of cultural domination has assumed

---

*This was the official state religion of Persia, introduced by the prophet Zoroaster around 1000 BCE. He preached the concept of monotheism, the duality of good and evil, messianic redemption, final judgement, heaven and hell and the idea of a kind, loving and forgiving God. Man's salvation in the afterlife was attained through the practicing of good thoughts, good words and good deeds. Many of these concepts had a profound influence on Judaism, Christianity and Islam.

prime importance and the divisions between both these cultural forms has become more marked. The Pahlavi regime sought to define Iran by the glories of ancient Persia, whereas the Islamic Republic has exalted Islam. Both are incomplete cultural pictures in that each interpretation denies the complex and interlocking nature of two traditions that exist within the Iranian national psyche. The cultural weapon assumes prime importance in the arsenal of a state whose main aim is to socialize people into accepting the legitimacy of state domination. In this sense it can be said to have "greater potency than economic tools because it affects the soul of a community.[2]"

Islamic cinema can be seen to have its origins in the larger historical development of Islamic art (or more specifically, as will become evident, a unique type that can be referred to as Persian-Islamic art), which itself must be placed within the context of the changed post-revolutionary ideological atmosphere and the institutionalization of culture that saw all activity brought under government control, either through legislation, force or censorship.

According to Robert Graham, "Culture is just another tool of the political system in Iran and survives only where it is allied to the system."[3] Under such circumstances culture becomes merely a manipulative plaything for those in power, and as a result, exists in a complete vacuum. Such an analysis, though, tends to ignore the depth of feeling that Iranians have toward their culture, as well as it neglects the Iranian ability to assimilate foreign influences and adapt to changing contexts. This phenomenon arises from the cultural perception that Iranians have of themselves, as they see themselves as the protectors of an ancient culture and as the custodians of the Shia sect of Islam. As a result Iranians consider their culture uniquely rich and different, and experience it with an unusual and deeply felt sensitivity. This sense of difference can be found in the Iranian reaction to the introduction of Islam in the seventh century: "The cultural superiority of the Iranians and their pride in their institutions remained to stamp the cultural and artistic future of Islamic Iran with a character quite different from that of any of the other Muslim countries."[4] This difference is built on the cultural duality of Persia and Islam. The former derives from the legacy of the first Persian empire (550-334 BCE) and its belief and faith in the just ruler, the established monotheism of the Zoroastrian religion, and the art and architecture as evidenced in the ancient city of Persepolis. The challenge to this system came in the seventh century with the arrival of nomadic Arab tribesmen armed with the newly acquired faith of Islam, preaching ideals of unity and equality. Iranians embraced this new religion not as a new set of beliefs that defined all that came before it as polytheistic ignorance but as one that was capable of appealing and conforming to many of their pre-Islamic beliefs, such as justice, equity and tolerance. Unlike others, such as the Egyptian and Mesopotamians, who had their culture and identity subsumed by the Arab conquest, Iranians retained their own language and a deep attachment to their pre-Islamic culture. Indeed, it was this culture that was to eventually conquer the Arabs as Persian art and knowledge formed the basis of the Golden Age of Islamic civilization that flourished between the eighth and eleventh centuries. However, it was not until the Safavid dynasty (1501-1722) and the establishment of Shia Islam as the official state religion that Iranians began to define themselves differently within the Islamic world. The acceptance of Shiism had much to do with the Persian elements inherent in this sect of Islam, which appealed to pre-Islamic traditions like the return of the savior on judgment day and the question of legitimacy and the right to rule. Furthermore, in contrast to the rigidity of Sunni Islam, Iranians imbued Shiism with a spirit of constant theological inquiry, believing that humans are able to engage in the interpretative reasoning of Islamic law and are therefore capable of deciphering and expounding on the tenets of the faith. Such a philosophical approach to religion expressed Iranians fascination with the world of ideas, the spiritual and mystical, and the meaningful ambiguity, allegory and emotion, found in Persian poetry. This entwining of the Persian language and traditions with Islam continued until the nineteenth and twentieth centuries, when Iran met the Christian West. It was here, most vividly exemplified by the revolution, that Persia and Islam began to separate and move to opposing, antagonistic camps, each seeking to deny or exorcise the other's existence in the attempt to wrestle control of the nation by redefining the culture and nature of Iranian-ness. Having defeated the Pahlavis' Persian cultural vision the Islamic Republic set about reclaiming and institutionalizing its version of the Iranian Islamic tradition.

## The Concept of Islamic Art

The notion of an Islamic art is uniquely difficult and problematic to define. Bearing no discernible formal and thematic traits that allow it to be classified generically as belonging to a particular artistic school it is more often defined as the antithesis of Western art, or by general and tacit consensus, the sum total of all art produced by Muslim artists, whether it can be deemed religious or not. This remains a rather simplistic and vague definition of the complex relationship between art and a religion that informs all aspects of spiritual and social life. It is the total order that Islam represents in relation to all planes of physical existence into which Islamic art seeks to insert itself as a sacred and esoteric form of divine expression in the service of God. The central arts of Islam are therefore generally seen as architecture and calligraphy with the former taking pride of place with the building of sanctuaries and places of worship and the latter acting as a perfect decorative geometric accompaniment.[5] These forms emphasize the functionality of art in the service of God and Islam and the unchanging relationship/equilibrium that exists between the artist and his work. The artist is not consumed by individual artistic creation but seeks to transform material, giving meaning and expression to those who use the objects in a spiritual union with the immensity and presence of God. The equilibrium and unchanging nature of this relationship is based on Islamic monotheism, which is the reason why Islamic art avoids certain means of expression such as the depiction of corporeal beings.* In this sense the arts are placed into a hierarchy of functions, defined and operating within the limits of holy scripture, and to be used for the dissemination of Islamic ideology and the expression of religiosity.

The main tenet of Islamic art focuses on the debate concerning the image and its reproduction. Abstract representation and decoration, consisting of arabesque, inscriptional and geometrical elements was the preferred method of representation, in opposition to the figurative forms of Western art.[6] Because God is seen as the sole creator of all things and has prescribed them with perfection, artists operated in a sphere of "religiously motivated Islamic iconoclasm, prohibiting the depiction of creatures—man and beast, who, unlike plants, carry a 'soul.'"[7] In this respect anti-iconography invites "man to fix his mind on something outside himself and project his soul onto an 'individualizing' form." However, no direct reference to image-making can be found in the Qur'an, the closest being allusions to idolatry,† that one who worships an image other than God makes one an unbeliever.[9] It is only in the sayings of the Prophet (*hadith*) that explicit reference is made prohibiting the making of such images and for punishment to be administered to the producers of such images.[10] This absence is perhaps the most striking feature of Islamic art but it is understandable given the contemplative and sacred nature of the art form. Indeed it was these notions and the refinement and development of the various arts such as calligraphy and architecture, which had been practiced and refined in Iran for many years, that found unique expression as Islam encountered the ancient arts of Persia and the art forms entered a golden age of civilization.

---

*Contrary to popular misconception, however, figural imagery is an important aspect of Islamic art. Such images occur primarily in secular and especially courtly arts and appear in a wide variety of media and in most periods and places in which Islam flourished. It is important to note, nevertheless, that representational imagery is almost invariably restricted to a private context. Figurative art is excluded from the decoration of religious monuments. This absence may be attributed to an Islamic antipathy toward anything that might be mistaken for idols or idolatry, which are explicitly forbidden by the Qur'an. "Introduction" to Islamic Art, Los Angeles County Museum of Art, http://www.lacma.org/islamic_art/intro.htm

†These are to be found in: Sura 2: 105; 135; Sura 4: 48; 51; 76; 116; Sura 5: 60; 82; Sura 6: 138; Sura 9: 1-17; 28; 36; 113; Sura 22: 17; Sura 35: 14; 40; Sura 48: 6. *The Koran*, translated by M. M. Pickthal.

## Persia and Islam, the Golden Age

It is worth noting that the coming of Islam did not immediately supplant the Persian pre-Islamic style of architecture that had managed to maintain a distinct character throughout the ages "in spite of the influx of large new population groups, of great historical upheavals and change of religions."[11] The merging of Persian and Arab ingredients resulted in the redefining and refining of the nature and basic architectural forms of the pre-Islamic ceremonial tombs and grand palaces of the former Achaemenid (550-334 BCE) and Sasanian (224-642 CE) rulers, replacing them with mosques that served as the focal point of the new religion. These new religious buildings were imbued with the Persian characteristics of precision, clarity and lucidity combined with a simplicity of construction offset by a lavish use of surface ornamentation and color. The Islamic ban on human representation meant that the corporeal representations of kings, soldiers and animals, found on many of the pre-Islamic bas-reliefs, tombs and palaces fell from favor and were replaced by non-representational forms such as calligraphy.

However, this did not mark a dramatic and abrupt shift from Persian architectural forms, as decoration in the form of mosaics and frescos were common and had become highly developed during the Sasanian period. This meant that it was in essence a perfect form and mode of expression in representing the glories of the new religion. Furthermore, the development of Iranian art exhibits a slow, steady stylistic progression, based more on the addition of layers and nuance than any abrupt changes in style. This is the reason why there is no dramatic break between pre-Islamic and Islamic art in Iran. The architectural style used to build the temples and palaces of the pre-Islamic period mixed with Islamic influences to produce a style that emphasized balance and scale and which was marked by a simple structural form (consisting of a courtyard and arcades, a lofty entrance portico and four *iwans*, or barrel-vaulted halls opening onto the courtyard) combined with lavish use of surface ornamentation and color. This combination of different elements into new cultural and artistic forms also reveals the age-old Persian ability to assimilate elements of foreign culture and to adapt them to their own specific needs or tastes.

Furthermore, the individualism and difference felt by Iranians in the face of their Arab invaders, who viewed all non-Arabs as inferior, drew them toward Shia Islam, which they felt held within it elements closer to the historical traditions of Persia and the deeply felt notions of Iranian nationalism, identity and cultural difference. Thus, assimilation was counterbalanced by the individualism and difference which was expressed in the desire to reflect, revive and make known the national and cultural identities that made Persians distinct from the bearers of the new religion. In cultural terms this conflict manifested itself within the *shuubiyah* movement.* Exemplified in the literature of the time, this movement focused on the merits and superiority of Persian cultural traditions over those of the Arabs, a debate that was to continue among Iranian intellectuals in the twentieth century. Perhaps the quintessential example of shuubiyah expression lay in the famous Iranian poet Ferdowsi's epic poem *Shahnameh*† (*Book of Kings*) where, at the poem's end, he chronicles the conflict between pre-Islamic Iranian identity and the Arab Muslims foreign beliefs,§ as in this lament uttered by a Persian general facing the oncoming Arab army:

> But for the Persians I will weep, and for
> The house of Sasan ruined by this war:
> Alas for their great crown and throne, for all
> The royal splendor, destined now to fall,
> To be fragmented by the Arabs' might....[13]

The ability to maintain this sense of identity and difference lay in the unique reverence and hallowed position that Iranians devote to poetry. At its core poetry, whether epic, lyrical or simple quatrains,** has defined national cultural and historical identity. Persian poetry provided and gave expression to the ambiguity of Persian culture and was a unique manifestation of an intense emotional intimacy in defining Iran and its relationship with Islam. In this regard Persian poetry while not

---

*The *shuubiya* movement emerged in the tenth century as the Persians sought to assert their own cultural identity against Arab-dominated Islam. Disparate groups of intellectuals, who discussed the merits of Persian over Arabic cultural traditions as well as Persia's place within the Islamic Empire, took the revitalized Persian language as the basis of their cultural awakening. With the coming of Islam, Middle Persian, referred to as Pahlavi, had been replaced by Arabic as the language of administration and culture. However, in the ninth century Pahlavi, which had remained in use primarily among the uneducated and the dying Zoroastrian priesthood, combined with the Arabic script to produce what has become the modern-day Persian language. The survival of Persian culture depended on the survival of the Persian language, and this was reflected in the work of poets such as Daqiqi, Rudaki, and most famously Ferdowsi, a devout defender of Persian national identity who is considered the savior of the Persian language with his epic, the *Shahnameh*.

†The *Shahnameh* is an epic poem containing over fifty thousand lines that took thirty-five years to write. It covers one thousand years of Iranian history from the genesis of the world right up to the invasion of Islam. Combining myth, fact and lore the poet poured the whole history of Iran into a long hymn to valor, wisdom, bravery and patriotism. The sweep and psychological depth of the Shahnameh is magnificent, covering moments of national triumph and failure, human courage and cruelty, blissful love and bitter grief. The Shahnameh is "nothing less than the history of the country and its people from the creation of the world up to the Arab conquest...the one indisputably great surviving cultural artifact that attempts to assert a continuity of collective memory across the moment of conquest; at the least it salvaged the pre-conquest legendary history of Iran and made it available to the Iranian people as a memorial of a great and distinctive civilization." Dick Davis, *Shahnameh: Persian Book of Kings*. See Davis' masterful translation of Ferdowsi's epic, the most complete version available in English.

§This conflict of cultures is a constant strand and preoccupation in Iranian intellectual thought throughout the centuries continuing until the twentieth century with the writings of such scholars as Shariati, Jalal Al-e Ahmad, and with Ayatollah Khomeini's famous declaration of "Neither East nor West."

**These quatrains, written by poets like Omar Khayyam, were made of *do-bayti* ("two-liners") which in combination comprised the more well known *rubai* (plural *rubaiyat*), and composed in a rhyme scheme of AABA, occasionally AAAA. With lines of varying length and prosody, the longer lines contained internal rhyme.

totally un-Islamic in character was not entirely Islamic either. This ambiguity gave rise to a form of poetic expression that found in the mysticism and spirituality of Sufism the ability to express these contrasting elements while at the same time appealing to the Iranian sense of historical difference that deepened after the invasion by the Arabs, whose customs and traditions the Iranians held in contempt.*

The place of Persian poetry, and in particular the *ghazal*† is of particular importance in relation to the development of the post-revolutionary "quality" cinema. Traditionally the ghazal deals with themes of love, ecstasy, freedom, humanity and sympathy for the problems of the ordinary man. The giant of this form is the poet Hafez, whose most famous work, *The Divan*, attempts to reflect the universality of the everyday in the search for the reality and love of God. This was not a search conducted within the restraints of conventional religion but derived from the freedom of a personal union with God in which God is seen as inherent in creation rather than transcending it. Indeed, a defining element in much Persian poetry is its ambiguity and the interplay between the spiritual and material worlds, which offers the reader multiple meanings built on an enigma that is ultimately unsolvable. This reflected the desire to achieve a personal and passionate union with the divine through a simultaneous detachment from the material world and the practice of sensual spirituality. Sufism allowed for the expression of Iranian difference within the rule-bound logic of Islam. It also allowed for the expression of certain themes, such as the futility of life in the face of inevitable death or the absurdity of man's existence in an inexplicable world, found in the pre-Islamic belief system and which were in contradistinction to the Islamic belief in God as man's raison d'être. Indeed, as will be shown, structurally and thematically, much Iranian cinema operates within the legacy of Persian poetry in its depiction of an ambiguity that encompasses a search for self and cultural identity located in a material and spiritual world of multifaceted metaphors, allegories and symbols. Films such as Makmalbaf's *Gabbeh* (1996) or Rakhshan Bani-Etemad's *The May Lady* (1998) exhibit many of these poetic attributes in creating complex inner tensions while at the same time serving as an affront to the monotheistic vision of the Islamic Republic by rendering Iranian culture and its representation as a contested and discordant space.[14] Filmmakers have looked to this poetic genealogy and sought to express it explicitly, as Abbas Kiarostami did in *The Wind Will Carry Us*

---

*This was a form of mysticism within Islam that appeared among devout ascetics during the Umayyad caliphate (660-750) as a reaction to the perceived worldliness and corruption of the ruling elite. Its central tenet is the rejection of materialism in the pursuit of a personal spiritual union with God through the hidden meanings held in the words of the faith.

The ghazal is a lyric poem of six to fifteen couplets linked by unity of thought and symbolism rather than a logical sequence of ideas. See Annemarie Schimmel, "Poetry and Calligraphy: Thoughts about Their Interrelation in Persian Culture" in *Highlights of Persian Art*.

(1999), which uses the poetry of Forugh Farrokhzad, or implicitly, as in Makhmalbaf's allusions to Omar Khayyam in *The Silence* (1998), in order to use an indigenous and readily identifiable cultural form that reflects the complexities of Iranian culture while at the same time standing as a bulwark against those who enforce a dominating, restrictive vision of official culture. These age-old tensions, arising from the clash of Persia and Islam have fostered a Persian-Islamic art form that sought to challenge absolutist depictions of Iranian culture. But how has this tension between Persia and Islam manifested itself under the strict ideological controls of the Islamic Republic, which has attempted to depict Iranian culture in purely Islamic terms?

### Islam, Representation and the Cinematic Image

The Islamic prohibition on image-making was never strictly adhered to in the case of cinema, a phenomenon exaggerated in Iran by the existence of an expressive Persian cultural influence. In fact, acceptance of the photographic image can be found within the rubric of religious justification. In this context the filmic image is seen as a sign and not a creation by virtue of the fact that it lacks spatial characteristics and therefore does not impart a soul to things. This precedent is set by a hadith: "Angels do not enter a house where an image is stored except if it is a sign on fabric" which justifies "photography, and in the same way, 'moving images,' as a shadow, reinforcing the power of God, the creator, rather than competing with it."[15] Rather, religious resistance to cinema arose in relation to issues of morality.

During and since the revolution the media was used by Islamic clerics to achieve their goals while at the same time held up as a signifier of the ills of the ancien régime and its excessive modernization and Western influence. The following statement by Ayatollah Khomeini is a telling revelation of that contradiction, and also outlines the media's role in the Islamic Republic, as part of the complete ideological transformation and Islamicization of all aspects of society which began to speed up with the closing of universities and colleges in the summer of 1980:

> Radio and television...have lawful intellectual benefits from the point of view of Islam. Their lawful benefits are acceptable such as news and the sermons over the radio and showing lawful things for education, or the showing of articles and aquatic and terrestrial wonders of creation on television. However, unlawful things such as the broadcast of songs and music and propagation of such unlawful things as counter-Islamic laws and the extolling of a traitor and a tyrant and spreading the voids and the presentation of those things which corrupt a society's morals and shakes their beliefs are unlawful and [it] is a sin.[16]

At issue here is the creation and definition of all aspects of society in Islamic terms. This necessitated a complete overhaul of the education system and the revision of history in order to reinforce the legitimacy of the new regime. The government began to control the propagation of historical truth "to give itself populistic as well as religious legitimacy," to isolate and marginalize its opponents and "to reduce complex ideological issues to simple personality conflicts in which one side epitomizes goodness, the other wickedness."[17] The universities, long seen as a hotbed of political protest and secular and oppositional ideologies, were identified as the primary targets of the Islamicization process and were submitted to a process of ideological restructuring that became known as the *Jihad-e Daneshgahi* (University Crusade). At the basic level this process disregarded Iran's pre-Islamic past and glorified its Islamic heritage, and sought to replace all Western values and culture with their Islamic counterparts.[18] In essence this reflected the attempt to apply the political-ideological orientation of the Khomeini regime to the arena of education with the express purpose of creating obedient Islamic citizens. Its main aims were: strengthening students' beliefs with respect to the basic theological tenets of Twelver Shia Islam; the promotion of sacred values like the family, Islamic brotherhood, socioeconomic justice, respect for the law, and the virtues of education; the promotion of ideas such as pan-Islamism and political independence, strengthening the nation's defense capabilities through military training on campuses; sparking a spirit of investigation and innovation in scientific as well as cultural and Islamic fields.[19]

In order to implement this system school textbooks were rewritten reflecting the ideological orientation of the new regime. The pre-revolutionary textbooks depicted politics as distinct from religion, economics as the development of modern values and institutions in tune with Western scientific and cultural development. By contrast the Islamic Republic's pedagogical emphasis decreed that religion and politics were conjoined, economics was taught in relation to concepts of justice and equality, and history emphasized the role of the clergy and preached a strong anti-imperialist message.[20] This resulted in the systematic transformation of education into an instrument charged with the replication of official thought patterns at all levels of institutional learning. Particular attention was paid, firstly, to teaching students "the main religious principles and the ideal pattern of state-citizen relation," before moving on to more complicated notions such as "the concept of velayat-e faqih and the overall leadership role of the clergy," and finally emphasizing "the basic foreign policy orientation of the Islamic Republic," which usually involved castigation of the West.[21] The result of this policy was that, by the time the government started incrementally to reopen schools and universities in October 1981, the education system was infrastructurally and intellectually devastated. The ideological purges had seen more than sixty thousand teachers lose their jobs because of their political beliefs[22] (the seriousness of which was further heightened by the post-revolutionary population explosion), an overall lowering of the quality of education, and had succeeded in creating a system in which students were rewarded according to revolutionary and Islamic credentials rather than academic merit. Similarly the regime began to use the media as the prime means of disseminating and propounding its ideological message in the Islamicization of the country and as a bulwark against the perceived dangers of a Western cultural invasion. This is an issue that has remained a constant concern for the leaders of the Islamic Republic and one, given the proliferation of satellite broadcasting and the uncontrollable environment of the internet, that has become more pressing as the present Supreme Leader, Ayatollah Khamenei, has expressed: "The enemy carries out its cultural onslaught against the Islamic Republic of Iran in an organized way. If our response is not organized, the danger of the enemy's onslaught increases. Therefore, this issue must be addressed seriously and all component bodies must cooperate and use various methods to neutralize the cultural onslaught of the enemy."[23] One of the leading elements in this drive to propagate Islamic ideology and counteract the perceived hostility of Western culture was the Islamic restructuring of the domestic film industry.

### The First Step Toward a New Cinema

The first step toward an Islamic (or more accurately an Islamicized) cinema was to bring all aspects of the medium under government control. This meant institutionalizing all facets of the filmmaking process, including issues of creativity and artistic freedom. Article 175 of the constitution calls on the Islamic Republic's Radio and Television Service to disseminate and observe Islamic norms and work in the service of the country's interests.[24] Toward this end the 1981 Censorship Act laid down the boundaries of what was permissible under the new system. The legislation essentially forbade the depiction of romantic relationships or physical contact between male and female characters/ actors, music and dance were banned, women had to adhere to an Islamic dress code (*hejab*) on screen and any shots depicting the curvature of their bodies or of a sexual nature were strictly outlawed. Other regulations prohibited any material that subverted or insulted Islam, the Islamic Republic, or the principles of velayat-e faqih, the Leadership Council or qualified mojtaheds.* In July 1982 the Majles ratified a

---

*In 1993 the government publicly released a full list of regulations governing film content. This was reproduced in the Iranian journal *Film*, March/April 1993: 41, and appeared in translated form in *Middle East Watch*, August 1993: 30-31.

general "Guideline to Govern the Policies of the Iranian National Radio and Television," which sought to legalize the doctrines of Ayatollah Khomeini with respect to the operation of the mass media. According to this directive the precepts of Islam govern all programming and the media is to adhere to and promote the principles of independence, freedom and the Islamic Republic, as well as giving "widespread expression to the ideas of the jurist/leader, that is Ayatollah Khomeini, and his constitutional successors."[15] Thus, the legally established function of the media was the propagation of the ideological, political, social and cultural objectives of the new Islamic state.

Overall responsibility for the film industry in Iran fell under the auspices of the Ministry of Culture and Islamic Guidance, which was charged with the enforcement and regulation of government policy and the centralization of state control. They in turn established the Farabi Cinema Foundation in 1983 to control local film production. Founded as a semi-autonomous group with government assistance, its members, "who combined their concern for the endangered art of film with impeccable Muslim credentials,"[26] proclaimed its task as "setting the parameters of cinematic activities...to provide opportunities and filmmaking equipment, take on the role of leasing out film supplies, and offer financial credit."[27] It has basically been through the efforts of Farabi that the domestic film industry was revived and its reputation enhanced, especially through its aggressive marketing in international festivals. But in reality Farabi acts as the government's arm for controlling the cinema industry in Iran and maintaining its Islamic character. The Foundation for the Oppressed, an autonomous religious foundation established by Khomeini as a charitable institution to look after the needs of the poor, also involved itself in cinema.* Until the 1990s it was the largest owner of theaters in the country and produced a significant number of films in the 1980s, including Makhmalbaf's *The Cyclist* (1989). Another public institution that became involved in film production was the Arts Center of the Islamic Propaganda Organization. They were primarily concerned with promoting war films and those that extolled the virtues of the Islamic regime. The Arts Center was also responsible for financing a number of Makhmalbaf's early films: *Nasuh's Repentance,* (1982), *Two Sightless Eyes* (1983), and *Boycott* (1985). In addition to these institutions the Ministry of Culture and Islamic Guidance established a proliferation of councils charged with the supervision, production and censorship of film:

---

*This largest of the foundations (*bonyads*) set up after the revolution to promote economic justice it was originally charged with the task of managing the land, assets and property of the shah's Pahlavi Foundation. The Foundation for the Oppressed now controls an estimated twelve billion dollars in assets and touches most aspects of economic life in Iran, owning global shipping lines, chemical plants, construction factories, hotels, apartments and soft drink companies. It is among the biggest economic complexes in the Middle East operating as a huge state-protected, tax-exempt institution.

1. The Council of Screenplay Inspection is responsible for reviewing and approving a submitted short synopsis of the screenplay of the proposed film. If this is approved it is then passed to the,

2. Council for Issuing a Production Permit. The director must submit a full working version of the completed script to the council for approval. Furthermore, a full list of cast and crew must also be submitted to the council before a production permit can be issued and shooting can begin.

3. The Council of Film Reviewing. This council reviews the completed film and has the power to reject, accept or require modifications to be made. If the film is finally approved the council awards it a viewing permit according to a four-grade system (A, B, C or D). In essence this system acts as a final, subtle means of censorship in that "grading is based largely on an assessment of what is aesthetically valid and ideologically correct rather than on any objective quality standard."[28] The grade that a film receives determines the exposure it will receive, its access to advertising resources and promotion, and its ticket price.

An example of this last form of surreptitious censorship can be seen in the case of the veteran director Bahram Bayzai's* film *Bashu, the Little Stranger* (1986). The film tells the story of a single mother in rural northern Iran who takes in a young boy from the south who has escaped the Iraqi war after seeing his family killed. The film was banned in Iran until 1990 for what was deemed its anti-war message. However, a more plausible explanation could be seen to lie in Bayzai's focus on aspects of Persian rather than Islamic culture, his strong female characters and his compassionate desire to reflect the ethnic and linguistic diversity of Iran, all of which have been constant elements in his work throughout his career. After the war with Iraq, desire to reflect a more liberal society, and the film's critical acclaim abroad,† finally allowed it onto Iranian screens. However, a low-grade rating gave the film poor exposure and allowed Farabi to declare that it was a financial failure in the main urban center of Tehran.[29]

Finally, films that have received official approval and made it to the screen may have their showings terminated in response to criticism from the government-affiliated press. Two of Mohsen Makhmalbaf's films, *Time of Love* (1991) and *Nights of the Zayandeh-Rud* (1991), were banned following protests by the main government newspapers, *Kayhan, Resalat, Jomhouri-ye Islami* and *Arbar,* at the Ninth Fajr Film Festival in Tehran,

---

*Bayzai is one of Iran's most accomplished film directors. Emerging from the vanguard of the 1960s he was, and continues to be, active in the fields of literature and theater, publishing some twenty plays before directing his first feature film in 1971. A committed approach to reflecting the social and political problems affecting Iran has meant that Bayzai's work has encountered problems with the authorities from both the Pahlavi and Islamic regimes.

†It received the First Prize at the Festival of "Art et Essai" Films for Children in Aubervilles, France, in 1990.

which attacked these films for their frank depiction of human love and what were perceived to be its attack on Islamic values (see Chapter 5). Such was the influence of this centralized and censorial apparatus that in the first four years after the revolution a total of forty films were made, of which twenty-three were banned by the authorities.[30]

## The "Islamic Man"

The Islamicization process was an undertaking by the ruling clergy to create a new society subordinate to their authority and, through the elimination of all oppositional ideologies and discourses, to submit all aspects of life in Iran to an Islamic conformity for the purpose of consolidating power. This Islamic ideology "substituted for the secular and nationalist ideas of previous decades a new ideology, that of Islamic revolution."[31] However, it was simply not enough to Islamicize the institutional and organizational apparatus of the state. These changes, if they were to have a meaningful impact and effect real socialization, would have to extend to the level of the psychology of the individual. In other words, the Islamic Republic required servile Islamic citizens.

In order to transform the populace into a subservient reflection of the clerical system the regime conceived the notion of *Homo islamicus*,[32] whose defining characteristics were an "absolute submission to the will of God as communicated by the velayat-e faqih."[33] This drive to create the Islamic man and elevate him to a new level of consciousness bears comparison to similar undertakings in other revolutionary societies.* The Cuban revolution sought to create a new man from a strong sense of morality and social consciousness, putting revolutionary ideals into practice in order to effect a spiritual rebirth that would free man from alienation through the dignity and liberty of labor.† In this respect the Cuban revolution was attempting to create a new citizen and society through an imported ideological system, socialism, previously alien to Cuban society. However, the fundamental difference in the case of revolutionary Iran lay in the fact that the new society, and by extension the creation of the new Islamic Man, was being built on a reappraisal of a familiar indigenous cultural form, Islam, which was some fourteen hundred years old and deeply embedded in the consciousness of the people. This, bolstered by the absence of oppositional voices and the complete monopolization of the media, allowed for the identifiable dissemination of this cultural form to the majority of the population. The cinematic manifestation of this Islamic culture led to the promotion

---

*I use the term "man" to highlight the fact that this socialization process and its cultural manifestation through Shia symbolism emanated from a patriarchal perspective that addressed men primarily. Furthermore, it serves to highlight the fact that the imposition of clerical culture was appropriated differently according to gender.

†For further elaboration on this point see Che Guevara, "Notes on Man and Socialism in Cuba," *Che Guevara Speaks: Selected Speeches and Writings*, 121-139.

and proliferation of a worldview that centered on the individual and virtuous Muslim male standing firm against corruption and promoted an ascetic philosophy of life built on the value of sacrifice and martyrdom (particularly in the war films that emerged during the conflict with Iraq) in the service of God and Islam.

Psychologically-rounded characterizations were jettisoned in favor of one-dimensional characters who merely served as mouthpieces for the Islamic regime. Through tight official control and the codes of censorship, cinema was employed as a means of socializing the populace along officially sanctioned Islamic lines. In other words art, personal expression and the ability to explore the panorama of Iranian culture became subjugated to the promotion of clerical ideology rather than a means of freely expressing aesthetic concerns or attempting to understand the complexities of life, society and the human condition. Makhmalbaf, as a zealous advocate of the new regime, sought in his early work to place his art at the service of promoting the new ideology. His early films are thus very much concerned with the creation and promotion of the virtuous Islamic man and are therefore part of the drive to create an "Islamic cinema" for the socialization of the population.

### An Islamic Quartet: *Nasuh's Repentance, Two Sightless Eyes, Fleeing from Evil to God* and *Boycott*

Makhmalbaf's early films are works of a devout religious and revolutionary zealot with an ardent belief in the righteousness of Islamic ideology and the ethos of the new theocratic regime. Produced under the auspices of the Islamic Propaganda Organization, whose proclaimed objectives were "presenting Islamic ideology through artistic media and challenging artists whose ideas and modes of expression are not harmonious with those of the organization,"[34] these films are uncompromising, propagandist and ideologically committed to the perpetuation of the Islamic Republic. As works of art they are extremely wanting, on just about every level—plot, mise en scéne, acting, montage and overall conception. Stylistically they resemble a series of interconnected talking heads expounding official ideology and a Manichean view of the world, in a tone that is pedantic, moralistic and sermonizing, and in which the message is more important than the medium. Aware of these shortcomings, Makhmalbaf has spoken of his early works as "aridly religious," governed by prejudice and chiefly concerned with moral and political issues: "These first works were very much influenced by my religious beliefs then, and they are clearly the works of a person without a background in film."[35] Despite the fact that these films may be artistically risible, they are extremely important elements of the ideological debate structuring the cultural and political undertakings of the new regime and its efforts to create and implement its vision of a new society. Furthermore, they serve as referential interventions in these debates and examples of a centrally controlled propagandist media in the service of a state socializing the populace along correct Islamic lines. Makhmalbaf's early films bear many similarities to the thoughts of Ayatollah Khomeini and Ayatollah Motahari in their creation of the Islamic man and a just society. Indeed, all three films are simplistic and dogmatic treatises exhorting man to follow a path to God.

*Nasuh's Repentance* is based on one man's attempt to atone for the misdeeds of his past and his subsequent search for forgiveness.* *Two Sightless Eyes* shows the righteous man's faith in God rewarded with a miraculous intervention that cures his ill son. *Fleeing from Evil to God* tells the story of five men in search of salvation and victory over the temptations of the body. Satan manages to deceive four of them but the fifth, a true believer, survives and achieves purity.†

## Cinema in the Name of God the Compassionate, the Merciful—the Path to God

The path to God is depicted in these films not merely as spiritual or religious action but as a revolutionary discourse based on doctrinal and ideological teachings directed toward the needs of the historical moment in instigating and guiding sociopolitical change. The framework for this socialization/Islamicization process resides in the notion of the individual journey along the path to perfection. The conversion of the individual forms the first part of a greater undertaking in accomplishing social and political change: "We cannot change our country unless we reform ourselves. If you want your country to be independent begin with yourself."[36] Within the context of a religious revolutionary discourse and the aim of placing art at the service of proclaiming the virtues of the new regime Makmalbaf's early films polemicize the path to perfection. Taken together, his first three films are structured as a journey in which the main characters search for meaning in a relationship with God that changes them as individuals and provides the first step in changing society. In this respect the path is portrayed as a form of personal jihad that serves the Islamic Republic and draws the individual closer to God. This journey involves forsaking the domain of human limitations and moving toward God in the search for truth. In doing so, the individual learns from God the concepts of love, anger and compassion, as well as the ability to witness them in other people. Having

---

*The script for this film was adapted from the writings of Ayatollah Motahari and Ayatollah Dastgheyb. The latter was the Friday mosque speaker in Shiraz who, during the height of the revolution, called on religious devotees to destroy the ancient ruins of Persepolis, deeming them un-Islamic. He is also remembered for his pronouncements on sexual matters.

†The scenario for this film was taken from Majlesi's seventeenth-century encyclopedia of Shia Islam, *Bahar al-Anwar*.

witnessed the omnipotence of God the final part of the individual's transformation lies in taking the message of God to others, directing them on the path to perfection, with a view to changing the basis and structure of society through the creation of a community of believers.

The thematic progression of Makhmalbaf's three early films, and the position of the revolutionary cinema itself, functions as a type of culturally manifested spiritual guide marking the path to perfection. In *Nasuh's Repentance* the approach to God is evident in the main character's spiritual rebirth and realization that forgiveness comes from God, not man, following the Qur'anic dictate, "But whoso repenteth after his wrongdoing and amendth, Lo! Allah will relent toward him. Lo! Allah is forgiving, merciful."[37] Having received forgiveness and having witnessed the compassion of God he dedicates himself to the service of the Islamic Republic and spreading God's message. *Two Sightless Eyes* portrays the drama of man in the presence of the compassion and love of God, who rewards the faith of the righteous man by revealing his mysteries in the form of a miracle. *Fleeing from Evil to God* shows a virtuous man, having survived Satanic temptation through his faith, return to preach the message of this newfound faith to his community.

Exhorting man to individual change predicated on a knowledge and reunion with the mysteries of God would seem to suggest the existence of free will in attaining a personal, unmediated union with the almighty. The mystical philosophy of *irfan*, "which encompasses the possibility of unity with the divine one and universal self" gives credence to the potential for human perfection in God.[38] However, the "attribution to man of an active—though implicit—agency of an instrumental role in the outcome of a dialectical opposition between the possibilities of Good and Evil"[39] offers a point of conflict with the all-encompassing ideology of the Islamic Republic (particularly the cornerstone of the regime, the concept of velayat-e faqih). Agency or expression of free will are tempered by limitations, and can act as only one of many factors in social and political transformation, which, in Iran, are designed and directed by the clerical rulers. The free will possessed by man, then, is mediated as the path to perfection and only made known to the individual through the intervention and guidance of the *ulama*, the body of learned clerics. The Constitution of the Islamic Republic makes this point clear: "The exalted dignity and worth of the human being and its freedom accompanied with its responsibility"[40] is based on "continuous *ijithad* [exercise of reason in interpreting Islamic law] by qualified jurists on the basis of the Qur'an."[41] The high-ranking clergy are the vice regents of God on earth, imparting and translating God's mysteries to the people. In other words, it is the necessity of the political agenda and the expediency of the historical moment, as determined by these clerics, that act as limitations and disclaimers to any notions of unbridled free will. Motahari, one of the theoretical architects of this societal construct, delineates these restrictions, declaring, "Man must know his own limitations and weaknesses to know how great God is," and it is the ability of human beings to construct themselves through such self-knowledge "which enables them to shape their future and that of society."[42] Thus the Islamic revolutionary man is located in a mythological definition of the world derived from the word of God as laid down in the Qur'an and interpreted by vice regents on earth: "He hath placed you as viceroys of the earth and hath exalted some of you in rank above others, that he may try you by (the test of) that which He hath given you."[43] What this means in the institutional theocracy of the Islamic Republic is deference to the figure of the faqih and the ulama and that human free will is free will in the service of the state, as arbitrated by the faqih and ulama.

*Nasuh's Repentance* and *Two Sightless Eyes* exemplify the call to submit to the will of the revolution and Islamic Republic. In the former, Loft Ali Khan's search for forgiveness from one of his neighbors is rebuffed with the imperative, "You should not be asking for my forgiveness, you should be asking yourself, 'Have I done my duty to Khomeini, have I done my duty to Iran?'" He eventually achieves salvation by submitting to the religious guidance of a cleric and service at his local mosque, where his son, having devoted his life to the revolution and the subsequent war, provides an example of the righteous man. Similarly in *Two Sightless Eyes* it is the righteous man, in this instance contrasted with an unprincipled leftist teacher and a greedy merchant, who, having given his son to the cause of the Islamic Republic in the war with Iraq, is the recipient of God's blessing, a cure for his blind child. In this way the cinema conveys official ideology through a mixed message of individual action exhorted by a Qur'anic authority and directed by the clergy. Makhmalbaf's early work attempted to transmit religious authority and ideology into a collective political force that could be harnessed for revolutionary purposes. But propagating this message called for a delicate balancing act in making them Islamically viable and historically relevant while navigating the contentious notions of free will and collective responsibility. And these notions were built on a myth that promoted a false view of human action: the freedom of the individual to change oneself through God and the consequent ability to alter actively the course of history. This, though, belies a contradiction between submitting oneself to the eternal truth of God and to the will of his supposed vice regents on earth, the clergy, for it is only they who are capable of leading the people to the promised land. For the clergy this promised land is the Islamic Republic whose perpetuation and legitimacy is incumbent on informing the people of their collective duty to ensure its survival. The clear and hypocritical contradiction between free will and submission sits at the heart of the notion of the Islamic man, and it would be explored and challenged by Makhmalbaf in later films.

## Boycott

*Boycott* (1985) stands as the most accomplished film of Makhmalbaf's Islamic period. Despite being deeply committed to the ideals of the Islamic regime, and reflecting official historical and ideological perspectives, the film exhibits certain elements of doubt regarding the belief in an absolute politics or ideology, and begins to suspect their role in the destruction and depersonalization of the individual. However, the main aim of the film is to attack those, in particular the Left, perceived to be enemies of the state and Islam. In this respect, despite being set in the clandestine world of pre-revolutionary opposition to the shah, it draws comparison to the reign of terror conducted against the Left, especially the Mojahedin-e Khalq-e Iran, in the immediate years after the revolution, and as such acts as a form of official propaganda. Within the generic codes of Islamic cinema *Boycott* can be classified as a "crime does not pay" film, attacking not just the villainy of the former regime, but also those now deemed enemies of the Islamic Republic. Furthermore, the film's historical revisionism reveal cracks and gaps that allow for the possibility of a reading that casts doubt on the new regime's methodology in enforcing ideological conformity and control.

### Islamicization and the Attack on the Left

Set in the years before the 1979 revolution, *Boycott* tells the story of Valeh, a young anti-shah activist who forsakes his family for the cause of leftist politics. His arrest and imprisonment cause great hardship on his wife. Valeh's acquaintance with his Marxist colleagues in jail forces him to rethink his ideology, which he renounces before being taken away and executed by the authorities.

The campaign waged by the Islamic regime against the "corrupting influence" and "treachery"[44] of Marxist thought marked the final stage in the clerics' total control of power. The assumption and consolidation of this power was achieved through both propaganda and harsh repressive measures, to rid the state of the last voices of opposition to clerical rule. In the period initially following the revolution many parties and organizations of the Left, including the Tudeh (Iranian Communist Party) and the Mojahedin, supported the new Islamic regime on the basis of its radical agenda and anti-imperialism. But once it became clear that the new regime was more concerned with the foundation of a theocratic state and subsequent cultural revolution, (rather than demanding a reappraisal of the ownership and means of production, or the establishment of democratic institutions) support turned to opposition and this opposition was met with repression. This took the form of violent mass arrests and executions as well as the deployment of the media in a propaganda campaign that attempted to vilify the Left and erase them from history. In his ambition for absolute power Khomeini revised history to extirpate the Left's contribution in bringing about the fall of the shah, declaring that, "[The Left] did not contribute anything. They did not help the revolution at all.... They were not decisive in the victory, they were not responsible, they did not contribute anything.... The people fought for Islam."[45] Other religious leaders like Ayatollah Golpayegani declared the Left to be the most dangerous threat to Islam and warned people to be on the lookout for atheistic communists pretending to be revolutionary Muslims.[46] This onslaught continued in the media and through Revolutionary Tribunals, which in one case blamed Marxists for causing the notorious 1978 fire in the Rex cinema in Abadan.[47] These verbal attacks were bolstered by a vicious campaign of terror that was to last for almost another four years, resulting in violent sieges, street confrontations and bombings, all of which claimed the lives of over twelve thousand political dissidents.

*Boycott*, then, can be seen as a piece of public media that espoused official ideology in order to castigate the regime's enemies through the socialization of a mass audience. In the film Valeh, on entering prison, states, "I now doubt the principles I had held for a long time. I began with the postulate, 'I fight therefore I am.' But now I doubt whether I really exist and therefore I don't care to fight. One needs a philosophy in order to fight." Later on he says to his Marxist comrades in jail, "I know all of you have robbed me of my faith and gave me nothing in return. Let me tell you I am doubtful of all ideology, of politics, of you, of myself, of everything and everybody." When he is being told to die like a hero for the cause of socialism and the obliteration of imperialism, he admits that, "Imperialism and socialism are the same to a dead person." The issue at stake here is the abandonment of the self in the service of empty ideals. These empty ideals have in turn deprived the individual of his belief in a greater power or reality—Islam—which reflects his true cultural identity and offers meaning and salvation. Furthermore, it highlights the tension between an all-consuming ideology, in this case Marxism, that robs the individual of free will, as opposed to Islam, which offers the possibility, if not the reality as defined in the Islamic Republic, of a transformation of the self through attaining a union with God.

The structure that the prisoners impose on all activities is a totalitarian and despotic system of conformity that espouses a nihilistic and anti-human ideology. As Makhmalbaf presents it, this ideology robs the individual of his sense of self and leads to the destruction of his humanity. One of the prisoners is continuously painting his own self-portrait, a search for an identity that has been subsumed in ideology, and in another scene a prisoner is murdered by his comrades for acting and thinking outside acceptable "dialectical and scientific" thought patterns. This depiction of socialist doctrine is instructive on two counts. Firstly, despite the rhetorical and superficial depiction of Marxism in *Boycott* certain points are pertinent with regard to the development of the Left in Iran. One of the main reasons posited for its historical failures, apart from relentless state repression both before and after the revolution, has been its often-demonstrated undemocratic means of dealing with internal ideological opposition. This arose for the most part from an adherence by Iranian communists to a Stalinist ideology that failed to respect the rights of individual members in internal disputes and resulted in serious party differences, resolved either by silencing ideological opponents or purging them.[48] Part of that ideological legacy was an attachment to Bolshevism and a belief in the leading role of a professional vanguard revolutionary party, allied with a deep attachment to Moscow, which prevented Iranian communists from adapting to and recognizing the realities and particularities of Iranian society.

The internecine ideological debates that take place within the hierarchy that the prisoners create for themselves highlight this rigid conformity. Secondly, the critique of the anti-humanist Marxism espoused by the characters of *Boycott* reverberates with Ayatollah Motahari's call for an Islamic ideological alternative. Motahari proposed that Marxism's materialistic determinism belittles man by denying him of an interior being and a conscience. By contrast Islam presents man with a grand destiny as the chosen creation of God, capable of knowing the ineffable. In this respect Motahari contrasts what he sees as the pessimism of Marxism with "Qur'anic optimism and man's noble destiny under the one compared to his role as the instrument of blind determinism on the other."[49] Makhmalbaf accentuates this existential division in the contrast between Valeh's death and martyrdom of the Islamic militants, Ali and Fatemeh, at the start of the film. Their deaths in a shoot-out are presented melodramatically, with swelling music and stirring action sequences using frantic cross-cutting, multiple close-ups and subjective camera angles. They die noble deaths as martyrs, attaining paradise in a hail of bullets for a higher cause. By contrast, Valeh's death for the "future of socialism" is presented as an entry into nothingness, a non-existence to which he asks the question, "What will happen to my family?" and finds the answer himself: "Ideology has no answer for that question."

Makhmalbaf was following the official line in presenting an ideology opposite to Islam, in this case Marxism, as corrupt. His method of denigrating opposing dogmas in Boycott takes the form of historical revisionism, where the Left is portrayed as alien to Iranian culture and as having contributed nothing to the revolution. However, the question of free will and the dehumanization/depersonalization of the individual in the face of an all-consuming ideology becomes more explicit in this film, and somewhat undermines this notion. Whereas in Makhmalbaf's other films of this era the individual had been an obedient servant searching for and finding God with a view to changing himself and his society, in *Boycott* death is the reward for blind faith in ideology. Valeh's questioning of ideology and his actions throughout the film, as well as the deaths of Ali and Fatemeh, are personalized to an extent not seen before in Makhmalbaf's films. Their actions and deaths are not presented exclusively in abstract terms in the service of ideals, but are depicted as having consequences on a personal level. The prime locus of this concern is shown in the effect that these actions have on the family. The deaths of Ali and Fatemeh are counterpointed by the pathos of their crying child, while the consequences of Valeh's political activities are shown in the ramifications they have for his wife and child: she is interrogated by the authorities, has to sell her personal possessions to survive while Valeh is in prison and their newborn child will lose his father. While on the one hand such juxtaposing is an attempt to give a human and personal point of identification to the political sloganeering it establishes a hierarchy of ideologies while at the same time questioning whether death in the service of an ideal is worthwhile.

## The Ideological Use of the Media

The scene of Valeh's trial in *Boycott*, (he is arrested for producing and disseminating Marxist literature) provides a cinematically self-reflexive take on the media's role as ideological propaganda. The attendees in the public gallery at the court are all military personnel who change into civilian clothes in order for a partisan media to transmit a manufactured picture to the nation of a populace in support of the models of state, the rule of law and the actions of its rulers. This point is made clearer when, during the course of the trial, Valeh rises to make his plea. The director of the television crew filming the unfolding events calls cut, refusing to record Valeh's defense. Here Makhmalbaf reveals the media, in this case Pahlavi state apparatus, as merely the ideological tool of those in power, primarily concerned with portraying the unquestionable righteousness of the court and the laws and the functioning of civil society. But while *Boycott*'s explicit aim is to castigate the former regime's unscrupulous control of media content, it is implicit within the structure of the film, here acting as a mirror to the court television crew and their broadcast, that these are the very same methods the Islamic regime uses to present an irreproachable image of itself; the only difference is the ideological setting. This complex intertextuality and its interpretation—the use of the media by the former regime to manipulate its audience and prosecute its enemies within a film that may be seen as part of the present regime's ideological campaign to prosecute its enemies—reveals the comparison of a common enemy dealt with through similar means with the shared aim of enforcing acquiescence to the will of the state by eliminating all dissenting voices. Makhmalbaf's loose adaptation and portrayal of historical subjects through the application of a particular ideological agenda leads to an implicit undermining and arbitrary reinterpretation of history. This is particularly germane when present political considerations determine the functioning of the modes of representation and their interpretation of the past and when historical revisionism sets in motion unexpected countercurrents of meaning.

In this respect *Boycott* is the first step in Makhmalbaf's increasingly complex interaction with and questioning of the world around him. Gone is the simplistic division of good and evil, the militant indignation and moral preaching have been toned down and Makhmalbaf seems to be issuing the first strains of a more tolerant humanism, a feature that was to mark his work from this point on. The essence of this change is wrought from the tension between the specifics of espousing official rhetoric and the generalities of a concern about the effects of ideology on the individual. While attacking the Marxist and extolling the Islamic man Makhmalbaf does attempt to transcend abstractions by personalizing these notions; he problematizes their consequences, eliciting sympathy for the individuals who become enmeshed in these categories. This personalized questioning of the "reality" behind the image was to be examined further in later films such as *The Peddler* (1989), which looked at the exploitation/creation of the image of the suffering poor as a source of emulation, or *The Marriage of the Blessed* (1989) which looked at the harshness of life for a returning war hero. Thus Makhmalbaf's Islamic films are a form of exorcism, as the filmmaker came to see cinema as a means of working out personal and artistic ideas. Film provided Makhmalbaf with a means of meditating on the notions of rhetoric and social realities as the former became an intellectually limiting and questionable, if not bankrupt, way of representing life in the Islamic Republic. Such an analysis provides evidence not only of nascent elements of doubt in Makhmalbaf's work, but the beginning of an awareness of the complexity of ideology. Makhmalbaf has himself stated that *Boycott* represents a critique of fascism and that the film stands is a work of transition between his Islamic films and the more socially critical films that were to follow, exemplifying his loss of faith in the new regime.[50] *Boycott* oscillates between a localized ideological dedication and a universalized doubt as to the merits of grand ideological themes. It also presages Makhmalbaf's subsequent artistic development and preoccupations, in particular his questioning of absolutes, his search for a reinstatement of the individual and his recognition of the fractured nature of truth and reality.

The idea of an "Islamic cinema" does not have a claim to some pre-defined, unique essence, or readily possess definable formal traits that set it apart from all other forms of cinema. Makhmalbaf's films of this period (1982-1985) are telling examples, with their melodramatic and stock generic elements, which contain an unsubtle message that preached "moral values, often via didactic slogans and aphorisms superficially woven into the dialogue or shrill rhetoric orated by characters."[51] The attempts to define the purpose and characteristics of an Islamic cinema have been at best vague, and a more accurate term would be an "Islamicized cinema," which formed a part of the Islamic regime's overarching strategy to control all aspects of society through ideological transformation. As the Deputy for Cinematographic Affairs at the time, Mehdi Kalhor, stated, "Cultural tradition forms the jumping board for the serious filmmakers who are witnesses to the most exciting period in the history of this country. They are experiencing almost at first-hand heroic acts of courage and self-sacrifice. It is therefore their duty to set to work and act as candid chroniclers of this glorious moment."[52] Toward that end all stages of the filmmaking process were brought under centralized government control, and the Islamicized cinema can therefore be defined under the rubric of propagating official Islamic ideology and the strict control of morality. The former meant expounding the sociopolitical ideology of the regime by functioning in the same way as the revised education system. In addition, the strict control and enforcement of a moral code has given cinema in Iran its uniquely "Islamic" appearance. However, this has been cast in an unnatural and superficial light, with the so-called "Islamic" character of films reflected by the absence of intimacy between the sexes and the regulations governing the appearance of women, resulting in an absence strangely filled by sermonizing and the omnipresence of the Islamic man. Makhmalbaf's first three films, *Nasuh's Repentance, Two Sightless Eyes* and *Fleeing from Evil to Good* serve as good examples of Islamicized cinema in their religious fervor and dedication to the virtues of the Islamic Republic. However, with the emergence of *Boycott* we witness the first signs of an artist in transition. Here is the filmmaker trying to express a more faithful picture of social realities and beginning to explore and engage with the medium as an expressive and meaningful art form, rather than subjugating it to official rhetoric. It remains in the coming chapters to see how Makhmalbaf and Iranian cinema in general would progress and develop throughout the years of altered political, social and cultural contexts, and how the Islamic regime dealt with these changes on the domestic front, and increasingly, the international stage.

# 4 | THE STATE OF THE NATION

The first decade of the Islamic revolution, from the toppling of the shah to the death of Ayatollah Khomeini in 1989, could be considered one of the most tumultuous eras in Iran's long history. During this time Iran experienced "the catastrophic problems of war, lack of reasonable planning, intensifying economic crises, inflation, stagnation and unemployment, corruption in sections of the ruling regime, housing problems, low incomes, and political, economic and social insecurity."[1] Having assumed absolute power the clerics had set about the task of governing, with the aim of perpetuating clerical rule and fully implementing Khomeini's revolutionary ideology, "neo-Shiism," a policy by which the tenets of the faith constitute the rules of government and members of the *ulama* exercise authority as the political elite. However, throughout this period the regime was not so obstinate as to refuse to adapt, and it showed itself very adroit at modifying its attitude as expediency dictated in its multifaceted application of cultural norms. Thus the nation's internal revolution through the Islamicization process slowed somewhat as focus was shifted to economic concerns and the international arena and the second tenet of Khomeini's revolutionary ideology—exporting the revolution.

The eight-year war with Iraq (1980-88)* was the all-consuming event of the first ten years of clerical rule and formed the backdrop against which all ideological, social, political and economic issues were to be argued and defined. The war was not only a military conflict; it was also an ideological struggle that distracted from domestic concerns and provided the clerics with a new lease on life and "a platform from which to

---

*The Iran-Iraq war began when Iraqi forces invaded Iran in September 1980. The causes of the conflict are historically complex but essentially the dispute arose when the Iraqi leader Saddam Hussein attempted to gain control of the disputed Shatt al-Arab waterway (Arvand Rud in Persian) and to position Iraq as the main power in the Middle East. Fearing that the revolutionary rhetoric emanating from Iran would incite Iraq's Shia population to rebel (other countries with sizeable Shia populations, such as Bahrain and Pakistan, also feared the spread of revolution from Iran) and sensing that the Islamic Republic was weak and disorganized he decided to attack, hoping that a quick victory and the collapse of the Islamic Republic would ensue.

rejuvenate the drive for national unity and Islamic revolution."[2] Once
again it was cloaked in the ideology of Shia Islam. Ayatollah Khomeini
described the conflict as a holy war (*jihad*) being waged against an "infidel" (Saddam Hussein) in defense of Islam: "They [Iraqi forces] have
attacked Islam and we have to defend Islam. Our weapon is faith, our
armory is Islam and with the weapons of faith and Islam we shall succeed."[3] The invocation of religious ideology saw the emergence once
again of the potent Shia symbols and themes of martyrdom and self-
sacrifice.* By referring to Saddam Hussein as Yazid—the Sunni caliph
responsible for the massacre at Karbala and the death of Hossein—in
the same way that they had referred to the shah, the clerics were
attempting once again to channel the cultural and religious-historical
sentiments of the people, this time against an external enemy. Thus the
ruling elite were able to further reinforce their power domestically by
rallying the nation behind a common cause, and also to postpone decisions on pressing socioeconomic issues. And it provided a platform for
pursuing Khomeini's other aim, the export of the revolution: "Islam is a
sacred trust from God to ourselves and the Iranian nation must grow in
power and resolution until it has vouchsafed Islam to the entire world."[4]
However, in elevating the war to a spiritual battle, Khomeini was privileging what he saw as the needs of Islam over those of Iran. In doing so he
was merely following Islamic doctrine for which the idea of a nation is
totally foreign, the community of which is not founded on nationalistic
notions of race or myth but on a community of believers (*umma*).[5] Khomeini's new Islamic ideology "substituted for the secular and nationalist
ideas of earlier decades a new ideology, that of Islamic revolution. The
legitimacy of the Islamic Republic therefore required a depreciation of
those other trends."[6] The repercussions for the Iranian nation and the
future of the Islamic state were to be immense and far-reaching.

### Nation versus Islam

The conflict between those who supported a nationalistic policy and
those who backed a strictly Islamic state formed the basis of a political
debate that eventually split the ruling clerics into two opposing camps
composed of Islamic radicals and pragmatists/moderates. This division
characterized the future political development and progress of the state
and permeated all levels of Iranian society. The realm of culture did not
remain immune for very long and indeed became an arena for the conflict between these opposing political factions. Of prime importance

---

*The notion of martyrdom as a lofty ideal and the path to God is described in the Qur'an. "Think not of those,
who are slain in the way of Allah, as dead. Nay, they are living. With their Lord they have provision." Sura
3, verse 169, in *The Koran,* translated by M. M. Pickthall, 76. Many Iranians wholeheartedly embraced
martyrdom during the Iran-Iraq war. Indeed many of the Iranian troops used in human wave offenses were
distributed with keys prior to battle in order to open the gates of heaven upon being martyred.

in this regard was the position and control of the cinematic medium. And, "due to its wide reach and its impact, cinema was in the forefront of discussions and skirmishes among the domestic political wings."[7] Makhmalbaf, in an open letter to the media protesting the censorship and prosecution of his work in public, recognized the role cinema played in the tug-of-war in the Iranian government: "The writer of these columns knows well that these arguments have nothing to do with him. The fight is over nothing other than the struggles between the different factions who seek power."[8]

In fact, threats to the Islamic Republic came not from those usually deemed the enemies of clerical rule but from within the clergy itself. What prevented these disputes from erupting into open war was the desire not to destabilize the state or jeopardize the clerics' position of power in conjunction with the unifying and exalted position and reverence in which Khomeini was held. In spite of the calls for unity, different ideological subsystems existed, and could be tolerated "among true believers as long as they remained loyal followers of Imam Khomeini."[9] The clerics still relied on the loyalty of the mostazafin as the basis of their support but even here a split was discernible. A system of equivocation began to operate whereby the leadership used an increasingly hollow rhetoric as an assurance of their devotion and commitment to the cause of the mostazafin while in reality an ideological shift had taken place as the government sought to align itself more and more with the middle class, in a bid to establish the mosque and the bazaar as the twin pillars of the state. This alignment arose from financial necessity as the regime's focus turned from issues of culture to those of economics, (although the latter was still argued in ideological terms), in a bid to bolster a shattered economy, keep the country fighting and offset rising social tensions. Furthermore, the revolutionary call for an "Islamic economics" built on the ideas of justice for the dispossessed and explained through sharia was becoming increasingly marginalized and unrealistic under the realities and hardship of conflict.

The war with Iraq cost Iran heavily. An estimated 262,000 people lost their lives, the nations spent between seventy-four and ninety billion dollars, not counting the indirect loss of oil revenue and the destruction of infrastructure and agriculture, all of which amounted to a toll of around $627 billion.[10] This merely served to exacerbate the failure of the Islamic regime to deal effectively with the multitude of economic and social problems besetting the country. The official rate of urban unemployment had risen from 7.1 percent in 1976 to 14.1 percent in 1986,[11] a figure made worse by a growing population that contributed a further 400,000 job seekers to its ranks each year. Inflation had risen from 9.9 percent in 1978 to a high of 28.9 percent in 1988,[12] with the gross domestic product falling by an average of 1.3 per cent per annum over the same period.[13] Furthermore, "by the end of the decade, the revolution had not even radically changed the distribution of wealth. Ten percent of the people owned sixty-four percent of the wealth. Despite the teachings of Islam that proclaims the meek to be the most noble, in Iran it was the wealthy who were the most admired."[14] In essence this reflected the failure of much Third-World populism in attempting to advocate a system of non-alignment operating between socialism and capitalism (Khomeini's oft-repeated phrase "Neither East nor West but Islam") when in reality it merely served to combine different aspects of the established economic systems as expediency dictated; radicalism began to be replaced by a creeping realism, and the question as to which should take precedent, Iran or Islam was repeated. Indeed, Iran's revolutionary decade has been characterized as one in which considerable instability, the breakdown of law and order, and a widespread feeling of insecurity among the population "eroded business confidence" and "resulted in little capital investment and a brain drain."[15] The ruling elite looked to the middle class as the means of offsetting and alleviating the country's dire economic conditions. However, in doing so the clergy were fundamentally altering the ideological basis of the Islamic Republic in displacing the dispossessed, the social bedrock of the new regime and one of their main sources of support, in favor of an economic alliance with the other main source of support, the *bazaari* middle classes.

### The Changing Class Orientation of the Islamic State

At the height of the Iran-Iraq war Khomeini declared 1983–84 to be "the year of the mostazafin," going on to state his alarm at the gulf separating what he termed the "shanty dwellers" (*kukh neshin*) from the "palace dwellers" (*kakh neshin*), warning that if the mentality of the "palace dwellers" prevailed the revolution would be in danger.[16] However, by the fourth year of Islamic rule the dispossessed had become the disenfranchised. The "owners of the revolution" suffered most from the economic constraints of war and also filled the increasing number of coffins coming back from the front, yet had experienced little or none of the benefits promised them by the revolution.* Their voices of discontent were prevented from becoming a dangerous political threat to the established order by two main factors. Firstly, Iran's oil income, despite the war, was still significant and, combined with rationing and

---

*Khomeini was well aware of this: "To which class of society do these heroic fighters of the battlefield belong? Do you find even one person among them who is related to persons who have large capital or had some power in the past? If you find one we will give you a prize. But you won't." *Tehran Times*, February 10, 1982: 6. It is worth noting that in January 1983 Khomeini, recognizing the need for unity and the growing (financial) importance of the middle classes, was at pains to stress the historical link between the clergy and the bazaaris and to express his gratitude for their support in offering their sons and finances to the war effort. *Jomhouri Islami*, January, 31 1983.

the systematic discouragement of materialism, managed to maintain a sufficient supply of basic necessities. The second factor lay in the person of Khomeini himself, who still commanded zealous support from the people and was politically astute in achieving some measure of national complacency. This latter point is clearly evidenced in his ideological restructuring of society from a "dichotomous image of society" to a "trichotomous" one, that recognized the existence and contribution of the middle classes.[17] Khomeini acknowledged this change explicitly, stating that "the revolution will remain secure as long as the parliament and the government are manned by members of the middle classes."[18]

However, the drive by the leaders of the Islamic Republic to establish a close relationship with the bazaar and the mosque did not represent a total betrayal of revolutionary ideals, per se. Rather it was a reflection of the chameleon-like nature of the Islamic regime to use traditional alliances as circumstances dictated. In seeking to engage with the middle classes the clergy were merely seeking to emphasize an alliance between bazaar and mosque that had historically operated in Iran as the two most influential social centers of power whose authority rested on the socioeconomic cultural bonds between them. This alliance has traditionally been built on a similarity in ideological outlook and a system of mutual need that saw each group give shape, sustenance and authority to the other. The bazaaris, with their involvement in petty trade, production and traditional banking, are by nature conservative and tend to align themselves with an Islamic cultural worldview that serves primarily to protect their commercial interests. In this regard most oppose what they perceive to be Western dependency and the spread of Western values.

Bound by close family, commercial and cultural ties the bazaaris sought social standing and social capital in their relationship of mutual coexistence with the clergy. The high proportion of religious taxes and gifts to the clergy for charitable, religious and political purposes that came from the bazaar helped to cement the political bond between the two groups. In addition these financial ties were enhanced by the close communicative apparatus of the bazaar such as the *hay'at* (association), which gathered together merchants and clergy in informal "religious meetings" to network, discuss mutual problems and decide on strategic action. This alliance has been the main focal point of opposition leadership and all anti-government movements in Iran from 1891 to 1979. Society now moved from an antagonistic revolutionary dichotomy to a tripartite state of post-revolutionary semi-harmony, and the term mostazafin ceased to be an economic category, becoming instead a fetishized term denoting any hard-core supporters of the regime. However, the dispossessed, despite their economic hardships, still provide the bedrock of support and the foot-soldiers of the Islamic regime. The revolution, and more particularly the figure of Khomeini, had given the masses, if not an improvement in their material well-being, a sense of integrity, collective identity and an elevated standing in society. The cultural attributes extolled by the Islamic Republic (anti-Westernism, Islamic virtues and religious servitude) were in accord with the interests of the dispossessed. In this respect, given the shifting economic and political-ideological alliance and reorientation of the state, the sense of deprivation, at least in cultural terms, of the dispossessed has not been severely felt and the regime has maintained their support through the skillful use of rhetoric in empathizing with and acknowledging their sacrifice on the war front fighting to preserve Islam and the Islamic Republic. The cinema was to prove one of the most important cultural vehicles for depicting these sacrifices, reinforcing the regime's commitment to the cause of the dispossessed and the commitment of the dispossessed to Islam and the Islamic Republic.

## The Media: Control and Interpellation*

In Khomeini's call to furthering the revolution, cinema was once again cited as a key element in the political process: "Our devout wish [is] to save our youth, to save our future from these dens of corruption. We are going to take our youths away from the corrupting pleasures of the flesh. We drive them out of the cinemas and away from the dream machine and take them to the battlefields where they make real contributions, where they can place their lives on the line to defeat the enemy and defend our nation…. We will take them and arm them and send them to the battlefields. This is the kind of freedom that we need in this country."[19] Despite the rhetoric, and its apparent hypocrisy and contradiction, the clerics soon discovered the usefulness of the cinema as an essential tool in their desire to consolidate and reproduce Islamic (clerical) hegemony, a need brought into sharper focus by the exigencies of war. However, some of the militancy was toned down as people grew tired of the constant preaching and the Islamicization process was refocused in deference to the pressing needs of war. Khomeini, himself, moderated his view somewhat by declaring that television should become a "popular university" of the people carrying the message of revolution to the masses, but warned that no "un-educational" programs be broadcast in the future.[20] He also advised the clerics not to press down "too hard" on the people and to "refrain from extremism."[21] The Speaker of the Majles also began to criticize the harshness of many of the government's

---

*The Marxist cultural theorist Louis Althusser coined the term interpellation. According to his definition ideology is seen as a lived material practice—rituals, customs, patterns of behavior, ways of thinking. The term itself refers to the way in which individuals are "hailed." Althusser uses the analogy of an individual being hailed by a police officer. When the individual turns he or she has been interpellated, i.e. become a subject of the police officer's discourse or constructed by these material practices of ideology as subjects.

reforms, calling for more entertainment and sports programs rather than strictly religious ones to be made for public consumption.[22]

Censorship of the media, however, did not disappear. The 1985 Media Bill, in addition to the regulations already in existence, decreed that any publication deemed to contain material that could be construed as disrespectful to Islam or the religious leaders or that was seen as immoral would be banned. The terms of this bill were reiterated three years later in August, 1988, by The High Council of Cultural Revolution,* which went on to add that any material described as socially or politically divisive or likely to undermine the unity of the nation, promote corrupt Western values, or advocate sexual freedom or feminist issues would also be banned. The year 1988, though, did see some loosening of the previous strictures on film, albeit for reasons less openhanded than it would seem. For example, filmmakers were no longer forced to receive script approval from the Council of Screenplay Inspection before beginning a film project, although it has been said that "authorities came to the conclusion that the current criteria and standards were already known to filmmakers, while the Reviewing Council, which issues release permits, could always exert sufficient control and supervision."[23] The delicate balancing act needed to maintain a sense of unity among opposing factions can be seen from the fact that these measures, which gave the government sweeping powers of control, were, in fact, counterbalanced by a few voices of moderatism.

However, these changes should not be misunderstood as heralding a new cultural glasnost. Their primary aim was, yet again, to seek a balance between the demands of moderates and radicals in maintaining unity within the government. Indeed, if any of the attitudes were translated into practice at all they caused no more than a changing degree in the intensity of revolutionary fervor, with the ultimate aim still the creation of a new form of Islamic lifestyle and the maintenance of revolutionary zeal during a period of war. Criticism of the regime when it did emerge was either silenced or, like much else in the Islamic Republic, closely supervised and mediated. The tentative voices of criticism, which did begin to emerge near the end of the decade and which were to become louder after the death of Khomeini in 1989, constituted more subtle analysis than outright criticism of conditions in the country. This meant that where voices of discontent emerged they made sure they did not attack Islam, the government or the clergy directly. In such instances where negative criticism occurred it was immediately countered by pro-government forces.†

---

*This was the organization set up by Khomeini one year after the revolution to "revise" (Islamicize) the educational system.
  †An example of this process can be clearly seen when the *Hamshahri* newspaper claimed in an edition, dated 11 April 1993, that it had come to the conclusion that faith and religion were matters of personal and

As the war with Iraq consumed the country's attentions, the division between radicals and moderates within the government became more pronounced and "the discrepancies between the revolution's grand promises and the harsh realities of living under its rule were beginning to be aired in the Iranian press and parliament."[24] The division between radical and moderate political forces extended to all sections of society and was seen in the cinema in the discernible split between a "populist cinema,"* which affirmed post-revolutionary Islamic values, and a more critical form of cinema that began to engage with these values in a critique of social conditions under the Islamic regime.[25] Indeed, the employment of cultural forms was no longer primarily concerned with the spreading of official ideology but was being used in a bid to counteract the emergence of criticism, build unity and consensus, and keep the country fighting in the face of an external enemy that was depicted as threatening Islam and the future of the Islamic Republic. The "official" films of the time for the most part reveal cinema as a propagandist tool and call to arms in the war with Iraq while at the same time reflecting the political radical/moderate split. Thus, Iranian cinema found itself caught between the desire of those in power to retain it as an instrument of control and those who recognized that a freer form of debate and expression was necessary to avoid a backlash against a revolution that had plunged the country into internecine war and further economic and social instability. This division is crucial to understanding the evolution of Iranian film in a decade of war and revolution, and nowhere were these contradictory strains more discernible than in the cinema of Mohsen Makhmalbaf.

### Cinema at War

As has been shown, during the first decade of Islamic rule keeping the country running and fighting in the war with Iraq were the prime concerns of the Iranian leadership. In such an atmosphere difficulties arose at the nexus of art and politics. Mohammad Beheshti, the Managing Director of the Farabi Cinema Foundation (FCF), summed it up: "In a sense, our government authorities were wrong in their estimation and expectation of the film medium. Starting with the premise that significant social phenomena usually entail the emergence of artistic creations of great impact and magnitude, they expected the extraordinary events

---

spiritual perspectives and could not and should not be imposed as a matter of government policy. These assertions were immediately countered by the pro-government press as being pro-Western and seeking to undermine the revolution. See Homa Omid, *Islam and the Post-Revolutionary State in Iran*, 172-174.

*The Managing Director of the Farabi Cinema Foundation remarked, "When a filmmaker introduces a miscreant, say a police officer, teacher, et cetera it has to be seen whether he is criticizing an individual or the system as a whole. If the latter is the case then he has to be stopped." Interview with *Film Monthly*, Tehran, June 1984.

that occurred in the country to bring in their wake artistic creations of comparable significance. But when we do not have artists inspired by the revolution dunces take over, and when they make films on the war, their works turn out to be worthless reels."[26] At the time, it would seem that revolutionary zeal and support for the regime were more important factors in filmmaking than were artistic or intellectual creativity, which were generally treated with suspicion. It has been said that "preserving the revolutionary morale—whether in time of war or peace—constitutes the basic moral principle of Iranian cinema."[27] This assessment is duly borne out by the figures, which show that during the war period "a total of fifty-six feature fiction films about the war were made [with most of them emphasizing] action and violence over sensitivity and psychological depth."[28] Furthermore, on the thematic level it must be noted that, "although war led to an increase in the quantity of films, which emphasize Islamic values of martyrdom and self-sacrifice, it negatively affected the quality of films, which, by and large, have been limited to circulating clichés and slogans."[29] The war film, The Cinema for the Sacred Defense, was a genre in Iranian cinema that emerged only after the revolution. This new cinematic form was generally seen to have "nothing new to say or no distinguished features to put forward,"[30] as technical ability and intellectual depth were substituted by unsubtle official sloganeering in support of Islam and the Islamic Republic. In this regard they did succeed in providing the perfect format for the portrayal of the Islamic man as the stoic defender of the faith as well as reproducing Shia cultural forms such as martyrdom and sacrifice.

Beyond the Islamic rhetoric of martyrdom and the propagandizing of the Islamic man the truth of the war lay in the social and physical hardships visited on the people, particularly the mostazafin. It was here that certain directors began to use the war film as a means of subverting the genre (at least in its Iranian manifestation) and using it as a means with which to criticize and analyze the problems besetting Iranian society. Central here was the depiction of the mostazafin as the personification of the Islamic man and mouthpiece of the regime in what became known as *basiji* films. The *basij*, (Mobilization of the Oppressed) a popular reserve controlled by the Islamic Guards Corps, were largely uneducated men and boys drawn from the poorest sections of society who proved to be the most ardent supporters of the revolution. During the war with Iraq they were organized "into poorly trained and equipped infantry units which were often used in Iran's human wave assaults."[31] The basiji formed the prototype for the ideal Islamic man fighting injustice, but paradoxically provided the rhetorical framework with which to question the shortcomings of the regime. They basiji films came to represent a sub-genre within Iranian cinema, and the examples of the "war returnee, *basiji*, coming to terms with the many failures of the revolution"[32] appear in many in Iranian films: Ebrahim Hatamikia's, *Az Karkheh ta Rhine* (*From Karkheh to Rhine,* 1993) or Mohsen Makhmalbaf's *Marriage of the Blessed* (1989). Makhmalbaf's films that, more than any others, embodied the contradictions between the thematic representations of an official and critical cinema, as he moved from Islamic idealist to social critic. As a result, Makhmalbaf, the regime's most trusted and respected filmmaker at this time, was subjected to censorship and mounting criticism from the hard-liners "as he presented vivid and critical portrayals of the effects of abject poverty, and the disillusionment of soldiers with the Iran-Iraq war.[33]"

## Makhmalbaf's Mostazafin Trilogy

Makhmalbaf's Mostazafin Trilogy inaugurated his second period of artistic development, and focuses primarily on the themes of social justice. This trio of films marked not only a formal but also an intellectual break from his previous work, setting aside the sermonizing about the Islamic man to investigate critically the problems facing the country and to examine the possibility of creating a new cinematic language with which to articulate these concerns. These three films—*Dastforush* (*The Peddler,* 1987), *Bicycleran* (*The Cyclist,* 1989) and *Arusi-ye Khuban* (*Marriage of the Blessed,* 1989)*—are symptomatic of Makhmalbaf's enhanced awareness of the realities of the world around him and his desire to express the complexities of these realities, and also reveal a change in the cinema and society of the time. The Islamicization process had begun to slow somewhat as people became weary of constant sermonizing, which was reflected in the poor quality and repetitive nature of many films. Furthermore, the authorities had come to realize, through the experience of the war movies, that forcing subjects upon filmmakers resulted in poor-quality films that had merely adapted, in this case, the generic formula of the Hollywood war film and infused it with propagandist statements and officially sanctioned religious sentiment. Film audiences tired of these cookie-cutter movies as they did of the regime's relentless proselytizing. In fact when the war ended in 1988 the "happy ending" was no longer a prerequisite and this allowed many filmmakers to depict critically the harsh realities and social hardships arising from the years of bitter conflict. Nonetheless, the carrot-and-stick approach to supporting and controlling cinematic output maintained a strong grip on the artistic avenues of criticism, and the division between the "in-group" and the "out-group," which acted "as the yardstick for the managers and officials to support or refuse to support those active in

---

*I refer to these films as the Mostazafin Trilogy because they focus on the plight of the oppressed masses of people (mostazafin) who formed the vanguard of the revolution and the main centers of support and legitimation for the Islamic regime.

different areas" still served as the means of containing dissenting voices within acceptable parameters.[34]

For his part, Makhmalbaf, at this time, was a member of the in-group. In fact, when *The Peddler* was released Makhmalbaf was considered a "film director as well as a theoretician for the super-structure of the Islamic Republic."[35] It was this privileged position that allowed him the space and opportunity to voice his criticisms within the narrow confines of dissent then permissible in Iran. But Makhmalbaf transgressed, and quickly the insider became the outsider as he continued to develop artistically and intellectually, and moved further away from his initial role as dogmatic and moral polemicist.[36]

## The Evolution of an Artist

Makhmalbaf's *Mostazafin* trilogy marks the first stage in his maturity as an artist and with his critical engagement with Iranian society after the revolution. These films have been called "troubled, lyrical arias about human suffering in contemporary Iran that attack social problems, urban squalor, social cruelty and crime in *The Peddler*; capitalist exploitation in *The Cyclist*; and the nervous condition of a traumatized veteran of the Iran-Iraq war in *The Marriage of the Blessed*, with an unrelenting hallucinatory fury."[37] While these issues unite the films of the trilogy at a thematic level, stylistically they are linked by formal experimentation and the search for an appropriate cinematic language of expression, as well as a questioning of that language, engaged in a dialectics of how to represent Iranian society. This signals the beginning of a constant element in Makhmalbaf's work, the existence of Iran and cinema as separate but constantly entwining entities each asking questions of the other.

Makhmalbaf uses a number of different forms in depicting his critical social engagement and each film is in a sense a working-out of problems of the self, society and the visual language of representation. Thus we are presented with "the disturbing 'film noir' *The Peddler*, his iconoclastic *Marriage of the Blessed*, or his powerful *The Cyclist*, a plea for the world's refugees and its deprived."[38] The portrayal of the darker sides of society and human nature, or the representation of human dignity in the face of suffering, is still very much influenced by a religious perspective. This religious perspective is of crucial importance as it forms another of the touchstones of Makhmalbaf's work—his changing relationship with God. He may have turned his back on the dogmatism and religious zealotry of his earlier work but he has not turned his back on God; he has only moved away from the particular representation of God promulgated by the Islamic Republic. The theological debate continues throughout his work, and is one that has taken on greater complexity: "I am more religious now than I was earlier," Makhmalbaf said at the time, "But my idea of God has become broader."[39] The

Mostazafin trilogy follows the doubts raised by *Boycott*. Central in this regard is a more balanced and critical treatment of social realities, the exploration and questioning of a variety of visual forms in depicting these realities and a continual process of attempting to understand the individual and his relationship with God.

### The Peddler

*The Peddler* consists of three tenuously linked episodes dealing with different aspects of the harsh daily lives of the poorest members of Iranian society, the mostazafin. The first episode tells the story of a couple living in the slums of Tehran with their four children, each of whom has a physical handicap. The wife has just given birth again, and fearing that the same fate awaits the newborn child the parents attempt unsuccessfully to abandon it at various places around town—the mosque, the house of a wealthy man—in the hope of offering the child the chance of a better life. The second episode tells the story of a scatterbrained, deluded and infantile man who cares for his aging and senile mother. While out collecting his mother's pension he is knocked down by a car and robbed. On returning to the flat it becomes apparent that his mother has died but he seems oblivious to this and continues his chores and monologues as if she were still alive. The final episode concerns a young hustler/peddler selling shirts at the bazaar for a criminal gang. In a flashback it is revealed that he has been a witness to a murder that was carried out by two members of the gang. Fearing that he will talk, the peddler is brought to a teahouse to meet the leader of the gang, who takes him to a deserted warehouse. The peddler, fearing for his life, tries to escape only to be caught and executed by the gang.

Episode one sets out to document the poverty and desperation of those forgotten by the revolution, and it reveals a process of formal experimentation. Virtually all of the segment is realistic, with no unusual camera set-ups or lighting effects and with fairly sparse dialogue.[40] The film starts with the stark portrayal of a family living in abject poverty in a disused and decrepit bus on the outskirts of a shanty-town. The images of poverty are harsh and presented as matter-of-fact. However, this realism is undercut by the use of metaphoric allusions and associations. In the first instance the birth of the child is cross-cut with the birth of a cow. Later on in the film when the mother, Hanieh, goes to feed the child while in the mosque the scene is intercut with an image of a calf suckling, after which the father says, "In God we trust." The association between the physical actions (birth, breast feeding) of humans and animals is on the one hand an attempt to show how poverty deprives the individual of human dignity and becomes merely an existence of survival but also, in its specific references to the cow, a religious allusion that structures and counterpoints the entire narrative. The key to this lies in Sura 2, "The Cow," verse 233, "Mothers shall suckle their children for two whole years.... The duty of feeding and clothing nursing mothers in a seemly manner is upon the father.... A mother should not be made to suffer because of her child.... If they desire to wean the child by mutual consent and after consultation it is no sin for them; and if ye wish to give your children out to nurse, it is no sin for you, provided that you pay what is due from you in kindness." This contains the general narrative of the first episode, in which the father, unable to provide for his wife and fearful of the child becoming physically handicapped, decides to leave it to the care of others so that it will have the possibility of a better life. In doing so he and his wife first arrive at the hospital. Here the realist mode gives way to a type of surrealism as the film moves into a hospital for sick, abandoned and mentally ill children. The camera whirls constantly, tracking, panning and zooming in a hallucinatory trance that emphasizes, somewhat unsubtly, the grotesqueness of the surroundings and the despair, tragedy and hopelessness of the unfortunate inhabitants of the hospital ward through the subjective point of view of the mother. The alternating style within the first part of the film is not so much an abrupt shift but more of a logical process that serves to foreshadow the increased prevalence of fantasy, surreal and unexpected stylistic and tonal shifts that will take place in the following episodes. As Makhmalbaf explains, "In *The Peddler* I change my style very slowly in the film. I don't confine myself to a particular style.... The anxiety about form is evident in all my films. I have always liked the experimental cinema. It is in search of unknown and undeveloped topics."[41] However, the springboard for the experimental anxiety has as its starting point realism, from which all other forms emanate.

The realist/documentary mode has allowed Makhmalbaf, and indeed much of the critical Iranian cinema as a whole, to capture society with greater faith to the texture of life in Iran.[42] While realism is seen as socially committed and constitutes a reclamation of space— thereby engaging in the subversive act of restoring "things to their real place and meaning"[43]—it certainly has limits. Realism, though it offers the appearance and promise of the real, is not an objective end in itself, because it never neutrally renders reality, as it is based more on the notions of subjective response and personal discovery. The filmmaker, then, has to define constantly not just his relationship with his subject but also the means by which he represents that subject matter.[44] The concept of realism is generally, theoretically at least, associated with the maintenance of liberal and democratic values from the point of view that it is the spectator who is given the space to interpret the director's filming of "reality" and is therefore an active co-creator of meaning. The concept of realism does not refer simply to the objective and neutral rendering of reality but is in actual fact a complex interaction of competing discourses and modes of interpretation. Makhmalbaf is aware of the volatility of the realist aesthetic and seeks to subvert any essentialist notions by combining an ardent social program with an aesthetic in which realist elements (episode one of *The Peddler*) give way to subjective surrealism (episode two) before combining both elements (episode three) that mixes freshness with an overall sense of chaos, but crucially is caught in a process of constant self-criticism. Realism opens up the necessary space for experimentation, but a belief that a distinction exists between realism and the real also allows a departure from traditional modes of representation: "Sometimes we talk about form and say that it is realistic but sometimes we mean the realistic or naturalistic content of the film...reality is a prison."[45] For Makhmalbaf realism inevitably leads to the surreal, and he states that *The Peddler* consists of many documentary-style scenes, which for him act as a way of transcending or mimicking real life: "I try to work in the genre of documentary realism in order to create a sort of symbolism, in coming toward surrealism."[46]

## The Changing Face of God

The combination of the real and the surreal has antecedents in a more culturally specific place of origin—the many facets of Islam. According to Makhmalbaf, this aspect of his work is influenced by the Qur'an: "Just as in our holy text the human and the divine coexist, so in my stories the real and the surreal may be found side by side," and this is very much at the heart of Makhmalbaf's narrative and formal technique.[47] These elements are reconciled in the last section of the film, when God's angels visit the dying peddler. In this scene we are presented with an action-sequence chase structured by furious cross-cutting as the peddler is pursued by members of the gang. The peddler is eventually caught and killed. However, before he dies the audience is privy to a fantasy sequence in which he imagines his escape. He jumps through an ornate window through which a bright light is streaming before being picked up by a car without a driver, on the back of which is tied a large clock, which then speeds off before dumping him on the side of the street. There he meets the dead, including the person whose death he witnessed at the start of the episode and who has now inadvertently caused the peddler's own death. The thriller mode here yields to the esoteric as we are presented with death not as finality but as a rebirth, captured in the final image of the scene, a fetus revolving in a jar. It is a startling and contemplative image where the visitation of angels upon death engender the beginning of new life and a return to God, reflecting the Qur'anic passage: "Wait they for naught else that Allah should come unto them in the shadows of the clouds with angels? Then the case will be already judged. All cases go back to Allah (for judgement)."[48] Here religious form and content coalesce, as the intended message of *The Peddler*, according to Makhmalbaf, is to convey the message that "God is the Light and therefore the source of all life, we come from the Light and we will go back to Him. Death is an eventual return to the Light, while our life on earth is the deciding factor which determines the quality of our life after death."[49] This notion of death as a form of rebirth is also prevalent in episode two, entitled, "The Birth of an Old Lady," in which her death is seen as a release from the suffering and cruelty of this world.

This is the evidence of a more socially critical stance, albeit one that is tempered by the limits of a remaining attachment to an Islamic ideology that sees the solution to social problems within faith in God. While *The Peddler* fails to tackle or apportion blame for the causes of the plight of the poor it does take the first step toward treating the subject of social problems. From the point of view of the Islamic state, revealing the plight and realities of life for the majority of the dispossessed betrays the broken promises of the revolution. Furthermore, a more personalized and organic reading of religious tolerance moves toward questioning a religious dogma that has alienated itself from the populace in its functioning as a form of socialization. It also serves as a tacit questioning of the revolution, for the dispossessed—who were the children and soldiers of the revolution—were not experiencing an improvement in their lot. In *The Peddler*, Makhmalbaf rejects official Islamic rhetoric for a more sophisticated interpretation of man's relationship with God, one that is more in line with the traditional teachings of the Qur'an and is imbued with a certain compassion and humanism that is at odds with the all-encompassing and institutional Islam promoted by the authorities.

*The Peddler* also highlights certain trends that had emerged in Iranian society at the time. The first and last episodes, being situated for the most part in the mosque and the bazaar, identify these two institutions as the cornerstones of Iranian society. The couple in episode one leave their child in the mosque only to discover that it is being exploited by beggars to receive extra alms. They then go to the bazaar and place it beside some businessmen in the mosque there, who ignore it and continue talking about the price and quality of pistachio nuts. In episode three the bazaar for its part is depicted as a squalid den of corruption and murder, stylistically rendered at the beginning of the sequence where the selling of goods is cross-cut with a lamb having its throat cut. These traditional centers of money and power are seen to be callous to the plight of the mostazafin, who were merely paid lip service by official rhetoric (this in a time when the government had begun actively seeking the support of the bazaaris and the middle classes).

The couple in episode one finally leave their child at the house of a wealthy family. However, the final image of the episode shows the child in a hospital for mentally ill and abandoned children, presumably placed there by the wealthy family to which it was abandoned in the hope of a better future. The camera cranes up and pulls out from the child lying helplessly on a bed amid the hysterical laughter and cries of the hospital inmates. The dehumanization of people by poverty and the harshness and cruelty of a society that it has created, far from a revolutionary utopia, is further emphasized in episode. In the second episode, in the scene where the infantile young man is knocked down by a car we see him bundled into the back of a car on the promise of being taken to hospital only to be robbed by the car's inhabitants. Then the couple from episode one appear and take the groceries that the injured man had left on the street. Makhmalbaf attacks the lack of concern about the situation of the poor and the increasing accumulation of wealth by certain classes and capitalism in general. Paradoxically this put Makhmalbaf in line with the orthodox rhetoric of those in power, who constantly preached on the evils of materialism usury and hoarding (Khomeini's oft-repeated phrase "We will drag all capitalists to the court of justice"). In this sense the film operates in the space between official rhetoric and policy, and thus is able to levy criticism at both simultaneously. Taking up the regime's vituperative critique of wealth, *The Peddler* reveals the hollowness of that rhetoric, at the same time condemning, with a realistic take on life in Iran, the intentions and results of the revolution as guided by an elite clerical oligarchy.

### The Cyclist

*The Cyclist* tells the poignant story of Nasim, an Afghan well digger who is desperate to raise money to pay for his ill wife's hospital treatment. With work poorly paid and hard to come by and having been a cycling champion in Afghanistan he accepts a proposal by a businessman to promote him as an Afghan superman who will cycle nonstop for seven consecutive days. Cycling around in a circle in the center of the town square his endeavor attracts the attention of a number of different groups: downtrodden citizens and other Afghan immigrants who see hope for their own plight in the figure of Nasim; shady businessmen and hucksters, who place bets on the spectacle; and government officials who see him as a security threat. Having completed the task, Nasim, an image of resignation and hopelessness, and of exploitation by the end of the film, continues to keep on cycling.

*The Cyclist* continues to develop the social criticism begun in *The Peddler* by examining "many questions about Iran's inadequate economic structure, the nation's vicious circle of poverty and the absurd lengths financially desperate people will go to"[50] in a more coherent, structured, and focused way. Makhmalbaf himself has stated that this trilogy of films "are a critique of capitalism and its effect on our society."[51] In this instance the effects are brought into sharp focus by Makhmalbaf's representation of the hopelessness and despair of the underprivileged by depicting the plight of an Afghan refugee. This choice of central character is significant for a number of reasons, most notably Makhmalbaf's desire to reflect the multicultural and ethnic diversity that makes up the Iranian nation,* and this is a preoccupation that becomes more pronounced in his later work, particularly with regard to the issue of the Afghans.† While this can be seen as a development of Makhmalbaf's portrayal of universal humanity, it also displays the strong tendency, somewhat unique to the films that appeared after the revolution, to reflect Iran's multicultural population. Previous to the revolution, cinema tended to reflect a homogenous Tehrani bias.[51] The new trend served as an affront to the homogenous picture of a united nation put forward in the rhetoric of the ruling clerics, who "constantly stressed that no ethnic distinctions existed within the Muslim community."[52]

However, the attitude toward minorities must be considered within the context of the ideological shift that was taking place in the Islamic Republic at the time, which saw a move toward a more socially inclusive model of society preaching harmony among the classes. This policy extended to minorities such as Khomeini's recognition of the contribution of Jews in the struggle against the shah and the granting of certain concessions to Armenians.[53] The shift in policy was based on the need to maintain unity during the war with Iraq as well as to avoid antagonizing minorities (such as the Kurds in Iran), which might cause them to ally themselves with the enemy or seek autonomy. The concessions to Iran's hybrid culture was also reflected in the desire to paint a more conciliatory profile for foreign policy, by presenting a moderate program and acting as a peaceful arbitrator, to export the revolution by example rather than by force. This was shown by Iran's intervention as an impartial mediator in the conflict between Armenia and Azerbaijan, in order to prevent an Azerbaijani alliance with Turkey that would have had serious and destabilizing consequences for Iran given their own large Azerbaijani population.

---

*Only half the population of Iran is of Persian descent, one-fourth are ethnic Azerbaijanis with the rest consisting of ethnic tribes and ethnic minorities such as the Baluchi, the Bakhtiari, and the Qashqai. At the time Iran also had some two million refugees—more than any other country in the world —mostly Afghan and Iraqi Kurds. See Fen Montaigne, "Iran Testing the Waters of Reform," *National Geographic*, July 1999: 12–13.

†In part three of *The Peddler* there is a short scene in which two Afghan refugees are accused by the police of committing the killing witnessed by the peddler. Makhmalbaf's most recent film *Kandahar* (2001) deals with the issue of Afghan refugees fleeing the Taliban regime in Afghanistan. He followed this film with a plea to the Iranian government and the international community at large to take notice of the plight, and act on behalf of, the Afghan people (BBC Persian World Service, June 18, 2001). This commitment to the situation of the Afghans is also seen in Makhmalbaf's short film *Afghan Alphabet* (2001), which focused on the efforts of young Afghan girls in the border villages between Iran and Afghanistan to receive an education denied them under the Taliban.

While the government was attempting to promote the idea of class harmony Makhmalbaf was once again attempting to show the deep divisions that still existed in Iranian society. The bulk of *The Cyclist* is located in the bazaar, the center of middle-class trade and commerce, presented as a place of corruption and exploitation. Here we have the epitome of the dispossessed cycling around in circles while merchants and businessmen get rich exploiting him. This is rendered cinematically by Makhmalbaf's creation of a claustrophobic atmosphere through expressionistic lighting (where corrupt deals take place in the shadows or in the enclosed spaces of cars or cellar rooms) and increased use of a moving camera in constructing circular imagery that depicts the banality, repetition and pointlessness of Nasim's undertaking. Iran is presented as a fractured country where the masses are still searching for justice, despite the revolution. In fact the dispossessed are not just exploited financially in the film but also ideologically. During Nasim's endurance test a number of socially marginal groups, prisoners, the elderly and lepers, are brought to witness the spectacle and lectured to as an example of a lesson in life. They are told that "happiness lies within us" and that "man lives with his hopes, it is only the spiritual leprosy that is incurable" and that Nasim is a figure of hope and respectability deserving of praise. The overriding cynicism of the film shows the poor and forgotten enmeshed in the rhetoric of the Islamic man; his figure is placed before them as a means of offsetting the misery of their own lives.

In this regard the logic is drawn to absurd lengths, as the suffering and struggle of the exploited Nasim is presented as something to aspire to for those even further down the social ladder. The atmosphere of exploitation is pervasive, and stretches from the bazaaris right up to the official level as the governor fears that the event is drawing together too many disgruntled groups who may cause a threat to the social order. The governor then offers the Afghan workers higher wages and work digging holes in the desert far away from the circus spectacle. Thus there is an inherent tension between the need to create heroes to which, in the absence of tangible improved social conditions, the mostazafin are encouraged to aspire and to prevent these role models from becoming a rallying point for the expression of discontent. Placing *The Cyclist* within the dominant sociopolitical discourse of official nationhood in Iran "serves to challenge the homogenizing and monological narratives that have been served up as the real ones, thereby undoing the totalizing proclivities reflected in traditional history-making."[54] Makhmalbaf has enmeshed himself in an official version of history and nation while struggling to find ways of voicing alternative or dissenting narratives within this cultural straitjacket. In this regard, *The Peddler* must be seen as opening up the question of cinema as a means of treating social issues, while *The Cyclist* combines this in a more focused way with an attempt to open a space around the ideas of Iran and Iranian-ness—in this instance an Iran beset by the exploitation, poverty and despair of the marginalized. The final image of the film shows Nasim having completed his task and being praised as a figure of emulation by the media that has gathered to witness the final stages of his ride. But he is unable to stop and continues to pedal around in circles. This makes clear that despite a momentary release from his predicament Nasim will continue to suffer the hardships of an unjust and unequal system. Rhetoric can attempt to disguise but cannot fully hide the bitterness and inequalities of a society in which people have been betrayed by the broken promises of a revolution that pledged much but offered little. These elements came together in the last film of the trilogy, *Marriage of the Blessed*, to produce what can be seen as Makhmalbaf's most accomplished film until that time.

## Marriage of the Blessed

*Marriage of the Blessed* was Makhmalbaf's most successful film of the time in terms of technical and formal adventurousness and the scope and complexity of its thematic concerns. It tells the story of Haji, a basiji photographer who returns from the war suffering from shell shock and unable to assimilate into a society that he sees as rife with poverty, corruption, and injustice.

Three lines of graffiti scrawled on a wall and shot from a moving car, framed against the hood ornament of the vehicle (a Mercedes-Benz, the ultimate symbol of affluence and Western capitalism) form the opening scene, and set the tone: the first, "Volunteer combatant a lion in battlefields a victim in towns" is ironically contrasted with two quotes of hollow revolutionary rhetoric, from Ayatollah Khomeini: "The country belongs to the shanty dwellers" and "We shall drag all capitalists to the court of justice." *Marriage of the Blessed* is a dense and visually complex film. It first presents a simple sequence of events—the shell-shocked photographer who cannot settle into society after his experience in the Iran-Iraq war. The depiction of his trauma can be seen as a symbol of the greater national condition, in that it is "detached from its basic medical condition and looked at not only as the result of the war, but of everything that led to it and is still unresolved—crime poverty and women's conditions, in Iran."[55] Haji's suffering is depicted both physically—he suffers fits from memories of the battlefield—and mentally, by what he sees as the betrayal of the ideals that he fought for, justice and equality, and their displacement by the greed and corruption of Iranian society. In the scene in the marriage registry office Haji overhears two men making exploitative land deals, which induces a violent hallucination: Haji begins to use his crutch as a gun, believing himself back on the battlefield. Here and throughout, Makhmalbaf casts an angry and satirical eye on the modern-day revolutionary hero and his betrayal by the empty promises of the revolution, while at the same time mocking the Iranian-Islamic model of rectitude.[56] The Islamic man, as Makhmalbaf shows him in Haji, is no longer a virtuous figure defending Islam and standing firm against corruption, but rather a traumatized zombie whose idealism has been crushed, whose sacrifices have proved pointless and who sees the promised utopian society as nothing but hollow rhetoric usurped by the corrupt and wealthy.

The one-dimensional archetypes of Makhmalbaf's Islamic period have been replaced by a fractured character who is a lightning rod for the suffering of a generation faced with an internecine revolution and then war. In the case of style an urgent social agenda links method and subject to produce (as well as showing the process of production) an aesthetic that attains the "beauty of truth."[57] Makhmalbaf's stylistic adventurousness combines a passionate vision with disarrayed glimpses of natural and unnatural ravages in an attempt to engage what actually exists in a non-judgmental way.

## The Interrogation of the Image

In *Marriage of the Blessed,* memory structures the present through the recovery and rehabilitation of the confrontational and disputed space of cultural representation. The site of conflict in *Marriage of the Blessed* is the camera and the image. Memory is the only meaningful remnant the film's characters possess, the only thing that is left to them after the disordering of their values as a result of the revolution and war. Haji's betrothed, Mehri, shows him a series of photographs of their childhood in an attempt to rehabilitate him and draw them closer together through their shared past. Remembrance and the construction of reality through the image is a preoccupation of the film, which is constantly questioning how, by whom and why images are constructed. In one startling scene, Haji, while taking photographs around the city, imagines he sees crowds of fanatical demonstrators waving fists and placards, shouting, "Down with USA!" He raises his camera to his eye, clicks to take the picture and the imagined scene disappears. The stereotypical image of Iran, as created by the Islamic Republic and portrayed in the West, disappears in an indigenous reclamation of space that provides the artist with the opportunity to construct a more truthful representation of Iranian reality. Indeed, this questioning of representation and the attempt to recapture and situate it within complex and disputed contexts is something of a subversive act in challenging not only the monotheist dogma of official culture but also highlighting the way in which it hides and suppresses a multitude of different meanings that are set loose once the cultural space is reclaimed by showing the artifice and manufactured nature of image construction.

Film and the image have shaped Haji's past to such an extent that he attempts to construct his present through the camera. The war is over and the camera must turn to the emerging postwar society and the myriad social problems that were denied or ignored in the Islamic Republic because of the preoccupation with the war with Iraq. A newspaper editor, upon offering Haji a job, tells him, "This is much more complex than the front where you train your gun on the enemy and shoot." He then goes on to suggest, "Focus on shortcomings, but preserve a balanced view" (this can also be seen as a comment on the proliferation of poor quality propagandist films that appeared during the war, the genre that Makhmalbaf subverts in *Marriage of the Blessed*). As Haji goes to photograph the "real" Iran (one beset by poverty and social problems like drug addiction and homelessness) Makhmalbaf himself seems only too aware that "realism" and documentary "truth" are confined by the limits of individual response and personal discovery. In a telling scene, Makhmalbaf and his crew appear on screen, and a policeman halts shooting of the film, asking if they have permission to shoot. Fact and fiction become blurred as artistic expression and official constraint collide in a film that demands a questioning of the mode and means of representation. In this instance Makhmalbaf and Haji meld into one as both are governed by the need to document the real in attempting to find their country and themselves. The question of aesthetics and politics is located in this crossbreeding of fact and fiction where "aesthetically relevant terms are currently negotiated on the no-man's land of creativity where ferocious facts have to accommodate the workings of a noble fantasy." These "ferocious facts" are attested to when Haji goes into Tehran's drug-infested slums to document the lives of the destitute shanty dwellers. When the pictures that he takes are eventually censored by the newspaper, the editor remarks that, "You can't solve social problems with a couple of photographs." Makhmalbaf knows this only too well and steers clear of pedantic value judgments, through the almost obsessive foregrounding and reflexive self-consciousness to which the camera/image is constantly subjected. He strips away the artifice of film by showing the means of production, such as Makhmalbaf and his crew appearing on screen. This also challenges the normally invisible role of the camera itself, as people look directly into the lens throughout Haji's photo reportage, questioning the objective or hermetically sealed rendering of reality.

In this respect *Marriage of the Blessed* may be seen (as far as it is socially and politically committed) to be an investigation of the director-camera-image relationship. The foregrounding of the artifice of image construction reveals the complexities and problems of depicting reality.

In one scene Haji learns that his pictures of the plight of the poor have not been published because the newspaper decided instead to publish an inoffensive picture of a sunflower, which Haji took at the end of his odyssey through the shantytowns. This not only represents the difficulty and frustration of the search for "truth" (and may also be seen as a coded comment on Islamic revolutionary ideals, as the tulip, *laleh*, is the Shia symbol of martyrdom) but also provides a commentary on the frustrations experienced by filmmakers themselves in trying to make critical, socially engaged films that are not necessarily in accordance with the wishes of the regime. When Haji learns of the newspaper editor's "censorship" of his photos, he starts to have another seizure, this time while driving his motorcycle. What the viewer then sees is a series of iris shots from Haji's point of view.* He has now become inseparable from, and the physical embodiment of, the camera, constructed and defined through the image; he is literally the "anxious eye of the revolution."

The link between subject and object (in this case between image and audience) is most startlingly presented in a straight-to-camera long take at Mehri's photo exhibition. The exhibition features photographs taken by women covering all facets of womanhood in Iranian society (young girls, derelicts, *chador*-clad women with guns). The camera remains static in a wide shot throughout the scene, acting as an image/photo/mirror and a direct link to the audience, as characters pass by and are questioned by an interviewer, before addressing the camera directly. Here the illusionist tendency of cinema is most effectively and self-consciously shattered and the spectator is forced into an analytic rather than a sympathetic relationship with the subject matter.

The exhibition scene also provides a glance at women in the Islamic Republic. One of the reasons Makhmalbaf is celebrated in Iran is for his "populist hard-hitting films championing the cause of the oppressed, particularly women,"[59] and here are portrayed a number of women and their different social roles. The presentation of women in Iranian films has been plagued with so much difficulty that they are generally reduced to subservient, simplistic, maternal roles or removed from stories altogether. In line with official ideology they are portrayed as modest and chaste role models and good mothers who raise God-fearing children ready to serve the Islamic Republic. *Marriage of the Blessed* subverts these notions by presenting a series of counter-images of women in the photographs displayed at the exhibition. There are a series of images of women holding machine guns, and prostitutes and destitute women begging in the streets, undermining the notion of women as the virtuous mothers of martyrs or the quiet inhabitants

---

*This refers to an adjustable diaphragm in the camera which opens or closes like an expanding or contracting circle, giving a similar effect on the screen. Very prevalent in silent cinema it gets its name from its resemblance to the iris of the human eye.

of inner rooms. The scene also highlights and questions the ambiguous and contradictory role of women in the Islamic Republic. The new regime had forced women into a more public role. The war with Iraq and the shortage of manpower diverted women into the workforce and it was to them that Khomeini appealed in urging their husbands and sons to volunteer for the front. Furthermore, the population explosion and the chronic economic situation had left many women no choice but to seek employment. Despite these seemingly progressive steps women's actions and freedoms within the public sphere were severely restricted and controlled. The central issue in this regard was that of enforced public dress and appearance, as the Islamic Republic again reinforced its role as the guardian of morality by regulating the interaction between the sexes in public. Moreover, women were deemed legally subservient to men, reflected in the laws that prevent women from initiating a divorce, that hold a woman's testimony in court worth half of a man's, and that prohibit a woman from leaving the country without her husband's written consent. As Makhmalbaf himself notes, "The chauvinist mentality is something very established in Iran. Even in our literature you can see that in the stories about lovers, the man is most often the real subject of the narrative, the whole story is based on him."[60] The photo exhibition where the chador-clad gun-toting militant in the service of the state is contrasted with those whom the regime has forgotten or abandoned or who are forced through circumstances to beg and work as prostitutes because of economic and social conditions.

**The Insider as Outsider**

Through the central character of Haji we are presented with the image of the insider as outsider. Makhmalbaf has referred to him as "a symbol of a generation in anger against that which they have not been able to have. It is the symbol of the generation of the revolution which searched for justice, but which now sees injustice."[61] The viewer is taken on a personal and physical journey through a ravaged and disillusioned society by an individual weighed down with memory. This creative understanding is predicated to a certain extent on a location, culturally, and in time and space, outside the object. Consequently new aspects and semantic depths are revealed about the complexities of culture and society. However this outsider-ness (as Makhmalbaf has also positioned himself) is as threatening as it is productive, both to the individual and the establishment as it questions the status quo (Haji finds this out through censorship, frustration and ultimately alienation). Yousef, one of Haji's war comrades, makes a speech at Haji and Mehri's wedding banquet that testifies to this fact: "Brother Haji's camera is the anxious eye of the revolution. He has a passionate mind and a sorrowful heart. Let us hear the remembrance of this sorrowful heart." The use of the word revolution here is crucial and is presented in an ironic way. The children of the revolution are now the dispossessed having seen their initial fervor and ideals frustrated and then thwarted. Here the utterance becomes an intense conflict between one's own experience and another promised, ideal world, be that imagined or forgotten. This is a situation symptomatic of the film itself, which sees the image, like the word, emanating from an individual as a product of the interaction of social forces.

## The Politics of Criticizing the System

Makhmalbaf satirizes the selfish materialism of the new class of entrepreneurs who have emerged since the revolution, seeking gain through exploitation in explicit contradiction to the expressed ideals of Islam. At the marriage registry office men secretly propose exploitative land deals, and in the bazaar Mehri's father grumbles over the price and quality of watermelons, an ironic echo of Ayatollah Khomeini's assertion, "We did not make this revolution for cheaper melons," while poverty abounds. These are men who have embraced the new capitalist vision with vigor, and know how to use its methods. Women reside outside of this system and the film shows the concomitant effect this has on them—destitution, begging in the slums, and in one scene, one of Haji's neighbors is forced to beg on the streets when her husband is taken away by the authorities, accused of criminal activities. Furthermore, the film calls into question the doctrinal teachings on which the Islamic Republic is based, as well as examining the desire to create an Islamic economics that sought to forbid such practices as "dealing in interest which takes advantage of others and permits an increase in the wealth of the lender of money without his working for it.... Neither are any sorts of commercial interests permitted to exploit people."[62] The Islamic Republic has preached an anti-materialist message based on the Qur'anic dictates of justice and the forbidding of usury, in an effort to alter behavioral norms by creating a humanistic and altruistic individual, and by extension society,[63] based on the Prophet's declaration "O ye who believe! Let not your wealth nor your children distract you from the remembrance of Allah. Those who do so, they are the losers."[64] Again, Makhmalbaf's cinematic discourse aligns him with official rhetoric while simultaneously exposing that rhetoric as hypocrisy. While Makhmalbaf does depict aspects of Iran that the regime would like to hide, he does it according to Islamic doctrine, as a lever with which to introduce certain unsavory themes surreptitiously. Indeed, Makhmalbaf himself attests to this by showing that the central character of the film does not signify an opposition to the established order but rather stands as someone who believes in justice and the revolution that he took part in. What the film is attempting to examine is the betrayal of the revolutionary ideals and a call for the existing system to make good on its promises—the reform of the system, not its overthrow. This is a critique that is mirrored in the debate of how to represent a complex situation given the complexity of the image itself, its multiplicity of connoted meanings and representations. In the scene at Haji and Mehri's wedding feast Haji is taking photographs of children playing and the film cuts to images of starving children shown earlier in the film and which Haji had taken on photo assignments before the war in various parts of the world. Later, in his wedding speech, Haji invites the guests to "eat the food robbed from the poor." He is once again trapped by the connotation of meaning and memory. The ideals of justice, equality and the search for a better society that he believed in and attempted to document and highlight with his camera have proved illusory. He is trapped among his images and high-minded ideals to which he has devoted his life and is unable to adapt them to the realities of the present. In other words his whole belief system has been destroyed and revealed as hollow rhetoric, and has alienated him from a society that seems to have moved on. The film renders this alienation stylistically near the end in a zoom-in and rack-focus on the bars in the hospital as he Haji talks to Mehri, following his breakdown at the wedding. He is mentally and physically imprisoned and resignedly tells Mehri that the middle-class materialism and capitalist exploitation practiced by people like her father will "defeat the revolution from the inside." This serves as a prelude for the film's closing scene.

At the end of the film Haji escapes from the hospital and begins to live on the streets, becoming in the process the subject of someone else's photographic reportage, as does Mehri, who goes in search of him. Thus, in a neat reversal the photographer becomes the photographed—the creator of the image is now the image. The attempt to uncover a "reality" behind official rhetoric, the betrayal of ideals and the inability to accept the realities of the present has resulted in a voyage of self-discovery. For Haji this has resulted in frustration, alienation and censorship. The complexities involved in constructing images of reality in an attempt to uncover the truth have, in a sense, failed Haji. The only way for him to come to terms with his past and present, and to discover this truth, is actually to live the image that he believes in and to retain his beliefs through disengagement from the society that is alien to him.

The film ends with a high-angle shot of Tehran as gunfire fades into music. It is a contemplative image. In a society scarred by war and a gripped by social problems how are artists to approach the representation and interrogation of these problems? According to Abbas Kiarostami, "The only thing that art can do is encourage the audience to think, to ponder meaning…as directors we have no right to pronounce judgments. Our mission is to raise issues."[65] However, Makhmalbaf's is a more active and at times polemic cinema. His progression from the didacticism of his Islamic period is reflected in a more thoughtful and complex approach to issues that are built on a process of constant self-examination and critical awareness of the constructed nature of meaning. The open-ended nature of *Marriage of the Blessed,* and the Mostazafin Trilogy as a whole, stand as the first serious engagement by a filmmaker of the complexities of the world around him in an attempt to explore the possibilities of the cinematic medium and a drive to educate the self in the working out of the individual's relationship to art, society and God.

# 5 | THE POETICS OF CONTEMPLATION

Ayatollah Khomeini's death marked the end of the radical phase of the revolution, as attention moved to reconstructing a country shattered by a decade of war and unrest. It was also a time in which Iranian cinema matured artistically and thematically, and emerged on the international stage to critical acclaim. Makhmalbaf's films during this period show a discernible shift, as they began a critical engagement with the medium of film, itself, along with attempts to develop a philosophical aesthetics of contemplation, which brought him into open conflict with the ruling authorities.

## Khomeini's Legacy

The first decade of the Islamic Republic came to an end on 3 June 1989 with the announcement of the death of its founder and spiritual leader Ayatollah Khomeini. What Khomeini left behind was a battle-scarred and war-weary nation,* a divided ruling elite, a shattered economy with mounting social problems, and a political system that had just lost the creator and embodiment of its raison d'être, the personification of the principle of velayat-e faqih. Indeed, Khomeini's legacy to Iran was characterized by "muddle and division, economic collapse and isolation" and a failure to create anything approximating the "ideal Islamic society."[1] However, those seeing in the death of Khomeini the demise of the Islamic Republic itself were to be sorely disappointed. The Khomeini decade had been marked by the elimination of all internal opposition groups and the consolidation of a religio-political system that provided for the perpetuation of clerical rule and as such, any dissonant voices,

---

*The hostilities of the eight-year war with Iraq ended in August 1988. However, peace negotiations dragged on and the war ended officially in August 1990 when Saddam Hussein signed the terms of a negotiated settlement, as laid down in UN Security Council Resolution 598. This was done more in a bid to guarantee Iranian neutrality before Iraq became embroiled in the 1991 Gulf War than in any desire to reach a final agreement. The legacy of the conflict still sours relations between the two countries as issues, such as the transfer of prisoners of war, remain unresolved.

or indeed calls for reform, could only come from within the system itself. Therefore, the struggle to fill the power vacuum created by the death of Khomeini was fought along differing ideological interpretations of the late ayatollah's legacy, which was seen as the legitimating basis of the right to rule that would dictate the future course of developments in all areas of Iranian society.

## The Second Republic

These political machinations began less than twenty-four hours after Khomeini's death, with former President of the Islamic Republic, Ali Khamenei, elevated to the rank of ayatollah and, somewhat controversially, decreed as the country's new Supreme Leader. The reorientation of the new ruling elite was completed some two months later when the former Speaker of the Majles, Ali Akbar Hashemi Rafsanjani, was elected as the country's new president. He declared economic reconstruction to be his top priority and pledged to move Iranian society toward liberalization, reform and an openness to the outside world. The new Rafsanjani-led administration, composed mainly of pragmatists (a loose coalition of conservatives and "reformed populists"), and which came to be known as the Second Republic, promised much and seemed to herald a radical departure from the previous decade and the old order of insularity, dogmatism and revolutionary rhetoric, with its promises to install equality, freedom and economic justice. However, despite this initial optimism many of Rafsanjani's proposed reforms were never effectively implemented, due to the internal factionalism of feuding ideologues, and his failure to properly address the state's structural problems. These factors were compounded by ideological disputes among the ruling elite as to the future direction of the state and the type of economic reforms that were to be pursued. Such disputes resulted in a political stalemate that jettisoned needed economic reforms and restructuring in favor of the status quo that primarily sought to serve the monetary interests of the elite and middle classes, resulting in a widening of the already large disparity of wealth in Iran.

The government of the Second Republic became increasingly paralyzed by open disputes between radicals and conservatives on all aspects concerning the direction of the state. Indeed, by the mid-1990s the conservative faction was in complete control, rendering the executive branch ineffective and smothering any debate on issues of reform or societal development that might threaten their privileged status. As always these debates and their consequences were played out and reflected in the cultural sphere as attention was focused once again on the preservation of "moral values." These were upheld through the censorship and control of the media and the press in propagating "Islamic values" against what was seen by those in power as the "cultural onslaught" of foreign influences. This situation led to the arrest of many intellectuals and writers as the conservatives sought to close all avenues of protest through the imposition of some of the harshest and most repressive measures seen since the early days of the revolution. By the end of Rafsanjani's final term in office in 1997 the country was "rife with corruption more extensive than during the Pahlavi Dynasty, paralyzed politically by irreconcilable factional disputes and sinking fast economically."[2]

### Cinema in the Era of Reconstruction

For the cinema, though, certain changes and advancements were discernible. The post-1989 period witnessed an increase in films of a higher quality, in both form and content. While Iranian films were aggressively being registered in international festivals, there was increased attention to the implementation of the financial, regulative, technical and production infrastructure needed for sustaining the high level of film output necessary to accommodate a swelling population and to offset the influx of the perceived evils of Western cultural imperialism. However, the underlying tensions between filmmakers and those in power lingered, with issues like censorship and the inescapable influence of the government on film production. As always there was a fine line between freedom of expression and official censorship, because "although political and social criticisms were not unknown in films, care was taken not to offend the clerical establishment or the religious doctrines and saints."[3] This situation had been developing since the latter part of the war with Iraq and came into sharper focus with the social and political changes that occurred in the country during the Second Republic. The development of the cinema of this period reveals a picture of oscillating and contrasting fortunes. Iranian cinema appeared on the world stage, due in no small part to its active and officially-sanctioned promotion abroad through the office of the Ministry of Islamic Culture and Guidance and the work of the Farabi Cinema Foundation. In a way, cinema evolved into a strand of government foreign policy, as a universally understood cultural product, designed to "export the revolution" through example rather than force. This reformulated policy also served the purpose of presenting a positive image of the Islamic regime abroad as it sought to open up to, and develop relations with, the outside world, not least in its attempts to attract foreign finance and investment for the massive postwar reconstruction program. While repression of free speech and censorship of artistic expression continued on the domestic front, these films (many of which were critical of the regime, or deemed "un-Islamic" and therefore banned from screens in Iran) became, unwittingly, the simultaneous voices of protest (in a restricted and controlled sense) and the promoters of a false cultural liberalism that the regime was keen to manufacture and show abroad even if the reality could not be further from the truth.

Throughout the lifetime of the Second Republic cinema, like the media and press, proceeded from an initial relaxing of restrictions in the early days of the new administration. After 1992, though, the parliament was purged of radical and reformist elements, and the conservatives consolidated their power and control. This change in leadership led to a severe crackdown on all dissident cultural expression and attacks on what was seen, by those in power, as nefarious foreign influences. Once again the clamor for reform and the course of the country's future development was being formulated in the cultural realm. However, this time circumstances had changed. The effects of globalization, the emergence of a new, educated and articulate elite, as well as the demands of an increasingly disgruntled youth population, meant that these demands could not go unheeded and that the traditional recourse to repressive measures could only go so far. The advent of satellite broadcasting began to open up a whole new world of possibilities to Iranians and by 1994 it was estimated by the Iranian press that more than two million people watched foreign broadcasts. Grand Ayatollah Araki voiced his concern about this new technology and what he saw as its ability to corrupt the youth and produce a counter-Islamic message, declaring that, "Installing satellite antennae opens the Islamic society to inroads of decadent foreign culture and the spread of ruinous diseases to Muslims and is forbidden."[4] As cinema was considered a more controllable medium those in power saw it as a bulwark against the more unpredictable satellite broadcasts. The changed intellectual and ideological environment and the agents driving the demands for change meant that reform was being called for and operating in the cultural realm through media to which the conservatives were finding it increasingly hard to adapt and respond.

The reasons for and implications of this turnaround are manifold. Slackening of the tempo and fervor of the drive to Islamicize the mass media was replaced after Khomeini's death by a transfer in emphasis to more pressing economic and social problems. The incessant sermonizing decreased to a certain degree as the government felt that it had begun to create "a backlash reducing the size of the audience and hence threatening the reach and effectiveness of the medium as a convenient ideological tool."[5] Furthermore, constitutional amendments had further increased the institutional role and power of the president, who along with the new Spiritual Leader of the Islamic Republic, Ayatollah Khamenei, was keen to portray a more "moderate" image of Islam and improve Iran's position on the world stage. Thus a rather nervous and unsure government sought to create a more liberal and diversified cultural policy in order to reach a wider audience.

## Makhmalbaf's Third Period

For Makhmalbaf this period was characterized by three stages of development that were in many ways a product of the aforementioned changing sociocultural climate. His first two films of the time, both of which were banned in Iran, seemed to confirm Makhmalbaf's transformation into one of the leading members of the outsider group of filmmakers: *Nobat-e Asheghi* (*Time of Love*, 1991) and *Shabha-ye Zayandeh-Rud* (*Nights of the Zayandeh-Rud*, 1991) continued in the socially committed vein of his Mostazafin Trilogy and also explored sensitive social issues such as adultery and physical love. In the next four films, *Nassereddin Shah, Actor-e Cinema* (*Once upon a Time, Cinema*, 1992), *Honarpisheh* (*The Actor*, 1993), *Salaam Cinema* (1995) and *Nun va Goldun* (*A Moment of Innocence*, 1996) Makhmalbaf explored history, the state, and cinematic language as a mode of artistic expression. In these films, and particularly in *Salaam Cinema* (1995) and *A Moment of Innocence* (1996), we see the full realization of the dialectic of cinema and Iran positioned as lenses in a state of constant reflection. *Gabbeh* (1996) brought this period to an end and heralded Makhmalbaf's emergence onto the world scene, though it also marked a change in aesthetics and form that was to influence his later work. Still preoccupied with the question of form Gabbeh saw Makhmalbaf dispense with the self-reflexivity of his previous work and attempt to break cinema down to its basic component parts, conjuring a more humanistic, poetic, and philosophical celebration of life.

## The 1989 Constitution and the New Power Structure

The foundation of the new emerging power structure lay in the 1989 amendments to the constitution. These changes were undertaken in a bid to ensure a smooth transition of power, bolster the legitimacy of the new ruling elite and create a framework in which the aims of the state (in this instance economic reform), rather than Islam, could be pursued without the stalemate that had plagued previous administrations. The complex and contradictory nature of the new reforms can be seen in the overarching importance of measures taken to reduce the power and influence of the faqih. The new constitution separated the charismatic authority of the faqih from the stated requirement that he be a *marja* (the highest source of religious emulation), redefining its role in purely rational terms. Rather than possessing divine piety and moral authority, as originally stated in the 1979 Constitution, the revised Article 109 stated that the new Supreme Leader should possess sufficient "scholarship as required for performing the functions of *mufti* (religious interpretation) in fields of *fiqh* (religious jurisprudence). In essence this relegated the faqih to a post of spiritual leader who no longer had to be a source of religious imitation but could be chosen from among any religious scholars who possessed the knowledge of Islamic law as well as political experience. However, the apparent weakening of the position of the faqih in spiritual standing was more than compensated by the extension, as laid down in Article 110, of his institutional powers, which included: assuming supreme command of the armed forces, responsibility for the issuance of decrees for national referenda and the ability to appoint, dismiss or accept the resignation of, among others, the supreme judicial authority and the head of national radio and television. This new definition of the faqih gave legitimacy to the appointment of Khamenei, who possessed neither the seniority of rank nor the principle of marja. It was also an attempt to place more authority in the hands of the president, which Article 60 achieved by expanding the role of the president, abolishing the post of prime minister.

The nature of the new appointment and the constitutional changes made to facilitate it had "unwittingly undermined the theological foundations of Khomeini's velayat-e faqih."[6] Given that the system of governance in the Islamic Republic is built on the rule of the jurist, the weakening of its powers inevitably creates questions about the legitimacy of the entire system. Furthermore, by separating the religious charisma of the marja from the faqih there arose the possibility that this charisma would be displaced onto the president* or to a marja outside the system, potentially leading to fractured and competing power bases. Despite these concerns the changes were designed to centralize power in the hands of the clergy by attempting to legislate and compensate for the absence of the unifying presence of Khomeini and to alleviate the stalemate of competing power relations† by concentrating power in the hands of the executive branch of government. This facilitated the proposed economic development plans and infrastructural renovation,

---

*This was something that Rafsanjani was keen to encourage due in no small part to his own vanity and his desire to protect his privileged interests, such as the family business the Rafsanjan Pistachio Producers' Cooperative, which is the largest pistachio enterprise in the country. Perhaps the full manifestation of this transfer of charismatic authority is seen in the adulation and elevated expectations that have been projected onto the person of the current president, Mohammad Khatami. This was contrasted with Rafsanjani's fate in the 2000 elections where he waged an advertisement drive and distributed some two million fliers during a campaign he expected to win easily, yet only squeaked into the last seat in Tehran by a slim majority, having captured just over twenty-five percent of the vote. He relinquished his seat prior to the parliament convening but as head of the Expediency Council he continues to wield power that is more often than not partisan, as in the decree that the new parliament under Khatami had no authority to investigate any institution or foundation under the purview of the Supreme Leader.

†This had been particularly acute between the Majles and the Council of Guardians (the body appointed to rule on the Islamic credentials of all bills passed by the parliament and to decree whether they should become law) with the latter essentially having veto power over all legislation. In a bid to solve the problem the Expediency Discernment Council was set up in 1988 with the power to override a veto by the Council of Guardians. Article 112 of the 1989 Constitutional review made the Expediency Discernment Council into a permanent body, to strengthen Rafsanjani's parliamentary hand. This was seen as a necessary step that would compensate for the absence of the authoritative interventionary presence of Khomeini, but in reality it has merely resulted in the further formalization and division of competing power sources.

making it possible to achieve them in a comprehensive and amenable manner. Furthermore, the reconstituted political structure would create an administration in which the republican and popular sources of legitimacy, rather than the Islamic sources, were increasingly emphasized.

## Cultural Glasnost?

The initial days of the Rafsanjani presidency offered much promise. The stated priority of economic reform was reflected in the makeup of the new cabinet, dominated by technocrats, no less than a third of whom were educated in the West, and who were charged with rebuilding the country's infrastructure after the devastation of the war years. They sought to instigate a recovery program that would expand the private sector and encourage the role of foreign investment under the direction of a series of five-year plans that began in 1990. This openness was also reflected in some tentative changes in the sociocultural sphere, like the legalization of chess (which had been banned for encouraging gambling) as well as the growth of the theater and arts and the revival of traditional Iranian classical music (which had been deemed un-Islamic). Perhaps of more significance was the recognition by Ayatollah Khamenei that the ruins of the ancient pre-Islamic monarchy at Persepolis were "a heritage of mankind that must be preserved."* This marked something of a cultural shift in the thinking of the clergy as the ancient ruins were more often considered as a symbol of corrupt monarchies and forever associated with the extravagance and arrogance of Mohammad Reza Shah.† It was also a tacit admission by the regime of the existence of the notion of an Iranian nation and that Iranian culture was Persian-Islamic in nature—both unintended recognitions that the all-consuming Islamicization policy of the previous decade had been less than successful. The press was also experiencing something of a renaissance with the number of journals and newspapers rising from 102 in 1988–89 to 369 in 1992–1993, many of which were critical of the new government.[7]

These developments may appear insignificant but they could not have been implemented "without the changes in the structure of power after Khomeini's death."[8] That there was no substantial structural change in the liberalization of Iranian society can be attributed primarily to the monolithic economic program and its developmental benefits that accrued to and strengthened the position of the mercantile bourgeoisie. In this regard Rafsanjani acted, despite the rhetoric, on the premise

---

*Rafsanjani went one step further in April 1991 when he visited Persepolis, calling on Iranians "to reinforce their national dignity." See Shireen T. Hunter, *Iran after Khomeini*, 94

†Mohammad Reza Shah, last shah of Iran, held an elaborate ceremony among the ancient ruins of Persepolis in 1971 to celebrate 2,500 years of monarchy, which statesmen from all over the world attended. The pomp and extravagance of the event was symbolic of an arrogant leader increasingly alienated from the general populous many of whom were living in conditions of poverty at the time.

that the need, and demands, for society to develop, and the subsequent establishment of channels of free expression and political protest, would become unnecessary and irrelevant if the economy improved. All factors were placed in the service and promotion of the economy, and the veneer of a liberal society was only useful insofar as it served economic purposes, for example the attraction of foreign investment or to reinforce the position of the ruling elite. Rafsanjani's policies of deregulation, privatization and integrating Iran into the capitalist world system resulted in fueling the profit-making spirit of private entrepreneurs.

Rafsanjani essentially succeeded in creating "a bourgeois republic dominated by a bureaucratic-authoritarian structure which sought to compensate for the loss of charismatic authority by establishing a political network founded on mercantile interests."[9] This was not an entirely new occurrence, as the shift toward appeasing the middle classes had begun under Khomeini as an expedient element for consolidating the locus of power in the bazaar and the mosque. Rafsanjani had merely extended the concept, and consequently elevated the role of the middle classes, developing it into a concrete political structure based on commercial power operating through a self-serving bureaucratic administration, dominated by himself. Indeed, it must also be noted that the authoritarian economic form of governance, which links "political despotism and economic oppression,"[10] has a long and pronounced history in Iran. The shah had tried to introduce modernization without modernity and the establishment of civil institutions, and was eventually overthrown, as were the Safavids and the Qajars, because despotism in Iran has historically prevented "a widely diffused power base from emerging,"[11] resulting in the alliance of disparate voices of protest through alternative channels—the example of the Islamic revolution itself. However, in the Second Republic emerging tensions were kept in check by economic safety valves, such as the exemption of essential imported foodstuffs from exchange rate fluctuations, which served the dual purpose of guaranteeing the support of the less privileged elements of society and of the powerful institutions and religious foundations that administered these goods for further economic reward.[12] These safety valves were reinforced by cultural manipulation, seen in the use of cinema during this period, which came to function as the regime's cultural ambassador abroad.

### Economic Reconstruction, Ideological Reorientation

Part of the new economic reconstruction plan required an opening up of the country in order to attract much-needed foreign loans. This was concomitant with proving to potential investors that a liberal and stable society, which actively encouraged investment, now existed within the country. Furthermore, the effects of globalization and new information technology meant that Iranian society was becoming increasingly exposed to outside influences that no longer made the pursuit of an isolationist policy realistic. The balancing act of those in power became one of trying to promote the veneer of a liberal, active and culturally open society and to prevent the spread of "Westoxification" and foreign influences that were seen as the driving force behind demands for increased freedom, democracy and a civil society that ultimately posed a threat to the position of the conservative and reactionary ruling clerical elite.

Rafsanjani had attempted to manipulate Khomeini's ideas in order "to legitimate a project that was economically liberal, politically authoritarian and philosophically traditional."[13] By the end of his first term in office he was finding this course more and more difficult to maintain and was increasingly pushed toward a more conservative strategy by conflicts that were emerging within the ruling elite. The isolation and removal of radical Majles deputies in 1992 by the conservative clerics was to prove a double-edged sword for Rafsanjani. While his political machinations had removed some of his harshest critics it forced him into an exclusive alliance with the conservative clerical establishment that left him no room to maneuver. The latter were supportive of the economic reform program, which proved beneficial to their financial interests, but were extremely hostile to any attempt to instigate any kind of political or cultural reforms. In pursuing this goal the conservatives began to eject reformers from those state institutions seen as necessary to imposing and controlling ideological obedience.

### Culture and Ideology Refocused

Iran's new strictly economic relationships with the outside world marked an ideological shift from Khomeini's desire and primary foreign policy objective to export the Islamic revolution abroad. He had proclaimed early on that "We should try hard to export our revolution to the world… because Islam does not regard various Islamic countries differently and is a supporter of all the oppressed…. If we remain in an enclosed environment we shall definitely face defeat…we [shall] confront the world with our ideology."[14] Given the failure of the war, this objective needed to be reconsidered in more pragmatic and less confrontational terms. What began was a reassessment and appropriation of the terms of Khomeini's objective in order to adapt it to changed circumstances and ideological needs. This in itself serves as an example of the competition among the ruling elite in the post-Khomeini era to lay claim to Khomeini's legacy, which had as its basic aim the legitimation of the right to rule and the successful implementation of policy. Furthermore, the other stated aims within Khomeini's speech—the role of "the oppressed" and the need to "confront the world with our ideology"—had also exhibited marked changes over the years. The former had seen a widening gap develop between rich and poor since the start of the revolution as well as a shift in emphasis by the ruling elite toward the needs and concerns of the middle classes, a fact confirmed with the mercantile bourgeois orientation of the Second Republic. However, the second point, which once again referred to the need to export the revolution in order for the revolution to survive and flourish, was to prove the more complex part of policy reorientation and revolved around a cultural-economic axis that exposed the deep differences of opinion among the ruling clerics.

### The Media and the Export of the Revolution

The changed ideological format of revolution export shifted from aggressive confrontation to the promotion of good examples (primarily through the use of the cultural medium), which it was hoped would be emulated abroad. For Rafsanjani, this was to be achieved, and could only be made possible, through economic success, which could be publicized and promoted through the use of new information technology and opportunities provided by the impact of globalization. The export of revolution by force was replaced by one of example, all actively promoted through strictly-controlled government media.* "The General Policies and Principles of the Voice and Vision Organization of the Islamic Republic of Iran" had clearly laid down the duties and obligations of the mass media by stating that it should endeavor to promote and uphold the principles of Islam, the velayat-e faqih and the policy of "Neither East nor West." Furthermore, the Ministry of Culture and Islamic Guidance was charged with formulating and carrying out these ideological policies both inside and outside of Iran. The ideological change in focus and circumstance was clearly reflected in the words of the Foreign Minister, Ali Akbar Velayati: "We must continue to export our revolution, but in cultural terms. The Western countries are doing the same thing. They export their culture, their way of thinking, through the mass media or universities where foreign students are taught."[15] Once again the cultural and the political became officially and inextricably linked. This influence was crucial for the new administration, as the absence of real and meaningful structural reform in the social and political arena meant that the illusion of a new liberal society was maintained through the tight control and selective promotion of ideologically servile cultural products.

### Iranian Cinema on the World Stage

The progress of Iranian cinema during this period reflected the changed and complex conditions of expedient revolutionary export.

---

*One such example of government-controlled media actively engaged in spreading the message of revolution was the establishment of a radio station on Kish Island in the Persian Gulf. This station broadcast Iranian propaganda to the Gulf region as well as to Egypt, Sudan, Saudi Arabia and Jordan urging revolution. See R. K. Ramazani, *Revolutionary Iran: Challenge and Response in the Middle East*.

In 1988, the year before Rafsanjani came to power, forty-seven Iranian films were screened in international film festivals and events around the world, winning a total of two awards. The following table shows the dramatic increase in their presence abroad during Rafsanjani's first term in office, 1989-1993:

| YEAR | NUMBER OF IRANIAN FILMS SHOWN IN FOREIGN FESTIVALS AND EVENTS | NUMBER OF AWARDS WON BY IRANIAN FILMS |
|---|---|---|
| 1989 | 88 | 17 |
| 1990 | 377 | 19 |
| 1991 | 291 | 22 |
| 1992 | 279 | 23 |
| 1993 | 415 | 26 |

Source: Mohammad-Mehdi Duagoo, "Government Policies," *Cinemaya: The Asian Film Quarterly*, no. 22 (Winter 1993-1994): 64-67.

The Farabi Cinema Foundation, operating under the auspices of the Ministry of Culture and Islamic Guidance, began to increase its centralized control of film by implementing a series of measures to promote aggressively Iranian cinema aggressively, in line with government policy.[16] These included the strict governmental control of imported and exported films and a system where the Ministry of Culture paid for the expenses of promoting "superior Iranian films" at the international level, only receiving repayment from producers when the films had been sold in foreign markets.[17] Furthermore, a whole arsenal of government facilities, advertisement, distribution, licensing and screening was placed in the service of promoting these so-called superior products. The desire to extend and promote cinema as an element of government policy operated through the apparatus that placed Iranian cinema on the international scene. According to Fakhreddin Anvar, undersecretary for cinema to the Minister of Culture and Islamic Guidance, the aim was in "changing foreign viewers' image of Iran and making them question their attitude about the country."[18]

In 1990 the Venice International Film Festival approached the Farabi Cinema Foundation (FCF) with a view to procuring a selection of films by the director Amir Naderi* in order to hold a retrospective of his work. The FCF agreed to release the films on the condition that

---

*Amir Naderi is one of Iran's foremost film directors. Having begun his career in the pre-revolutionary era he has found it increasingly difficult to make films under the Islamic regime because of his critical and highly allegorical style. He was refused production permits on numerous occasions and has had many of his works either banned or heavily censored, for example, *Water, Wind, Sand* (1984) was banned for five years before being released for screenings at international festivals only. Shortly after this film was made he was forced to leave Iran in order to continue making films. He settled in New York where he continues to live and make films.

the festival screen some thirty other films that had been produced or
financed by Farabi. These additional films were propagandist in nature,
serving the express aim of promoting the "achievements [of the Islamic
Republic] since the 1979 revolution...and propagating Shiite cultural
values."[19] In this way official cultural policy has allowed controversial
and critical films to act as the promoters of a heavily adulterated, false
image of the existence of a liberal and vibrant cultural atmosphere,
while simultaneously serving as a means through which the ideologically desired aims of the regime can be simultaneously pursued through
the release of films in tune with true Islamic values.*

Furthermore, it is interesting to note that the international promotion of Iranian cinema also reflected and enhanced the division
between an artistic and a commercial cinema with the former at the
vanguard of foreign promotion and the latter strictly limited to the
domestic market, thus giving foreign audiences a somewhat skewed
picture of the film industry in Iran. This division was illustrated by disputes within the political power structure concerning the nature and
implementation of government cultural policy, and the uncertainties
and fear of the potential power of these films. Ayatollah Khamenei
echoed these concerns, stating that, "It does not impress me if we win
foreign awards because these films often have dubious agendas."[20] To
avoid such uncertainties and to maintain tight control of the domestic cultural arena many of these films, while praised and lauded on
the international scene, were either censored or banned from Iranian
screens. This contradictory cultural policy in relation to domestic and
international audiences has served "to promote the misconception that
at least in the area of filmmaking, there is freedom of artistic expression
in the Islamic Republic."[21] Makhmalbaf's first two films produced during this era, *Time of Love* (1991) and *Nights of the Zayandeh-Rud* (1991)
are symptomatic and instructive in this case.†

## Censorship and the International Market

*Time of Love* and *Nights of the Zayandeh-Rud* caused a storm of protests
when they were screened at the Ninth Fajr International Film Festival
in Tehran in February 1991. They were attacked for their depictions
of physical love and critical commentary on society, which the govern-
ment-sponsored press saw as advocating corruption and fornication,
insulting the families of martyrs and serving to undermine the values

---

*See Behjat Riza'ee, *Persian Meditations*, for a more detailed discussion of this incident.

†These examples are in no way intended as exclusive and limited to one particular time period. Jafar
Panahi's film *The Circle* (2000), a hard-hitting social commentary on the constraints and difficulties faced
by women in Iranian society, was widely shown on Western screens but remains banned in Iran. This
illustrates the fact that the domestic/international debate continues under President Khatami's so-called
liberal government.

of the Islamic Revolution. For many in the establishment these films offered the latest evidence of Makhmalbaf's transformation from "an Islamically committed filmmaker [who] had finally crossed the hair's width…that separated the acceptable from the unacceptable."[22] The conservative elements within the government, most notably Ayatollah Ahmad Jannati, a leading member of the Council of Guardians, and Ali Akbar Nateq Nuri, speaker of the Majles, already alarmed at what they perceived to be a liberal cultural onslaught, added to the voices of condemnation. The films were promptly banned at home, although they were actively promoted on the international festival circuit where they were critically well received. Dimitri Eipides of the Toronto International Film Festival described Time of Love as "an intriguing commentary on the social order in Iran, expanding on the social criticism of Makhmalbaf's earlier works such as *The Peddler* and *Marriage of the Blessed.*"[23] In total these films were shown in thirteen international festivals.[24] Furthermore, the European distributor MK2 decided to distribute *Salaam Cinema* and *Gabbeh* after they were shown at the Cannes Film Festival in 1996.*

However, the issue of censorship and control was to have wider ramifications for the entire cultural field as the examples of *Time of Love* and *Nights of the Zayandeh-Rud* highlighted the growing tension and escalating scale of disputes between the reformist and conservative elements within the government. Makhmalbaf himself was acutely aware of the intimate connection between the cultural and the political, and responded to the public persecution of his work: "The fight is over nothing other than the struggles between the different factions who seek power. The person who has more might is right. It is clear from now who the loser in this dispute is. Very well, congratulations. Who is next?"[25]

Makmalbaf's comments speak to the complex functioning of art and protest in the Islamic Republic, which operates within a system of narrowly defined and officially sanctioned norms of behavior laid down by the ruling elite. On the one hand these films were seeking to challenge and undermine the authoritarianism and patrimonial system of governance while on the other they served the needs of government. The films that challenged the system were initially "tolerated by members of the political elite anxious for ammunition in their internecine contests" as well as being "useful for their own legitimacy, the legitimacy of the system and the image of the Islamic Republic abroad."[26] But such a relationship, built on expedient political and ideological requirements, was invariably volatile. These tensions came to a head with the parliamentary purges of radicals and reformists in 1992, which saw the assumption of

---

*MK2 is one of France's leading independent film companies. Established in 1974 MK2 produces, distributes, as well as exhibits films, through its own network of forty four cinemas in France.

conservative majority control in government that set about quashing criticism and intellectual freedom of expression by force. From this period on, "culture became the frontline for a broader existential conflict over the extent of freedom that would be tolerated in the Islamic Republic"[27] and once again the media was caught in the eye of the storm.

## Controlling the Voices of Dissent

In late 1992 the Minister of Culture and Islamic Guidance Mohammad Khatami was forced to resign by conservative politicians who felt that his policies had a corrupting effect on the country's youth population. Khatami was generally considered responsible for the rebirth of Iranian cinema, because he promoted a liberal policy that encouraged filmmakers to explore sensitive and, at times, controversial issues. Khatami's desire to distance cinema from official policy/propaganda was echoed in his declaration that "cinema is not the mosque.... If we transform cinema to such an extent that when one enters the theater one feels imposed upon...then we have deformed society."[28] Because of his stance, Khatami was replaced by the hard-line conservative Dr. Ali Larijani, who promised to instigate a cultural policy that would offset the perceived onslaught of Western cultural decadence and dominance with Islamic values. Larijani, referring to Iranian film production, remarked, "We must leave the door open for the doctrinaires and Hezbollahi filmmakers."[29] For cinema the changed ideological environment resulted in the necessary approval and more stringent examination of film scripts. Also the issuance of production and screening permits became more difficult to obtain. Bureaucratic and supervisory controls during production also increased. *

The conservatives' desire to reassert their control over the media continued unabated with the removal of Mohammad Hashemi Rafsanjani (the president's brother) as director of Iranian Broadcasting, the Voice and Vision Broadcasting Company, on the charges of promoting a liberal broadcasting policy, which the conservatives deemed pro-Western and in violation of Islamic values. He was replaced by Larijani whose vacant post at the Ministry of Culture and Islamic Guidance was filled by another Islamic hard-liner, Mostafa Mirsalim, who vowed only to give support to "those films that deal with topics such as the war with Iraq and the cultural onslaught."[30] By this time the three main bodies responsible for the implementation of cultural policy (the Ministry of Culture and Islamic Guidance, Iranian Broadcasting and the Organization for Islamic Propagation), were under the control of con-

---

*Makhmalbaf had a screenplay rejected for a proposed film on Iraq's occupation of Kuwait in 1990-91. The screenplay was rejected by the Council of Screenplay Inspection for portraying Iraq as too much of an aggressor, and Kuwait as too much of a victim, for portraying the West as liberators and not sufficiently depicting the innocence of the Shia people. See *Film*, May/June 1993: 20.

130

servatives. They began to implement their policy of promoting Islamic values and stopping the foreign cultural onslaught with the result that by the mid-1990s most reformist newspapers had been banned or closed down, hundreds of intellectuals and supposed dissidents had been imprisoned or executed and tens of thousands arrested for what the authorities called "social corruption." The film industry responded to the crackdown by publishing a petition, signed by over two hundred film directors and actors, calling on the government for a "cancellation or serious reduction in the straitjacket regulations and complicated methods of supervision."[31] The government responded by tightening controls and announcing a ban on the export of any film that portrayed a negative image of Iran. In an echo of the militant declarations made during the early drive to create an Islamic cinema, President Rafsanjani himself endorsed this conservative shift at the closing ceremony of the Twelfth Fajr Film Festival in 1994 by declaring, "If you directors make good films there will be no need for pulpits."[32] Once again cinema was publicly cast as the ideological mouthpiece of the state. Despite the imposition of these harsh measures the cultural battle showed no signs of abating and rather than being forced into silence, with each repressive measure artists and intellectuals responded with further arguments and debate. By this time a critical and socially engaged form of Iranian cinema had evolved into a mature and distinctive art form that was displaying recognizable thematic and aesthetic attributes, creating a situation in which "the Iranian government likes the fact that Iranian cinema has become popular abroad, but they are also afraid of its power."[33]

### Time of Love and Nights of the Zayandeh-Rud

Makhmalbaf's first two films of this period continue the engagement and questioning of social problems that began with his Mostazafin Trilogy. However, by then the focus had shifted from the economic to the personal and the exploration of freedom of individual choice and action in the face of social restrictions. These films examine the taboo subjects of human love, and stylistically they also mark something of a formal progression. Linear narrative and one-dimensional commentary have been jettisoned in favor of a multi-voice perspective and a fractured narrative exhibiting temporal and spatial disjunctions—for example the distinct episodic structure of Time of Love in which the same story is told from three different perspectives with the main protagonists exchanging roles in each section. This ruptured narrative is a product of the contentious and controversial nature of the subject matter, which influenced the shooting location in the hope of circumventing censorship constraints by setting it in different geographical and temporal surroundings (Time of Love was shot in Turkey, and Nights of the Zayandeh-Rud was set partly in the pre-revolutionary era) that attempt to distance and eschew, but yet cannot avoid, the immediate parallels with present circumstances.

*Time of Love* adopts an episodic structure that follows the consequences of a woman's extramarital affair on the participants of the love triangle. Presented as a tragic trilogy, all three episodes are variations on the same story, each with a different ending, which is further complicated by the two principal male characters exchanging the roles of the husband and lover from episode to episode. This transposition of roles and the repetitive but fractured sense of perspective allows for a meditation on their moral positions, the limits of individual responsibility and the pressures of social forces in determining and conditioning individual actions.

## Moral Perspectives

The film begins with an old man in a graveyard holding an empty birdcage, listening to the sound of birds in the wild as two lovers hold their illicit and clandestine meeting nearby. The audience is positioned within this private meeting through the old man's aural perspective and a series of fractured and claustrophobic close-ups that illustrate the tension on which the film revolves: the contrast between domesticity/capture and nature/freedom. People are enclosed and trapped throughout the film either in cluttered apartments, taxi cabs or by the constraints of society, which sees love in terms of economics—the girl in resignation and sadness tells her lover that happiness depends on having a taxi and finishing his army conscription. The poetic and idealistic notions of love and the ability to choose one's own destiny and happiness are tempered or negated by the expediency of reality and the expectations of society. However, the film illustrates that these worlds are not separate entities, but tend to overlap, influence and impinge on one another.

## Poetic Symbolism

The tragic and ethereal notions of love in this film are based on the symbols of Persian poetry. In Sufi literature, the sea and the prevalence of birds signify poetic love.* The sea is a symbol of eternal truth and love, and drowning in the sea connotes a reunion with God. In the first episode the lover takes a fish from the frying pan and rushes

---

*Sufism is a mystical form of Islam that rejects the constraints of conventional religion in order to pursue a more personal and spiritual union with God. It aims at a detachment from the material world through performance of rituals like meditation and fasting. A major influence on Persian poetry, Sufism expresses a deep, passionate and ecstatic love for the divine from a belief that God is inherent and knowable in creation rather than transcendent to it. This search for a personal union with God and its depiction in a poetic aesthetic was to become more pronounced in Makhmalbaf's work, particularly in the films *Gabbeh* (1996) and *The Silence* (1998), as he began to explore the complex nature of God, and depiction of God's existence in the world around him. *Time of Love* (1991) was Makhmalbaf's first film to frame social issues within the metaphors and allegories of Sufism.

to put it back in the sea where it quickly regains life and swims away, emphasizing the restorative power of the sea, love and its attendant freedom. At the end of the episode the cuckolded husband has killed his wife's lover and is sentenced to death by the court, which decrees, "The judge doesn't benefit from execution but society does. The court defends people's right to live. Nobody is allowed to take anybody's life except the law." The husband asks to be executed by being thrown to the sea, remarking, "For those who die at sea are reborn," reiterating the redemptive power of the sea, and demonstrating that while society (the court) administers punishment, only God can provide forgiveness. In the final scene of the first episode the wife commits suicide and bids goodbye to her lover in a dream. She goes to put the fish back in the sea but this time it is not revived. All that remains in the absence of the beloved and the belief in God is the emptiness of death.

The presence of birds throughout the film, heard on the soundtrack and seen in the actions of the old man who spies on the couple and records bird calls, signifies the duality of a happiness and despair mediated by reality through the use of culturally specific motifs. The line between the desire for freedom and the reality of an existence imposed by the limits of the cage operates in the cultural space between the Islamic and pre-Islamic Iranian symbolism of the bird. In the former peacocks, or composite birds, are depicted as the creatures of paradise that were, according to legend, expelled from the Garden of Eden along with Adam and Eve. Their mournful refrain is a reflection of their pain and grief at having left the heavenly garden. Pre-Islamic Iranian legends depict the bird as an omen of good having brought the sweet nectar of the gods down to earth. Their appearance in Persian literature generally symbolizes joy, good luck and happiness.[34] The lovers in the graveyard (or Adam and Eve after the fall, as it were), surrounded by the incessant bird chorus and trying to snatch fleeting moments of joy, are aware of but insulated momentarily from the harsh realities of life. These realities are shown by the economic and social constraints—the lover is a poor shoeshine who has yet to do his military service—that restrict the desire to escape with one's beloved to the freedom of the sea. Equally, the unhappiness engendered by marriage despite economic freedom is itself conditioned by social constraints, the social taboo of divorce for example, and it too prevents freedom to pursue individual desire.

The search for the ideal and a freedom of choice checked by the imposed barriers and rules of society, particularly on women, are also the hallmarks of Forugh Farrokhzad's poetry.* Filled with trapped protagonists and treatises on the search for individuality Farrokhzad

---

*Born in Tehran in 1934, and killed in a car crash at the age of thrity-two, Farrokhzad is widely regarded as the greatest Iranian woman poet and one of the most important artists in Iranian history. She was the first woman in Persian literature to write about female sexual desire, using her own volatile and crisis-ridden

**133**

presages not only *Time of Love* but also Makhmalbaf's development as an artist moving toward a more elemental political struggle for a personal identity. Furthermore, Makhmalbaf's own regard for Farrokhzad as a poet, her charisma and lack of innocence, and her refusal to accept traditional Iranian cultural norms, in this respect her unwillingness to accept patriarchy by promoting an alternative positive and feminist depiction of Iranian-ness, bears similarities to his exploration of the self interacting with and arising from specific social and political conditions. Furthermore, both, albeit toward different ends, have attempted in their work to marry the lyrical and the social through combining poetic themes with naked realism. Farrokhzad invokes the image of the bird in two poems that show a progression from resignation to despair. In "The Bird Was Only a Bird" she presents a picture of freedom restrained:

> The bird said, "What, scent! What sunshine! Ah!
> Spring has come
> And I shall go in search of a mate…"
>
> The bird flew through the sky…
> At the altitude of unknowingness
> And madly experienced
> Blue moments.
>
> The bird, Ah, was only a bird.*

In "The Bird Is Not to Die" the motif continues but the tone is darker, more somber:

> Lamps of relationship are dark.
> No one will introduce me
> To the sun
> No one will take me to the feast of sparrows.
> Remember flight.
> The bird is to die.

Episodes one and two of *Time of Love* evoke the sentiments of unfettered emotions and the hope for a future of possibilities tempered by one's responsibilities to the community and lives of others, as the desires

---

life as the source of much of her work. In 1962 she made a short film, *The House Is Black,* about the life of lepers. Combining documentary and poetic forms it is regarded as the first Iranian film of genuine artistic ambition and vision, and a precursor and influence on much Iranian film and filmmakers, including Makhmalbaf, that followed. See www.makhmalbaf.com.

*Both these poems are taken from Forugh Farrokhzad, *Another Birth Let us Believe in the Beginning of the Cold Season,* 64; 122.

and actions of the protagonists lead to death and despair. Makhmalbaf's film attempts to overcome this pessimism in the final episode through a plea for understanding in a humanist spirit of compromise.

## A Third Way

The final episode of *Time of Love* concludes with the husband allowing his wife to leave and marry her lover. Stating as his reason the realization that "I loved her. She's in love too. When I can be in love, then why can't she?" the scene is a call for tolerance and forgiveness and a belief in the ability of individuals to conduct their lives with propriety, far from the interference of state and social institutions. This call for a greater freedom of personal action and choice in a highly centralized society— where the divisions between the private and the public sphere are not clearly marked and moral guidance is seen as the preserve of government—presents something of a challenge to the accepted and decreed norms of Islamic law, which enforces harsh punishment for the crime of adultery.* Makhmalbaf's call for individuals to be afforded greater personal control over the decisions they make is not, as may appear, an affront to the veracity or authority of divine ordinances. It is a call for a more balanced and humane consideration of the complex reasons behind human behavior, rather than pursuing narrow-minded goals of achieving results according to a Manichean worldview. This dichotomy is delineated in the speech that the judge gives at the wedding ceremony: "We are not real characters.... You had to kill this man and I had to execute you.... All my life I've been performing a social role. I've stopped acting as a judge since I heard about your marriage. Judgments suit the person who thinks of the practical results of the criminal actions, not the reasons." However, Makhmalbaf further muddies the water at the end of the film by showing that freedom of choice is not without its costs and responsibilities. After the wedding the lover turns to his new wife and says, "We are united at last." "I'm still not happy," she replies. "Then what does happiness mean?" asks the lover. "I don't know, but I feel that my heart is still with him," she answers. This highlights a message that conflicts with the liberal tone of the film, that happiness is relative, unbridled love is not all and that kindness and forgiveness are equally important attributes, with each person accepting that individual actions have wider ramifications in the larger social arena.

### *Nights of the Zayandeh-Rud*

Set in three different periods before during and after the revolution, *Shabha-ye Zayandeh-Rud* (*Nights of the Zayandeh-Rud*, 1991) is a controversial and searing indictment of an Iranian society in which the choices

---

*The punishment for adultery according to Islamic law is stoning to death, although technically this requires four men, or three men and two women, to have witnessed the actual "crime."

facing the individual are filled with bitterness, hopelessness and despair. The film is essentially divided into two sections. The first, set in the immediate pre-revolutionary years, tells the story of a university professor with outspoken views on the shah and his society. He is interrogated by the shah's secret police, SAVAK, for his beliefs as the spirit of revolution begins to grip the streets. During an evening walk with his wife they are knocked down by a speeding car. She dies and he is confined to a wheelchair. Increasingly bitter and disillusioned he withdraws from life as the violence and protest of revolution rage around him. The second part of the film is situated in the post-revolutionary era, and the focus shifts to the university professor's daughter. She works in a hospital unit treating individuals who have attempted to commit suicide and she is in love with a veteran paralyzed as a result of injuries from the war with Iraq. Caught between personal desire and the oppressive expectations and pressures of society she finds herself deprived of the freedom of individual choice—her father refuses to let her marry the man of she loves—and seeing the trauma of a society through her work, she sinks into despair and hopelessness.

## The Personal and the Political

The film's central concern is the individual caught between the social and political pressures of the historical moment. Makhmalbaf by now has moved beyond his belief in the ideal progression along the path of perfection with the aim of becoming an active participant in effecting revolutionary change. The professor dissects society in his classroom, at one point telling his students that monarchy is an intrinsic part of Iranian culture and history but one that has been abused through the cult of personality worship of the monarch. Despite being situated in the era of the shah these comments resonate beyond the historical frame as the Islamic regime has taken the one component of Iranian culture, Shia Islam, and used it to create a determinist view of society under the cult of the monarchic faqih. An all-encompassing ideology does not allow dissonant voices, trivializes any notion of debate and depersonalizes the individual with rhetoric. The professor, after being interrogated by the secret police for his perceived anti-regime comments in the classroom, stops to buy a drink from a street stall before proceeding to smash the bottle in frustration, shouting, "I drink therefore I am." In this instance the efforts of those in power to promote an official way of thinking have deprived the individual of the essence of his being, the ability to formulate independent thought. The individual's position in that world is one of a depersonalized automaton functioning at the level of compulsive physical actions deprived of individual thought and therefore the essence of being. This alienation of the self becomes the basis for the depersonalization of society.

In the scene where he and his wife are knocked down by a car we are presented with a microcosm of a society that is uncaring, debased and soulless. A group of men pass the couple prior to the accident, and after, as they are lying prostrate on the road, no one comes to their aid. The revolution's spirit of collective action is shown to be a false myth replaced with the selfish actions of scattered, isolated and detached individuals. Faced with a seemingly soulless and unconcerned society, the professor decides to withdraw into the bitter isolation of the self. This he does, throwing his notes and research papers from the window of his apartment, a purging realization of the futility of his own thoughts and resistance in effecting change; he retreats to a detached position of observation. The sense of isolation is described cinematically through a pronounced use of wide shots and long takes. This functions in separating the individual in space and diverting the focus of attention away from the main characters, opening alternative spaces of contemplation and investigation through the distancing of the audience. The official apparatus of the state in enforcing its version of ideological conformity through the elimination of alternative, dissenting and nonconformist thought patterns has depersonalized the individual and conspired to rob him of his sense of free will. But paradoxically, by driving the professor into the misanthropic cell of isolationism it forces him closer to an evaluation of the self. And while the political robs the individual of any sense of self, without the individual the political is meaningless. In one particular scene we see the coalescing of these elements where the personal and the political converge in providing a subjective and personalized challenge to grand ideological claims.

From his window the professor looks down on the street battles and demonstrations of the revolution. The film cuts to a series of pictures of his wife in the apartment, which is followed by a shot outside of riots on the street. This is then followed by a shot of one of the protestors on the streets spraying a stencil of Ayatollah Khomeini's visage onto a wall, which is in turn cross-cut with pictures and paintings being thrown into the river. The inferred connection between the two scenes is clear: the influence of the image and the subjective but real meaning it signifies for the individual are the motivators to action, not the belief in abstract and distant ideological beliefs. For the professor, his belief in the image of his past paralyzes his present and renders his future hopeless. Furthermore, the cross-cutting between the Khomeini stencil and the objects being thrown into the river neatly encapsulates the changing social order. Here one image, clerics, is simply replacing another, king, to which the professor remains impassive and detached. This is a notion that Makhmalbaf pursues and critiques in the second part of the film, whereas in *The Marriage of the Blessed*, he documents the failed promises of a fractured post-revolutionary society through frustrated and scarred human relationships.

### The Disillusioned Generation

The second part of the film focuses on the professor's daughter in the years after the revolution, and life in a new society. Here the roles are somewhat reversed. Whereas the professor has withdrawn from society, choosing personal isolation over political intervention, his daughter has chosen social intervention by working at the hospital's suicide ward. However, she eventually becomes trapped in a prison of personal isolation as a result of the restrictions placed on women in Iran. In the professor's case the choice is made by the individual and highlights the personal basis of the political, but the daughter's situation reveals how politics functions in socializing and repressing the person by inhibiting freedom. The hospital ward provides a cross section of a generation—army officers, war heroes, young girls, all without hope, damaged by a revolution that promised much and delivered little. They see their only salvation and freedom in taking their own lives. In Iran, suicide is particularly prevalent among young women. One disturbing statistic shows that in the first six months of 1991 forty women killed themselves by self-immolation.[35] Although particularly acute among the female population, serious social discontent, given the burgeoning population, lack of employment opportunities and entertainment outlets, is widespread among the country's large youth population.*

The professor's daughter is faced with the dilemma of loving two men at the same time in a society where, despite the fact that women take an active role in society through increased employment and educational opportunities, their personal life choices and moral behavior are still restricted or strictly controlled by the state. During a conversation with one of her suitors in a restaurant she asks him if it is possible to love two people before confessing, "Maybe the heart has two corners, one for each of them....I wish I were a man then things would be easier." One of the men she loves is a paralyzed veteran from the Iran-Iraq war.

Gone now are the lofty ideals of martyrdom and the virtuous "Islamic man" standing firm against the infidel in the name of God. The norms of the patriarchal society even extend to the level of interpersonal relations as the professor forbids his daughter from engaging in a relationship with the disabled veteran. The sense of frustration and despair is all-pervasive. The girl prevented from pursuing the life she wants, goes to the bridge over the Zayandeh-Rud and sinks to her

---

*A particular problem has been the large increase in drug abuse, with the number of heroin users recorded at some three million in 1999. Furthermore, prostitution, as a result of the two million young women who have run away from home in Iran, has reached such high levels that the Majles has recently considered legalizing the practice in state run "houses of decency." BBC World Service Special Report July, 30 2002.

knees in sadness and resignation, covering her face with her chador. Her frustration and future are rendered cinematically by cutting from a close-up of her face to a high-angled long shot along the arches under the bridge. Through a series of jump cuts we see the girl walking alone, then walking with her suitor before disappearing to reveal an empty frame.* This is then followed by two more jump shots moving left to right and right to left as she pushes the disabled veteran in his wheelchair across the frame. This stylistic and surreal depiction of her thoughts reveals a series of choices—to be alone, to marry someone she doesn't love, or nothingness—that are pervaded by the image of the disabled veteran whom she is forbidden to marry. Nearby some street musicians sing a lament about the need to wait, that the future will come. This is a future that is depicted in oblique terms in the final scenes of the film. The girl, in her capacity as a counselor at the hospital, meets a widow whose husband was killed at the front and who has tried to commit suicide. Feeling powerless to help, the girl asks a doctor whether it is right to commit suicide in the face of overwhelming despair. This scene is followed by her meeting the disabled veteran by the banks of the Zayandeh-Rud where they conduct a mock marriage ceremony imbued with sadness and world-weariness when they see in each other that society has caused their present condition (he physically paralyzed by war, she paralyzed by her father's words) which will dictate their future. She hands him a bunch of tulips (the symbol of martyrdom) and he hands her one back before they exchange rings. He goes on to tell her that all the people he knew at the front are dead and that all the time during the war he was thinking of her, before asking, "When will we marry?" She replies elliptically that he should come to the bridge in order to achieve his wishes. They depart and she says goodbye to her friends.

The final shot of the film is a high-angled shot through an arch of the bridge as the moonlight glistens on the water. The veteran moves across the screen and turns to look out at the water. On the sound track we hear a song extolling the beauty of Isfahan—everywhere you look there is beauty and art in the world. The ending makes unclear whether the girl has committed suicide, or whether the couple will finally be together. The mournful refrain of the song, the contemplative, dreamlike beauty of the final shot and the solitude of the veteran, provide for a multitude of possible interpretations existing within the confluence of the beauty of art and the ugliness of life where each makes the other knowable.

---

*Jump cuts are elliptical cuts that appear to be interruptions of a single shot that omits part of the action. In this instance various figures change instantly against a constant background.

### Once Upon a Time, Cinema, The Actor and Salaam Cinema

This trilogy of films are Makhmalbaf's paean to film, exploration of various aspects of the cinematic medium and the relationship of the artist to
his work. They also exhibit a more reflective, celebratory and less controversial and confrontational stance than the previous two films of this
period. However, it is his experiences at the hands of the censors and
political authorities that influence and infuse the playfulness and frivol-
ity of this cinema-obsessed series with a sense of gravitas as Makhmalbaf
looks at issues like censorship, the culturally-created persona of the artist and the power of cinema to communicate and corrupt.

*Once Upon a Time, Cinema* is an intoxicating palimpsest of film's
arrival in Iran. It is a celebratory fantasy of a Western art form inserted
in an Eastern setting that jumps backward and forward across time and
space, conflates history and shatters the illusions of fact and fiction by
creating a fractured hyper-reality derived from and brought into being
by the creative ability of the cinema to reshape and give meaning to the
essence and emotions of life. The film, set during the reign of Nasir
al-Din Shah (1848-1896), tells the story of a monarch who is preju-
diced against cinema, but upon seeing his first film falls in love with
the heroine and abandons everything to become an actor.* The film
is inspired by the 1932 film *Haji Agha, Actor-e Cinema* (*Haji, the Movie
Actor*), directed by Ovanes Ohanian, which tells the story of a religious
man who is converted to the cause of cinema after attending a cinema
school and appearing in a film.

The tone and style of Makhmalbaf's film is encapsulated in the mix
of cinematic codes and forms and the playful engagement between Iranian cinematic and history. It dispenses with expected references and
meanings by offering multiple possibilities of interpretation through
the subjective and objective combination and separation of sight and
sound. The opening scene of the film shows the court cinematographer,
Ebrahim Khan, placing objects on the back of a cart. Included among
these objects is a large mirror (the symbol of cinema) in which his
beloved, Atieh (which means "future" in Persian), is reflected. The cinematographer wishes but is unable to marry Atieh because, as he states,
he is "married to the cinema." This scene is followed by documentary
archival footage of the Qajar royal family's ceremonial activities, with
cinematographer Ebrahim Khan's voiceover: "All is fair here. Pleni-
tude everywhere. But there is no atieh (future), not for my Atieh." The

---

*The false historical setting highlights this notion of an artistically created hyper-reality which pays no atten-
tion to factual accuracy as the cinema and the artist combine to construct their own sense of meaning
through the rearrangement of time and space. In fact cinema came to Iran during the reign of Mozaffar al-Din
Shah (1896-1906) when he purchased a cinematograph in Paris in July 1900 while on a trip to Europe. The
first indigenous Iranian film footage was filmed less than a month later when the court photographer, Mirza
Ebrahim Khan Akkasbashi, used the new equipment to record the shah's visit to Belgium on 18 August 1900.

play on the word atieh refers simultaneously to the fact that there is no future for this opulent monarchical system of governance, no future for this type of cinema—an instrument serving those in power—and no future for his personal relationship with Atieh. What follows is a narrative built on a disordered montage of consciously acknowledged indigenous influences (both cultural and political), which serves as a meditation on the development of Iranian cinema. Furthermore, cinema itself, through a process of reconstruction and reference, forms a meta-commentary on its own historical progress. Constant allusion to and repetition of reconstructed historical scenes within the narrative of the film show the historical progression of the medium but also how it has influenced and been subjected to the demands and dictates of the political and social system in which it operates.

One of Makhmalbaf's main points of reference in structuring the content and formal attributes of *Once Upon a Time Cinema* is Parviz Kimiavi's 1973 film *Mogholha* (*The Mongols*). After the opening sequence the court cinematographer is shown with his head in a guillotine, sentenced to death for the crime of "cinematography in the royal chambers." This is a direct reference to a similar shot in *The Mongols* where the frustrated director puts his head in a guillotine (Makhmalbaf underlines the point of reference by showing a group of Mongol riders pass through the shot). However, this is not merely an homage to cinematic influence but a recognition of similar thematic concerns, which still preoccupy Iranian cinema despite the changed temporal, ideological and political circumstances that separate the two films. *The Mongols* attempted to articulate a vision of Iran that contrasted an ancient civilization with modern-day mechanization and the rush of modernization by comparing the coming of television with the destructive Mongol invasion of the country in the thirteenth century. This derived from the ideological context of the time, with much of the intelligentsia articulating a concern about the shah's modernization programs and the increasing influence of Western cultural forms in Iran. In *Once Upon a Time Cinema*, Makhmalbaf for his part also attempts to show the influence of a foreign cultural form within a Persian setting. However, whereas Kimiavi was skeptical about the influence of television as a link between past and present, Makhmalbaf is more optimistic regarding the role of cinema and attempts to depict its essence as operating between the twin concepts of artistic freedom and the interference of those in power who would like to create a medium in their own image.

### Dictates of the State

The cinematographer is eventually saved from the guillotine by the court sorcerer, who in answer to the shah's question, "Of what purpose is cinema?" answers, "Grow rice should you intend to harvest in one

141

year. Plant trees to gain fruit in ten. Cultivate a person to develop in a hundred years. Cinematography cultivates people. The cinematographer relates his account." The cinematographer's solution is very similar to Ayatollah Khomeini's assertion that the media should be a university educating man to enjoin good and forbid evil. The question remains as to the ideological form and purpose underpinning this "cultivation." The film approaches this issue by using the guillotine as a metaphoric means of censoring the cinematographer's screenplays. Proposed scripts for films about a sultan prone to love and passion and an officer of justice "apt to press taxes on the peasants unjustly more than flesh and blood can take" are rejected on the basis that they are an insult to the sultan and a threat to the police department. Regimes may change but their fundamental preoccupations remain the same—the maintenance of power and the censoring of all criticism of those in power. As Mohammad Beheshti, managing director of Farabi until 1995, warned, "Criticism is not forbidden.... But when a filmmaker introduces a miscreant...it has to be clear whether he is criticizing an individual or the system as a whole. If the latter, then he must be stopped.[36]

By locating his film within an historical epoch in which cinema did not exist and then tracing its history, Makhmalbaf is drawing attention to the fact that censorship has been a constant element in government dealings with the cinema while at the same time avoiding direct confrontation with the current regime by creating an allegory in an historically impossible situation. Given the fact that his two previous films were the subject of censorship and severe government criticism this analysis does seem pertinent, and regardless of ideology both the pre- and post-revolutionary regimes have shown similar tendencies in suppressing political and social dissent. Since censorship was first introduced to Iran in the 1920s, formally institutionalized by the Pahlavi regime in the 1950s and reconfigured by the Islamic Republic in the 1980s, the unifying element has been regulation of the medium. Predictably, a series of laws for the functioning of cinema are drawn up in *Once Upon a Time Cinema:*

> "The Cinematographer must abstain from discontented remarks directed toward the person of the Sultan in any manner, explicit or indirect, brief or at length.
> "The script must not display any signs of insolence, anomie or insensibility toward the cavalry, the police, the Ministry of Justice, the Ruling Governors or their kin.
> "On failing to do so the regisseur shall be confined, his instruments confiscated, tribunal charges collected and public dignity defended."

An official of the court reads the decree, and the scene is inter-cut with a scene of the sultan and his harem watching cheaply made slapstick comedies of the *Abi va Rabi* type popular in Iran in the 1930s. Following the decrees the sultan allows cinema to be brought to the people, but due to the heavy restrictions, the film exhibited in public is a seemingly unending single shot of an old woman trying to thread a needle. Makhmalbaf's meaning is clear: censorship leads to a reduction in freedom of expression and a resulting drop in quality, with art being replaced by trite and low-grade productions. This is a situation lamented by many filmmakers in Iran, where "contrary to the belief held by many abroad, censorship does not lead to better films and more ingenious ways of filmmaking. What we need are less restrictions, not more, to be able to produce the films we want to make, not what we are allowed to make."[37] *Once Upon a Time, Cinema*, is a reaction by Makhmalbaf against his "own censorship woes...and struggle between authority and artistic freedom."[38] Furthermore, the playful aesthetic and meta-cinematic form that he employs allows him a mediated space in which to flout the censorship regulations, for example by showing women dancing in clips from Bollywood films and the exposure of women's hair in early films such as *Dokhtar-e Lor* (*The Lor Girl*, 1933).

### The Influence of Pre-Revolutionary Cinema

Despite the restrictions placed upon him the court cinematographer (who acts as Makhmalbaf's surrogate in the film) states his intention to make a film about "a person (the sultan) resentful of cinema.... The regisseur records his daily life. Upon seeing himself on the screen he makes amends with cinematography. I have named this script *Haji Agha, the Cinema Actor*" (the name of the first feature ever made in Iran). This film turns out to be *Once Upon a Time, Cinema*, which Makhmalbaf constructs as a work brought into existence and shaped by cinema itself, thus establishing a relationship where cinema is created by cinema and an interaction with history and reality. Both derive their meaning from the functioning of the other but the divisions between the two concepts are fluid and interchangeable. The conflation and inversion of the reality/art division begins with the sultan's obsession with the heroine (and by extension the cinema itself) from the film *The Lor Girl* (Iran's first sound film), which structures the narrative of the film and allows the cinema to create its own reflection of reality through its own historical artistic development. The division between the cinema and the "reality" of the sultan's court (which in this instance is further complicated as it must be seen as a film within a film of a film) is rendered obsolete as characters jump in and out of cameras, projectors and screens. As characters pass from one dimension to another the sultan remarks, "Was this a fancy or reality? Cinematography makes fancy of the real and shows the real to be a fancy." The reality of the court begins to resemble cinema by taking on the formal attributes of the early days of the medium as we witness speeded-up chase scenes, over-the-top acting styles and slapstick comedy, and the replacement of royal portraits with pictures of Charlie Chaplin. When the cinematograph is on, Golnar, the heroine of *The Lor Girl*, is on the screen, but when turned off she is in the palace. The sultan's obsessive imagination has replaced the projector in forming an alternative (cinematically-induced) version of reality.

However, this heightened sense of the creative reality is rendered through the projection of indigenous cultural products. Whereas the French New Wave of the 1950s and 1960s was underpinned by a love of American cinema, Makhmalbaf has sought to show that the local reality and sense of self is created through indigenous cultural forms, as manifest in his exclusive reference to Iranian films. It is only through the interaction of the historical, the political and the culturally specific that his art derives its primal essence and forms the starting point for the exploration of universal themes of understanding. In the film the sultan receives a letter from Amir Kabir* complaining, "Your Royal Highness, The State and Nation are devastated as the sultan is engaged with his Malijak and lady fair.† Only a hero can bring honor to this nation." The sultan replies in disgust, telling his courtiers to "Search our domain, provide us with the mightiest of our peasants to release Amir Kabir from the burden of our nation's honor." This exchange is then followed by a scene containing a number of clips from a series of Film Farsis showing the moody, muscular heroes engaged in a series of fights and confrontations.

The sultan has become so consumed by the cinema and the reality it has created for him that the only solution to the country's problems are the heroes of "cinema lati." The blurring of these lines becomes complete when the sultan decides to become an actor. Makhmalbaf adds a further dimension by conflating the star persona of the actor Ezatollah Entezami, who plays the part of the sultan, in another form of meta-cinematic commentary and construction, by getting him to take on the role of a cow, a reference to the role Entezami played in Dariush Mehrjui's groundbreaking film *Gav* (1968). Whereas Entezami's character Mashdi Hassan in *Gav* is driven to madness and despair by the loss of his cow, the sultan in *Once Upon a Time, Cinema* is driven to the point of insanity by his inability to differentiate the "real" from the "projection of the real" and his love for the unobtainable fantasy hero-

---

*Amir Kabir was appointed Chancellor to the Court of Naser al-Din Shah in 1848 and is credited with introducing many much needed reforms, including the balancing of state expenditures, the rebuilding of a strong army and the introduction of a modern education system, before his exile and execution, as a result of the political intrigue of his opponents, in 1851. He is seen by many Iranians to occupy a special place in their history as a result of his attempts to modernize the country and stand up to Western interference at a time when Iran was in a weakened state. See Abbas Amanat, *Pivot of the Universe: Nasir al-Din Shah and the Iranian Monarchy, 1831–1896*.

†Gholam Ali Aziz al-Soltan, a young man in the court, was a favorite and intimate of Nasir al-Din Shah and was referred to as Malijak. The term later came to be used for court jester-type favorites of shahs.

ine Golnar. Once again it is the cinematographer who is sentenced to death for insulting the "royal figure of the shah" by transforming him into a cow. This underlines the historical presence of censorship in Iranian cinema: *Gav* was famously banned by the shah's government at the time, which felt that it insulted the shah and his reform program by presenting a picture of Iran that was backward and poverty stricken.

The end of the film situates Iranian cinema within its present context. Kimiavi's *The Mongols* once again functions as a point of reference as Makhmalbaf recreates the scene in which an a iron gate materializes in the desert in front of a group of Mongol warriors, to which the Mongols pose the question, "What is cinema?" For Kimiavi the answer was Jean-Luc Godard but for Makhmalbaf it is the films that have been produced in Iran since the revolution. There then follows a celebratory and elative montage sequence featuring clips from various post-revolutionary films, emphasizing the presence of children, a wide spectrum of genres, war films, melodramas, and ending with a shot from Kiarostami's *"Where is the Friend's House?* (1987) that shows a young boy running up a zigzag path on the side of a hill. The final scene of the film shows the sultan dragging the cinematographer's possessions, including the mirror, on a cart through the snow, repeating the film's opening scene. The reflection in the mirror shows the cinematographer's beloved Atieh sitting on a bench. The sultan mistakes her for Golnar, to which she replies, "My name is Atieh. Did anyone ask after me on your way." The implication here is clear, that cinema in Iran can attain beauty, but if the control of the medium remains in the hands of those who wish to place restrictions on artistic expression and use it for their own ideological purposes then cinema and creativity is condemned.

### The Actor

*Honarpisheh* (*The Actor*, 1993) continues the cinematic chaos and frantic style of *Once Upon a Time, Cinema.* It tells the story of an actor (played by the Iranian film star Akbar Abdi) who wants to act in serious art films but is forced by his family's economic situation to star in low-grade commercial films. His plight is compounded by his unstable, neurotic and infertile wife, who becomes obsessed with having a baby. She finally convinces him to marry a second wife, a mute gypsy girl, in order to father a child. What ensues is a social farce that is both surreal and semi-tragic, satirical and comedic, and that touches on issues such as class differences, the culturally created persona of the artist, fame and wealth. The film has been described "as a bizarre portrayal of reality, or a realistic depiction of a bizarre situation...a painful encounter with an existential situation which seems to be shot through and through with irrationality." *The Actor* is also perhaps Makhmalbaf's most straightforwardly commercial film, employing well-known stars in

a linear narrative that combines elements of comedy and melodrama—
*The Actor* became the highest grossing film in Iran in 1993, breaking
the Iranian box office record with returns of some 505 million rials.[40]
Despite its commercial success, the film is one of Makhmalbaf's lesser
and least satisfying works, a film that jettisons the search for the simple
delights of life in favor of a life of tiny miseries, which are antithetical
to the general aims of his films.[41]

### The Essence of the Artist

Makhmalbaf has described *The Actor* as a further manifestation of his
search for an answer to the question "What is the truth?" *The Actor*
recounts "the story of a person who wants to become an artist but conditions won't allow him to."[42] Following the questions raised in *Once
Upon a Time, Cinema*, Akbar Abdi functions as Makhmalbaf's surrogate,
voicing his frustration about being prevented from making the films
that he wants to, and as a result being reduced to making commercial
and inoffensive new versions of the Film Farsi. The central preoccupation of Makhmalbaf's Cinema Trilogy is the relationship of the artist to
his work. Whereas *Once Upon a Time, Cinema* used the historical development of cinema in Iran as its template, *The Actor* situates the artist
within the framework of a contemporary setting in a search for an
understanding of the way in which art is derived from societal factors.
According to Makhmalbaf, "The main idea of this film…is the responsibility of artists toward their social surroundings…. My protagonist in
*The Actor* cannot choose the films he acts in. The film is looking for an
answer to the question, 'To what extent the artist is to be blamed for
this inability to choose?'"[43]

In other words art is created from the immediate conditions of the
social reality, the expectations of the public and the restrictions placed
on notions of artistic freedom and expression by those in positions of
power. In a central scene in the film Akbar's wife Simin jumps out of
their car following an argument, instigating a huge traffic jam. She,
in a mirror image of his frustration as an artist, is exasperated by her
inability to bear a child and thereby create the life/reality she desires.
Passersby stop to look at the ensuing argument between the couple,
believing it to be a film. They follow Akbar as he chases after his wife,
asking him what the title of the film is. This is a complex interaction of
the persona of Akbar Abdi, recognized as one of Iran's most famous
comedic actors, his part within the film that plays on this iconic status, trying to break free of this persona, and its interaction within the
"reality" of public expectation, though is unable to do so within and
outside the filmic narrative. Here the mixing of cinematic codes of reality and fiction is taken to almost impossible lengths, as Makhmalbaf
attempts to transcend the separation of both modes of representation

by employing a construct in which the two notions coexist seamlessly and problematize one another as forms of representation. In the scene where he argues with his wife the division between Akbar the Iranian film actor and Akbar the actor of the fiction film *The Actor* collapses as we are presented with a film within a film, both of which work in opposite directions. On the one hand we have the argument between Akbar and Simin as part of the narrative progression of the film *The Actor* while on the other hand we have passersby recognizing Akbar based on the preconceived interpretation of the scene as a comedy. Akbar, caught between the narrative of the film and the public's perception of what they perceive the narrative to be, sinks down in resignation and despair and responds to the crowd who have followed him and Simin, calling the film "a dog's life, a cow's life." Again this sets in motion another series of interpretations referring to his character's position within and interpretation of the narrative *of The Actor*, responding to the crowd who have created a film within a film while at the same time offering a commentary on the gilded cage in which the artist ultimately finds himself trapped. Makhmalbaf examines and questions the relationship of the real or authentic, and the control of these elements. In doing so he is attempting to examine the different ways in which art and cinema is perceived "and viewed in lived culture, a portrait of the audience which views the text [and inadvertently participates in creating it] and encourages the viewer to consider their own act of viewing."[44]

The fluid boundaries between reality and fiction in *The Actor* finally collapse into a system in which the artist is trapped in the prison of expectation, a puppet whose strings are pulled by other hands. The artist becomes a commodity, a construct, as much as his art, and is caught in a constant battle trying to define himself and his work in defiance of the straitjacket of an imposed role and image. At one point, Akbar, seeing a poster of himself advertising his next film, starts to hurl abuse at the image: "It's all your fault. What do you want from me? Get lost. Leave me alone. Everybody likes you, you shit. Nobody likes me. You sent these people to disturb my private life. You idiot. You've risen so high. I myself have been the cause. I'll bring you down myself. Leave me alone."

As a filmmaker Makhmalbaf has strived to create himself anew with films that reflect current social conditions interacting with a personal and developing intellectual consciousness. In placing himself within the debate between high and low art he has expressed his concern about the restrictions placed on artists and the subsequent production of compromised and low-quality work. Ironically these sentiments are expressed most aptly in a commercial film displaying a variety of different styles. It is this combination of the farcical, the surreal and the comedic that gives the film a disjointed and uncertain feel, and that is unable to hide the bitterness of tone, and successfully integrates elements of social commentary, such as class divisions, that are superficially treated and appear incongruous with the general aims of the film. Whereas the destitute in the slums of Tehran as shown in *The Peddler* were a cause for anger at injustice, those presented in *The Actor* (or more specifically the character of the gypsy girl chosen to bear Akbar's child) function as a means of showing that wealth does not necessarily equate to happiness and that people should be content and grateful with what they have. The division between the artist's life and the uncertain tone of the film as a whole is encapsulated in the final scene when Akbar picks up his wife from a hospital for the mentally ill. The scene is rather downbeat and open-ended, and uncertainty mixes with resignation. Akbar, unable to fulfill the ambitions of his artistic life, decides when taking his wife from the hospital (who in turn is unable to fulfill her life ambitions, to have a child, resulting in psychosis) to try and create a future from the elements of the reality that is his own life, which he has the ability to influence, rather than the one expected of him in front of the camera or on the cinema screen. The interaction between artistic and personal fulfillment and the bitter struggle to achieve either is in essence portrayed as an inevitable disappointment and is clearly a reflection of Makhmalbaf's own experiences at the time, when his work was being attacked and censored, and in his own personal life, as he had just lost his wife, to whom the film is dedicated, in a tragic household fire.

### Salaam Cinema

The final installment of Makhmalbaf's Cinema Trilogy is an ambiguous investigation of the director-actor relationship, the social power of cinema and its influence on the Iranian imagination, as well as both the cruelty and the ability of cinema to corrupt. Makhmalbaf draws attention to the abuse and corruption induced by absolute power, the unconditional acceptance of authority, the relationship of power and art, and the desperation and hopelessness of a people who will submit themselves to the humiliation and cruelty of the camera in the belief that it will provide them with solutions to their problems. By winding these various strands in a stylistic format of repetitive full frontal addresses to the camera, the artifice and illusion of cinema is stripped back and attention is refocused on the structural elements of the creative process. The effect is a self-reflexive text that constantly draws attention to its own signifying practices and its process of construction, by focusing on the relationship between the director and the actor, revealed as treading the fine line between the perception, manipulation and creation of alternate realities.

Salaam Cinema (1995) begins with the response to an advertisement that Makhmalbaf placed in a Tehran newspaper inviting people to audition for his latest project. Almost five thousand people turned up for these auditions, nearly causing a riot that forms the opening scene of the film. The rest of the film focuses on the screen tests of a number of these hopefuls who, in often cruel and manipulative ways, are asked to sing a song, cry on demand, mime a melodramatic death or simply talk about their lives or reasons for wanting to be in a film. The naked space in which the prospective actors and actresses are isolated, the relentless interrogation of the dispassionate camera and the gentle tyranny of Makhmalbaf as a director, combine self-analysis with a discreet dramatic structure that continues the examination of the cinematic form, its power, purpose and function within society.

## The Social Power of Cinema

The opening scene sets the tone for many of the film's thematic explorations. In it we see the camera placed on top of a car, filming the gathered masses, as it progresses slowly way toward the audition hall. Resembling a reverential, presidential-style motorcade the camera films the crowd below from on high, a position of godlike power. The scene is shot in a hand-held documentary style, with the camera posited as the recorder of the ensuing events. At the same time, in dialectical tension, it is also the catalyst that has brought events into being. In this respect it simultaneously establishes the camera as both a tyrant and unemotional documenter of events. The scene also shows, especially when the application for the auditions are thrown in the air and the crowd scrambles madly to grab them, people who are prepared to put their faith in the opportunities and possibilities that they believe cinema can offer them. The chaos outside with the camera as document/catalyst is contrasted with the calm, controlled atmosphere in the studio where the auditions take place and where the camera now becomes the tool of the director in documenting his provocation and interrogations.

The series of auditions alternate between comedic exercises and harmless play-acting to more emotionally-charged exercises of humiliation and manipulation in which performers are interrogated about their reasons for wanting to be artists. The answers range from the general to the specific and the personal, and one girl tells Makhmalbaf that she would like to be in a film so that her boyfriend in France can see her. In all these cases the performers are prepared to submit themselves to the will of the director and acquiesce to his every demand. The use of such harsh methods have been taken as a reflection of Makhmalbaf's personal view of cinema "as a kind of mass hysteria in which performers' self interests enable them to rationalize their masochistic submission to the sadistic authority of the director."[45] Specific cultural influences have given rise to such a situation. These influences can be seen in the traditional and historical structure of Iranian society, which has revolved around the general will being dictated by

**149**

a strong central and domineering figure, be that the person and cult of personality of the king or the father in the household. Moreover, such submission also reflects the sense of hopelessness and despair of a people that have been denied a role in society and are willing to place their faith in alternative structures of power: they suffer such degradations in the belief that film can offer them the possibility of a better life. Makhmalbaf himself has commented, "The soul of our people is in this film—their hope.... It shows that not much of a role has been given to them in society.... The distance between their hope and their hopelessness could be switched by one sentence."[46]

### The Distance Between Hope and Despair

The film begins a meditation on the morality of power when two girls begin to challenge Makhmalbaf's methods, calling them cruel and inhuman. Makhmalbaf responds by telling them, "If you stay you'll be an artist...if you leave you will be more humane." On hearing this the girls promptly turn to go, whereupon Makhmalbaf calls them back and offers them the opportunity to assume his position and direct the next set of auditions. Following their assumption of the director's chair the girls begin to replicate the same cruelty and dictatorial style that they had castigated Makhmalbaf for. This is quite a depressing and bitter conclusion on the functioning of power. On the one hand there are the majority who will follow blindly the decrees of the ruler and on the other a minority who when they do speak up against tyranny and corruption are themselves corrupted and merely repeat previous patterns of behavior.

Within the context of the time this is an oblique but prescient commentary on the performance of the Second Republic and the revolution in general, which started with high hopes, but preoccupied with the maintenance of power at all costs, degenerated into factionalism, corruption and inaction. The result was economic collapse and increasing enforcement of repressive social measures to stifle dissent. The sense of hopelessness of the degraded social milieu is clearly reflected in the cross section of those who applied to be in the film: eighty percent male applicants, nineteen percent female and one percent children. Of these eighty-three percent came from the capital and seventeen percent from the provinces. Twenty-eight percent of the applicants possessed a third-level education, thirty percent were high school graduates, forty percent had incomplete high school educations, one percent had only elementary school educations and one percent were illiterate. Finally, regarding employment, forty percent were government employees, twenty percent had independent jobs, ten percent were manual laborers and thirty percent were unemployed.[47] This broad sample of society on the one hand shows the esteem in which cinema is held in Iran and on the other hints at deeper cultural implications. Central is the notion of a society built on absolutes, an acceptance of one position or belief system as superior to all others, and an historical willingness to look for these elements in a leader. Makhmalbaf assumes this absolute role of tyrannical leadership in an attempt to draw a distinction between the individual who believes himself to be the bearer of the truth and the absence of dialogue that encourages thinking, analysis and discussion rather than blind faith. This is the ardent task of the artist, particularly in a society with little history of open debate and a large youth population denied any meaningful method of social and political intervention. As Makhmalbaf himself has stated, it is the task of art "to teach them [the youth] understanding, toleration and dialogue with those who do not share their inclinations and opinions."[48] This is the balance on which *Salaam Cinema* is based. The film is a non-judgmental depiction of the cruel tendencies of a fundamentalist society and a people's willingness to accept them. The film is stripped of its artifice, to call for greater critical analysis rather than blindly placing a belief in another individual.

*Salaam Cinema* looks into the space between the realities of people's lives and their perception of cinema's fictional construction of the real. This arises from the performances of the would-be actors and actresses that audition for parts. Here there is a distinction between those who are asked to perform a particular action cry, pretend to be shot, and those who are asked questions about their reasons for wanting to be in the film, or else to recount stories and events from their own lives. It is the stories of the everyday, brought into sharper focus by the histrionics of those who are asked to perform a particular role, and what they show of the lives of the people that forms the essence of the film. As Makhmalbaf comments, "We started shooting with a specific notion of reality and tried to bring out that reality by placing people in special circumstances. But they encountered us with a totally different kind of reality, which we tampered with and which we tried to return to them. I believe this process of give and take went on throughout the auditions and new aspects of reality were intermixed with make-believe. It is of course impossible to disentangle these two threads of the events."[49]

Stripping back the artifice of the creative process allows for the reconfiguring of its component parts and their recombination in different formats. In displaying its own signifying practices the film reveals itself not as a neutral rendering of external reality but as a producer of ideology; that ideology in turn can become all-encompassing and is easily reproduced. The artistic undertaking, then, must be a continuous questioning of the representation of reality, if the past is not simply to be reiterated.

## A Moment of Innocence

The central preoccupation of Makhmalbaf's third period is the study of the complex conditions governing peoples' lives, through multiple perspectives. By presenting a variety of conflicting voices Makhmalbaf attempts to open a space for public discourse, one that introduces certain problematic Iranian cultural traits, like individualism and the belief in absolute truths. Artistically and intellectually *A Moment of Innocence* stands as the most accomplished, complex and complete realization of this undertaking. It manages seamlessly to combine reality and art, fact and fiction, the personal and the political, in a rendering and examination of the historical moment as an interactive living site of past, present and future, wrought from memory, regret and possibility. It shows the power of film to intervene in the localized social arena of the personal in an attempt to reconstruct history and recast reality in a search for truth and meaning in life.

*Nun va Goldun* (*A Moment of Innocence*, 1996) is based on an event that occurred when Makhmalbaf was a teenager. As a member of a militant anti-shah group he tried to attack and disarm a policeman. The incident resulted in the stabbing of the policeman and Makhmalbaf being shot, arrested and sent to prison. Twenty years later the same policeman turned up at the casting sessions for *Salaam Cinema* hoping to become an actor. Though he refused to cast him in that film, Makhmalbaf convinced the cop that they should work together on a cinematic reconstruction of the tragic event that brought them together so many years ago. This sets in motion a dual narrative that follows the separate efforts of both Makhmalbaf and the policeman to find and coach the actors who will play their youthful selves. These different strands come together in the end with the reconstruction of the historical personal event.

### Idealism, Realism, Cinema and Reality

At the start of the film when Makhmalbaf is asked what his movie is about, he responds, "I want to recapture my youth with a camera." Similarly, the policeman says about acting and his reasons for doing the film, "I've been adrift for twenty years. I thought I'd rediscover my life. I wanted to act for the sake of my life." Their reasoning positions cinema, on the one hand, as a reclamation or document, giving voice specifically to forms of representation that act as "testimonies or agit-prop, film souvenirs of action or demonstration, film postcards to tell others 'I was here.'"[50] Yet the endeavor transcends the act of mere documentation, in order to unearth the complex reasons as to why one was there. Here Makhmalbaf performs an alternative film practice based on democratic principles, the avoidance of universalism and essentialism, the need to reclaim a social space and a practice located in the community, for the community, and speaking to the community. This mode's significance is that it establishes a space for dialogue while at the same time recognizing that this dialogue itself is never neutral or uncontested. The self-reflexive form of *A Moment of Innocence* reveals the hermetic conceit of narrative film, casting the reality it seeks to portray as a site of active intervention. Self-discovery and artistic self-reflexivity creatively drive *A Moment of Innocence*. This is made clear from the start where the cinematic devices are broken down into their elemental forms and exposed as active participants in the construction of meaning. The opening credits are spoken and written. We are constantly shown clapperboards to underline that this is a work in progress, a film about filmmaking, among other things. This dissection of the means of representation accommodates the heterogeneous voices—Makhmalbaf's and the policeman's—of personal memory, love and loss.

The dual narrative, which follows both the policeman and Makhmalbaf as they recreate their own versions of the same event, presents a subjective, personalized view of history where politics divides and art offers the possibility of reconciliation and a bridge to understanding within and across generations. This is rendered somewhat comically in the scene where the policeman goes to a tailor's shop to ask him to make a police uniform from the time of the shah. The tailor at first refuses—"Don't talk to me about that man"—but on learning that it is for a film agrees and begins to reminisce about the films he saw during that period. Talking fondly of a bygone era he enthuses about American film stars like as Kirk Douglas and John Wayne and recounts his memories of films such as *Spartacus* and *The Conqueror*. In this regard his personal memories of the pre-revolutionary era are filtered through the cinema; once again art has the power to bring people together, while politics promotes division. This seems to be the message of the film, as notions of truth and falsehood and the division between fact and fiction collapse in the search for common humanity. What is essential is not the actual occurrence of the event or its authentic existence but the necessity of conceiving, developing and depicting the process whereby each individual arrives at his own version of reality and truth. Makhmalbaf is setting out to create a fractured fictive truth rooted in reality.

At the beginning of the film the actor playing the young Makhmalbaf states that he wants to save mankind. This provides Makhmalbaf with a form of redemption through the realization that love and humanity are the essential elements governing human actions. Such a statement may appear obvious or even trite but it is arrived at through rigorous self-analysis and the questioning of a history that has depersonalized the individual by locating him as a mere functionary of ideology and politics. Makhmalbaf had wanted to disarm the policeman in order to use his gun to rob a royalist bank to fund anti-government activities. Makhmalbaf's own political activism is contrasted with the young Makhmalbaf who declares that he will use the money to "plant flowers in Africa or buy bread for the poor." The young Makhmalbaf asks if there is a better way to save mankind than stabbing a policeman. Makhmalbaf replies, "Is that how the youth of today talks?" He then tells the young Makhmalbaf that if people crowd around during the shoot he is to shout out anti-regime slogans. The young Makhmalbaf resolves instead to shout out a line from a book that his cousin, with whom he is in love, has given him: "Where there are trees there is life." The politics of the past has given way to the poetics of the present and the hopes for a future built on love rather than violence and destruction.

This reclamation of the past and the search for a lost love is also the driving force behind the policeman's attempt to reconstruct his personal history. In directing the young policeman he recounts how everyday a young girl would come to him while he was on guard duty in the bazaar and ask him the time. He fell in love with her and wanted to give her a flower as a sign of his affections but was prevented from doing so because Makhmalbaf stabbed him. Believing that if he had given her the flower he wouldn't have wasted twenty years of his life, he attempts to reconstruct the event from the perspective of reclaiming a love deprived him. However, during the reconstruction of the stabbing he learns that the girl was merely a decoy. He storms off the set declaring that the "real girl was false and this one [the actress playing the girl] is even more false." The rediscovery of a life that he thought would explain the last twenty years of his life has proven to be a lie. The alternative reality of possibilities that he had constructed in order to render the lived reality of disappointment bearable has been shattered and exposed as a myth. However, he returns to direct the young policeman in an effort to redress the shattered illusions of the past by telling him to shoot anyone who stops to speak to him. In a reversal of the Makhmalbaf sequence, where the debate is over replacing violence with love, the policeman seeks to replace his shattered illusion of love (the flower) with violence (the gun). In a final rehearsal before the scene is filmed the policeman directs the young policeman in how to shoot the young woman when she approaches.

The final reenactment of the stabbing scene in the bazaar shows the personal depictions of the past colliding with the interpretations of the present. Formally the scene is shot using a mobile camera that glides through the labyrinthine tunnels of a deserted bazaar. The fluid dreamlike movement down endless corridors is a manifestation of the tortuous search for memories in the tunnels of the past. The young actors play their allotted roles as directed only to refuse the denouement, refuse to repeat the past and refuse Makhmalbaf's and the policeman's subjective personalized interpretation of events. Previous to this the viewer has witnessed the exhaustively detailed reconstruction of the protagonists' personal histories: the "young actors mimic the characters they are playing to such an extent that they often seem to have assumed the older men's identities." Throughout this character development Makhmalbaf and the policeman appear constantly in the frame directing events. However, when the actual stabbing is finally reconstructed the scene is devoid of self-reflexive referents. In this respect it is the young actors themselves who are determining the outcome of the scene through an implicit form of self-direction that rejects their tutors' version of history. The last shot bears testament to this. In a freeze frame the young protagonists offer a flower and piece of bread to one another instead of violence and destruction. The shot connotes hope in the future and faith in a new generation not to repeat the mistakes of the past. It is an exercise in personal and political reconciliation and a call for tolerance that highlights the personal and complex nature of depicting history.

In this respect *A Moment of Innocence* is an ambitious and honest film that can be considered revolutionary. Here is a political art that operates on the level of the personal and that seeks to de-familiarize history by drawing its meaning from the inclusive differences between two worldviews and multiple art forms, but does so in such a way that appeals to the viewer's connections to these worlds. Thus new possibilities of interpretation are opened up. This new image is one in which the individual is an active creator rather than a detached participant passively fulfilling a predetermined role. Asking questions instead of giving answers, learning to listen to alternative opinions, and revealing the tyranny of absolutes, these are the modest, even self-effacing, revolutionary virtues of Makhmalbaf's practices in *A Moment of Innocence*. They rest on the assumption that works of art are created and controlled by the apparatus of society as much as by the individual artist. It is the awareness of this fact and the artist's ability to intervene actively and mediate this relationship through an elemental investigation of the constituent parts of the personal, the social, the political and the cultural, which allows for their reconstitution in constantly changing but critically engaged formats.

### Gabbeh

*Gabbeh* (1996), Makhmalbaf's last film of this period, marks a transition in his artistic and intellectual development. *Gabbeh* heralded his arrival on the international scene, and the emergence of a more tranquil, esoteric and poetic sensibility, rooted in a rural idyll. Eschewing direct social intervention for a contemplation of a personal and spiritual aesthetic set in a complex Persian cultural milieu, *Gabbeh* explores the nature of art in man's search for and relationship with God. Indeed, in this respect *Gabbeh* brings to the foreground elements that have been a constant though less fully explored cultural concern for Makhmalbaf. The specific and complex historic and cultural basis—and by extension the analytical frame of reference—is a Persian-Islamic sensibility. The recourse to a localized analysis is crucial to understanding *Gabbeh*, particularly in light of its success abroad—it became one of the first Iranian films to secure an extensive foreign distribution deal.* *Gabbeh* has also been co-opted as an Orientalist curiosity, or a technically beautiful exercise in form. At the center of this debate is the need for a method to approach critically the representation, reception and decoding of Iran and its cinema on the international stage. In other words how and to whom does the medium speak? For *Gabbeh* this is pertinent on two counts, given the problematic approaches and conclusions of most Western critics and also the fact that the film is a part of the trend of successful Iranian films in the West—that is, seen as part of a European art-house sensibility, exhibiting a slow, contemplative, poetic/realist sensibility located in a picture postcard and idyllic rural setting.† To many *Gabbeh* appears a packaging of a fabled Iran for tourists, a travel poster, fairytale substitute for the realities of life in the country,[52] a vague and uncritical picturesque work[53] or a critique of patriarchal culture and the censor of women's rights.[54] The problem with these analyses is that they take minor strands existing within the film and make them stand for the whole, ignoring the thematic development of Makhmalbaf's work and the myriad factors that surround his cinema. A more comprehensive and productive approach is one that defies the ethnographic interest in categorizing and classifying an aesthetic tourist desire for the exotic.[55] Refuting convenient categories makes possible a personal vision situated within the context of historically derived indigenous cultural forms, which despite their specificity allow for universal understanding.

*Gabbeh* tells the simple tale of a young woman from the nomadic Qashqai tribe, who, to be with her beloved, rebels against the traditional role of women in her tribe. Gabbeh is also the name of the distinctive coarse hand-knotted rugs made by the women of nomadic tribes, the patterns and designs of which tell a story inspired by the lives of their makers. From this simple premise emerges a film that combines life and art as reflections and determinants of one another, a film like the gabbeh rug itself, called into being by the "surrounding landscape and natural elements as well as folklore and fables recounted from time immemorial."[56] This background informs the examination of the nature of art and Makhmalbaf's personal, changing relationship

---

*Gabbeh* was released by the European distributor MK2 in France and Switzerland on World Cinema Day (26 June 1996) in twenty-three cities. This was the first time in French history that a non-French or non-American film received such a wide screening It was also the first Iranian film to secure such a large simultaneous release. See "Mohsen Makhmalbaf's *Gabbeh* Wins Awards," *Cinema '96*.

†In this regard it must be noted that despite the wide distribution and success that *Gabbeh* achieved internationally it was initially banned from Iranian screens.

with God. *Gabbeh* explores the artist's search for God and its expression in specific cultural forms. Makhmalbaf has taken and transformed this search into a quest for self-knowledge in approaching the divine through a process of artistic creation that is derived from, both in the historical and spiritual sense, the essence of God. The foundational basis of this self-knowledge is a formal and spiritual melding of Persian and Islamic art forms, which in this case is rendered through the complex communicative function of the Persian carpet.

## The Artistic Template of the Persian Carpet

The position of the carpet in Iranian cultural heritage is that of an art form based on the beauty of pattern as decoration. It is representative of a specifically Persian artistic mindset that exhibits "a strong predilection for embellishment and arabesque,"[57] and manages to encompass the main tenets of Islamic art with its "symmetrically arranged floral motifs, patterns of rectilinear shapes, arabesque systems, combinations of bright colors and little narrative or figural didactic content,"[58] into an expressive whole. Makhmalbaf uses these attributes as the formal means of constructing the style of the film, while at the same time attempting to go beyond the purely decorative by anthropomorphizing the gabbeh. The rug acts as visual narrator, deriving its essence and being from nature and life. It is a document reflecting and counterpointing human interaction with and transformation of the immediate environment, most clearly evidenced in the scene where we see a gabbeh being woven from the point of view of the weaver. The wool is being woven horizontally across strands hanging vertically, framed by a loom that looks onto a golden field of sown wheat whose upright growth is blown horizontal by the wind. This complex interaction of shape and framing highlights the very essence of Makhmalbaf's creative endeavor: God has created nature, nature is manipulated by the artist to create the gabbeh, the gabbeh creates the cinema, which is ultimately a meticulous form of creation wrought from the lives, landscape and culture of the people and reflected in their art.*

## The Search for God

Within this complex interaction of specific cultural production and imagery the spiritual/religious dimension of *Gabbeh* becomes visible. For Makhmalbaf, the artist seeks a closer union with God by recognizing that God is the sole creator of heaven and earth and that the artist merely transforms or rearranges elements that are imbued with God's essence. This process is reflected in the words of the Qur'an: "He hath

---

*Iran Darroudi has posited that Iranian cinema, due to a lack of a flourishing painting tradition, has been influenced by the Persian carpet, which itself is the essence of an Iranian national visual art form. See Iran Darroudi, "As Plain as Truth," *Film International*, Winter/Spring 1996.

created the heavens without supports that ye can see, and hath cast into the earth firm hills, so that it quake not with you; and he had dispersed therein all kinds of beasts. And We send down water from the sky and We cause (plants) of every godly kind to grow therein."[58] The notion that God has created and prescribed perfection in all things gives spiritual meaning not only to the work of the artist in transforming these raw materials but gives meaning to the objects themselves and those who use them. In this respect the work of art possesses functional (the transformative action of the artist) and spiritual (the perfection of all things created by God) dimensions that offer praise and recognition of the power of God each time the object is used or contemplated. The utilitarian and spiritual endeavor of the artist and his work, both of which are manifest in the gabbeh, approaches the essence of Islamic art, in which all acts of human creation uplift the soul to God in order to become "aware of His omnipotence in the creation of life and individuality."[59] Makhmalbaf delves further into the process of dual creation (by God and the artist) by examining its component elements and highlighting the function of the artist and the presence of God in his work through an examination of color.

In the film, Gabbeh's uncle after his wanderings returns to the tribe and goes into a school to quiz the children on their knowledge of the different colors. In the first instance he reaches out of the frame and pulls in two objects: poppies as an example of red, wheat as an example of yellow. He then points to the sky, "the blue of God's heaven," the sea, and the "yellow of the sun that lights the world." Each time he points his hand is transformed into the color of the object to which he refers. Finally he combines his blue hand and his yellow hand (water, sky and sun, the elements of God's creation) and creates green, physically denoted by the appearance of grass in his hands. The first two examples are given physicality while the last three are rendered essences—pure color—whose combination gives life. The next scene sees the women of the tribe using the natural elements to make dye for the wool of their gabbeh. Here, Makhmalbaf shows life as color, a beauty created by God through which the artist seeks to know God. The artist therefore considers beauty to be a divine quality and in creating beauty is joining with God in the perfection of the world.

### Life is Color

Makhmalbaf's meditations on color also exhibit his ongoing self-reflexive analysis of the formal properties and means of cinematic representation (a counterpoint for example, to the focus on sound in *A Time of Love*). It also refers to the specific cultural location of his work, which serves to counteract the film's categorization as a picturesque and packaged fable. The word for "color" in Persian has a another, peculiar usage, usually meant to refer to mode or manner, which in turn is given as the explanation of the Qur'anic reference to the "color" of God, which is taken to "denote the style, mode, spiritual shape of God."[60] This highlights the complex interaction of historical cultural forms in Iran where style and abstraction have traditionally been influenced by different devotional ties, from Zoroastrianism to certain forms of Islam such as Sufism, that have emphasized the compatibility of art, beauty, and spirituality. Throughout Persian history, a "close relationship has existed between the arts and the spiritual discipline deriving from the religion dominant in Persia at the time."[61]

The migrations of the tribe signify not only the artist's search for the divine but are also a reference to the two historical lifestyles of the Muslim world, the sedentary and the nomadic, the interaction of which is illustrated through the artistic evolution of the knotted carpet. The gabbeh represents a sedentary limit, frame and order, in contrast to the nomad's love of rhythm and infinite space. It is this living balance between stability and movement, and the exchange between these polarities, on which Islamic civilization lives and evolves. Throughout the film the gabbeh intervenes within this space as a commentary on life/reality and its depiction through art in the approximation of truth. Near the end of the film Gabbeh runs away from the tribe to be with her beloved and is pursued by her father. Two gunshots ring out. Her father returns to the camp saying that he has shot them both. He then throws a gabbeh on the ground that unfurls to reveal a scene of a man and woman escaping on horseback. Thus the gabbeh questions and provides a counterpoint to the validity of the father's story. The final scene confirms the claims of the gabbeh as we hear Gabbeh in a voiceover: "My father didn't kill us. That was just a rumor he started so my sisters wouldn't run away. So they would never answer the call of the wolf. That is why for forty years no one has heard the canary's song by a spring." The claims of art and its ability to question and document of the real, as well as its ability to reveal that which remains unsaid, are reinforced by the visuals that accompany Gabbeh's regret-tinged speech, when we see a gabbeh depicting a scene of a migrating tribe floating down a stream away from her, signifying all that she has left behind. Gabbeh's sense of regret at the end of the film once again reveals the effects of individual choice in the pursuit of passion and freedom, in this case at the expense of the family/community/society, all of which were depicted in different ways in *Boycott, Marriage of the Blessed* and *A Time of Love*.

## The Notion of the Beloved

During the course of the film Makhmalbaf has positioned the relationship between Gabbeh and her lover as an inverted depiction of the Persian literary notion of the beloved. Traditionally the beloved has been characterized as an ethereal woman of great beauty who is "unattainable, passive and silent, and the narrator has no desire to touch her as a physical touch would constitute a violation of the classical love relationship" (Ghanoonparvar, 1984: 15). In *Gabbeh* the beloved is the male (object) as seen through the eyes of a woman (subject) offering a means of release from the restrictive tribal structure. However, Gabbeh's freedom means isolation and a barren existence (reinforced by the fact that she is infertile and therefore incapable of having a family of her own), a sort of punishment and purgatory for allowing her own desires to surmount the needs of society and the maintenance of community. Her migration can be seen as restrictive rather than expansive, and is a clear echo of not just the migration of the tribe but also of women in general, as stated in the Qur'an; "Whoso migrateth for the cause of Allah will find much refuge and abundance in the earth, and whoso forsaketh his home, a fugitive unto Allah and His messenger, and death overtaketh him, his reward is then incumbent on Allah."[62] It also recalls the decision made by the protagonists in *Time of Love* that questions traditional societal mores and leaves doubt about the right course of action. Once again Makhmalbaf is walking a fine line between the desire to highlight the problems of male chauvinism in Iranian society and give voice to those denied freedom by it, while at the same time expressing a conservative religious belief in the strength and stability of the family/community that is very much in accordance with official ideology. For the Iranian artist, this is the fine line balanced between the expressible and the acceptable.

Makhmalbaf's cinema during his third period examines the microcosm of individual dilemmas at their most personal and emotional, projecting them onto a grand scale but remaining firmly located in their historical context. In this sense his cinema could be said to bear more than a passing resemblance to Cuban filmmaker Julio García Espinosa's idea of an "imperfect cinema," with its location in reality and its desire to "present a plurality of non-judgmental, non-prescriptive expositions of the problems faced by 'people who struggle' as a process."[63] However, such a definition is rendered somewhat problematic when attempting to explain the increasing complexity of Makhmalbaf's work, which has developed into a cinema that is derived simultaneously from reality and cinema itself (and indeed seeks to surpass both notions) and is in conflict with an all-pervasive and extraneous ideology from which he himself has emerged. Indeed, post-revolutionary Iranian cinema as a whole primarily is concerned with issues concerning the "legitimization of what constitutes the Iranian state and culture."[64] Makhmalbaf's cinema has participated in this debate by focusing on the human dimension and the interaction of human meanings transmitted through cultural traditions and embodied in social norms and institutions in the hope of opening up the eternal search for emancipation and justice. This search resides in a humanism that challenges the official neo-Shiism of the Islamic Republic. This, however, is not to suggest that the recourse to humanism is non-religious or anti-religious. Rather, the focus on the human, and its manifestation in Makhmalbaf's cinema, can be taken as a combination of thought and action about the concerns of people both in their social groups and individually. This concern recognizes the existence and importance of the spiritual but situates it as an organic phenomenon, not one handed down legislatively from the government. Focusing on the human, in an attempt to go beyond the structure of spiritualism and transcendental consciousness, not only questions man's relationship with God but draws man closer to God. This is achieved in a more personal and spiritual form of religion than the blind obedience of the Islamic Man demanded by the Islamic Republic, where the individual's relationship with God is only made possible by the intervention and mediation of the clergy. Given the entrenched system of government that the clerics have installed, social transformation can only occur within the theoretical battleground of Islamic ideology, criticism of which is forbidden. Therefore attention must be focused on the social and the suppressed Persian elements of the Iranian psyche in an attempt to open up an alternative space and mount a uniquely Iranian secular and moral affront to the official ideology, meanwhile attacking the source of its authority as well. It is this ideological tension, combined with the self-reflexive desire to unite the social and artistic that forms the ardent program of Makhmalbaf's cinema and provides its power.

# 6 | THE AESTHETICS OF REFORM

In 1997, at the end of Rafsanjani's tenure in power, Iran was a country in turmoil, and its economy was in freefall.* A ruling elite beset by corruption and inefficiency, Five-Year economic plans that had stalled, and were widely seen as ineffective, had merely resulted in widening the gap between rich and poor. The currency was devalued in 1993, development projects were shelved as the technocrats were ousted by conservatives, inflation was running at around thirty-five percent a year[1] and the Chamber of Commerce admitted that by 1996 up to forty percent of Iranians lived below the poverty line.[2] Rafsanjani's position as president had become ineffectual and isolated from the main locus of power, which was gathering within the alliance between the Supreme Leader Ayatollah Khamenei, the Speaker of the Majles Ali Akbar Nateq-Nouri and the dominant parliamentary grouping of conservative clerics, which effectively paralyzed the executive branch and stifled any debate on issues of reform. The early days of the revolution seemed to be back, with any form of dissent being harshly repressed. The Islamic system seemed to be near breaking point and parallels can be clearly seen with the situation that existed in the country at the time of the fall of the Pahlavi dynasty in 1979. This recourse to the narrative of Iranian history is instructive, not only as an example of the uniquely cyclical nature of events in Iranian history where "people are very strongly conditioned by their past, to such an extent that they act in patterns imposed by the past,"[3] but also provides a template from which to evaluate the post-Rafsanjani administration.

By the time of the new presidential elections in 1997 the voices clamoring for reform had reached a crescendo. Change, in some form, would have to occur if the Islamic system was to be prevented from

---

*The annual growth rate had fallen from eight percent in the early 1990s to one percent in 1996. Per capita GDP was below one thousand dollars a year and the economy was only creating two-fifths of the 700,000 jobs required annually to keep pace with the rising number of graduating students. See *The Financial Times*, May 2, 1997.

unraveling. The dissent that now being voiced was more persistent, articulate and coming from diffuse sources within the system, many of whom were children of the revolution now questioning the conduct of their parents. Thinkers such as Abdolkarim Soroush and Mohsen Kadivar, who were the most high-profile, public, and vociferous articulators of this growing social discontent, had begun to challenge the idea of authoritarian rule through a language that called for the recognition of individual rights, the establishment of a civil society and the need for a reappraisal of Islamic thought. These arguments called for a separation of Islam, and those who interpret it as a religion, from the center of power. These debates found eager recipients in the country's massive youth population (sixty-five percent of whom are under twenty-five years old[4]) who were increasingly alienated by the state's rhetoric and methods of repression. The tight controls that the ruling elite were able to enforce on domestic films and media were being undermined as Iran became increasingly enmeshed in the global economy. The availability of satellite television, despite parliamentary bans on it, and the development of the internet were exposing a new generation to the ideas and cultures of the outside world. This exposure was feeding the desire for change at home, which culminated in the election of the reformist liberal former Minister of Culture, Mohammad Khatami, in 1997 as the hoped-for figurehead of change that would herald the beginning of a new era of freedom, pluralism and democracy.

The former Minister of Culture and Islamic Guidance fought his election campaign on a policy platform that held as its priority the implementation of the rule of law and the development of a "civil society which would operate as a balance against the intrusions of the state, not only in the fields of politics and economics, but also on…the social and cultural aspects of life."[5] He also promised "greater social justice… administrative reform and a fairer distribution of wealth."[6] Khatami's reform program was seen as a radical break from the exclusive economic focus of the Second Republic. This shift of emphasis, which focused on the need for social and cultural change as a prerequisite for improving economic performance, seemed to offer the genuine possibility of a new reconstituted society, as the path to progress oscillated between "socially engaged visionaries and instrumental-bureaucratic functionaries."[7]

### Cinema in an Era of Reform

This period could be considered the pinnacle of post-revolutionary Iranian cinema, at least on the international stage, with Kiarostami's *The Taste of Cherry* winning the Palme d'Or at Cannes in 1997, followed by Samira Makhmalbaf winning the Jury Prize for *Blackboard* in 2000, along with Majid Majidi's *Children of Heaven* nominated for the Best Foreign Film award (the first Iranian film to do so) at the 1998 Academy

Awards. Artistically, however, it appeared that the medium had reached something of an impasse. Many films (particularly those shown abroad) began to exhibit formal and thematic repetitions—a focus on children, village life and beautiful landscapes, reducing them to formulaic post-card Orientalist curiosities that created "an imaginary space inhabited with strange natives."[8] The filmmaker Bahram Bayzai referred to this kind of cinema as "fake folklore…that makes it look as if Iran were a quiet country where everything is good, people are innocent, we have God…they are not real films but they present themselves as real."[9] The representation of Iran and Iranian-ness is a constant issue in the Iranian cultural debate and it has come into sharper focus given the current government's vaunting of Islamic democracy and the notion of a Persian-Islamic consciousness. But cultural representation must be viewed within the context of its historical antecedents and the broader issues of national culture and their discussion and reflection through art.

Makhmalbaf made two films during this period, *Sokut* (*The Silence*, 1998) and *Kandahar* (2001). These are a continuation and development of the poetic and aesthetic format that he had developed in *Gabbeh* and can be seen as part of the continued exploration and investigation of a humanism framed through Persian cultural forms. In this sense they describe aesthetic development derived from Persian poetry—particularly the works of Omar Khayyam and Forugh Farrokhzad—in approaching a Sufi mystical relationship with God. That is to say, these two films express a politics of the personal and the spiritual in discovering an individual form of piety and morality autonomous of institutional politics and ideology, yet firmly located within the contested spaces of Iranian culture.

### Realigning the Politics of Change

Khatami's "new" political and cultural directive in 1997 bore lineage to the cultural Islamicization undertaken in the first decade of the Islamic Republic, and in those terms looked like a return to the original aims of the revolution. Furthermore, this cultural emphasis is based on the notion that "identity" and identification in the Iranian sense is based on ideas of culture rather than nation, "a sense of Persian consciousness, of identity—*iraniyyat*—which runs throughout the country's history."[10] Khatami's civil society project must be seen, then, as an attempt to awaken this consciousness by laying claim to, appropriating and reinterpreting Khomeini's legacy. This is, itself, nothing new, as Rafsanjani had appropriated Khomeini's legacy, the constitution and the factional nature of the government to justify and pursue his economic goals. Indeed, the right to rule has been framed and debated within the need to justify all political undertakings according to the teachings and declarations of Khomeini. The basis and guarantor of this civil society lay in the full implementation of the 1979 Constitution, which in turn was cast as an historical narrative, and seen as but one stage of a movement that began with the calls for democracy during the 1906 Constitutional Revolution,* continued with the oil nationalization project of Mohammad Mossadegh that was defeated by the 1953 CIA- and MI6-backed coup† and culminated in the success of the 1979 revolution.

Although the Khatami era is still characterized by the struggle between conservatives and reformist elements in the ruling elite, this struggle has spilled over more visibly into the public arena with the tentative emergence of certain civic elements. For instance, increased freedom of the press has been able, to a certain extent, to set the agenda for their debates. However, the distinction between hard-liner/conservative and reformist/liberal needs to be qualified and treated with a certain amount of circumspection, because they can nonetheless be considered an inherent part of a hegemonic structure garnered to win support for the implementation of unpalatable policies by a regime operating according to the principle that the alternative is much worse. Furthermore, the shifting patterns of alliances within the Iranian political structure makes the application of such distinctions fraught with difficulty. These divisions are further called into question by the nature of the Islamic Republic's political system itself where "protean leadership makes a mockery of these false categories."[11]

Within the Iranian ruling elite these points are particularly salient. For example, in the economic sphere there exists little difference between the conservatives and reformists on the issue of policy implementation. While the reformists emphasize the need for social justice and the conservatives avidly promote the expansion of the free market, both sides support the liberalization of the economy and recognize the need to attract foreign investment. Furthermore, both sides recognize their mutual need for one another and the necessity of forming alliances if the Islamic system is to remain intact, as evidenced by the ritualistic patterns of political behavior that have developed in response to the public demonstrations of discontent that have occurred during Khatami's presidency.

The largest and most serious demonstrations and riots (those during the 1998 World Cup and the World Cup qualifying matches in 2001, and the violent student demonstrations in 1999) follow a clear pattern.‡

---

*Discontent with the corruption and mismanagement of the country by the ruling Qajar Dynasty as well as the increased territorial and economic interference in Iranian affairs by Britain and Russia led to the Constitutional Revolution. Instigated by an alliance of clergy, merchants and intellectuals it forced the shah to introduce the first constitution and parliament in order to limit the powers of the monarchy.

†See Chapter 1, page 15 n. ‡.

‡The student demonstrations in July 1999 occurred when the reformist newspaper *Salaam* was closed down. The protests after soccer matches have become a phenomenon in recent years with large public

Public discontent is met by the forces of state repression (usually a combination of the police, Revolutionary Guards, and unofficial forces, basij volunteers and Islamic vigilantes such as the Ansar-e Hezbollah, who see the defense of the Supreme Leader and the militant conservative values of the revolution as their raison d'être) and Khatami calling for calm, followed by the dissipation of the crisis and the formation of new alliances between the conservatives and reformists. Hard-fought changes to the social structure that are introduced are usually followed by a period of liberalization, then repression and a return to the status quo, with superficial changes introduced that pose little threat to the overall power structure.* Ayatollah Khamenei was quick to support Khatami and offer his pledge to cooperate following the attacks on student dormitories during the demonstrations in 1999.† Thus the demonstrations act as a safety valve while at the same time never seriously threatening the structure of the system and the locus of power. In fact in certain circumstances they have only further entrenched the position of the ruling elite through an uneasy alliance during times of crisis that seeks to maintain the ruling power structure at all costs in the suppression of periodic outbreaks of protest and dissent. In fact, one of the major weaknesses of these demonstrations is that they are more often than not spontaneous in nature, lacking an organized and clearly expressed mandate or set of demands through which to channel and articulate discontent.

### The Elements of a Civil Society

The cultural forces directing this discontent have been the press and the intelligentsia, pillars of dissent in any civil society and often the barometer by which the progress of reform and democracy is measured. The press and intelligentsia in Iran have traditionally filled the vacuum created by the absence of recognized oppositional political expression by informing, educating and extending political consciousness to the general public. Under Khatami the number of publications in circulation increased dramatically, and they not only became an

---

gatherings used as forums for political discontent. What is interesting to note is the change in the language of the protestors. In 1999, the chant was, in response to Khatami's conspicuous absence and silence, "Khatami where are you? Khatami what is your reaction?" *The Guardian*, July 17, 1999. In the aftermath of the 2001 World Cup qualifying matches, the chant changed to, "Khatami, do something or resign." *The Independent*, December 30, 2001.

*A group of students at the university in Yazd, when I asked them of the changes that had occurred under Khatami, remarked, "So headscarves are worn a little further back but what has that changed, nothing, things are still the same as they have always been." Author's research trip to Iran, September 2001.

†Following student demonstrations protesting the closure of *Salaam*, Islamic vigilantes, thought to be members of Ansar-e Hezbollah, entered student dormitories at Tehran University, assaulting students and destroying property. One person was killed and many were injured, and the event sparked a series of riots throughout the country, the worst seen since the revolution itself.

overt factor in political strategy but also began to set the terms of political dialogue by criticizing government actions or printing lectures and interviews of those criticizing the system and calling for reform. A new group of intellectuals, both lay and religious, began to emerge around issues of freedom, democracy and civil rights, finding a platform for the expression of their ideas in the resurgent press. The artistic community, many of whom had dealt with Khatami during his tenure as Minister of Culture, joined in this debate, and now offered their unconditional support to the new president. These included Makhmalbaf, who declared his allegiance publicly during the election campaign and was quickly followed by twenty-two other filmmakers who aligned with Khatami in an open letter to the press.* This new resurgent intellectual environment (despite having to operate under the constant fear of threats and intimidation) seemed to signal, or at least offer the possibility of, a new public oppositional alliance.

In Iranian society opposition to the state has traditionally come from a combination of the clergy, bazaar and members of the intelligentsia.† With the clergy's, and by association the bazaar (their position having being consolidated under Rafsanjani), assumption of power, and the purging, persecution and exile of many members of the intelligentsia, it would seem that the Islamic regime had succeeded in eliminating the threat of an oppositional alliance. However, a new confederation tentatively emerged from certain reform-minded elements within the clergy, a new intelligentsia seeking to discuss reformist issues in exclusively Persian-Islamic cultural terms, and a large disgruntled youth population that had its cultural and material expectations raised by the effects of globalization but constantly thwarted and unfulfilled by the strictures of the Islamic system. This last group was the largest and most vocal in their demands for reform. The youth and student population formed the core of Khatami's support and can be seen as the new mostazafin. This section of society has little recollection or experience of the shah and their discontent is directed solely at the Islamic Republic, because the Islamicization process has failed to socialize them as planned.

## The Politics of Change?

Despite the enthusiasm and hope engendered by the election of President Khatami in 1997, and despite the orientation of his policies,

*Many filmmakers also played an active part in Khatami's election campaign, producing a number of campaign films in a contest in which television proved integral. Khatami himself has also been the subject of a number of films, including Mohsen Makhmalbaf's forty-minute video film *Testing Democracy* (2000) and the acclaimed Iranian actress Fatemeh Motamed Aria's *A Man For All Reasons* (2001). It must be said, however, that neither of these were particularly informative or critically engaging.

†As happened in the 1979 revolution. See Ervand Abrahamian, "The Crowd in Iranian Politics, 1905-53" in *Iran: A Revolution in Turmoil*, for an historical analysis of the development and composition of mass oppositional forces in Iranian society.

Khatami was not the instigator of reform. The demands for change already existed in Iranian society, and became more acute following the failures and disillusionment of the Rafsanjani period.* In effect, Khatami attempted to articulate, manage and channel this social discontent into a political movement as a means of defusing or controlling it, in a bid to ensure that the Islamic system remained intact. Indeed, "what most distinguished the third republic from the two earlier phases—and what gave it the greatest prospect of enduring—was the fact that leadership increasingly came from the streets, not mosques or political offices."[12] In this respect Khatami operated with a dual perspective, responding to a popular mandate while simultaneously acting as a "safety valve"[13] employed by the ruling regime. It is certain that Khatami did not become president of the Islamic Republic in order to dismantle it, and Khatami has stated that, "The most important [issue]…is the preservation of the system and of our Islamic values…. What is a priority is that the system should be preserved, improved and strengthened…. It should be made strong and stable."[14]

The central tenet of Khatami's agenda was to preserve the Islamic system as established by Khomeini, aligning it with and implementing fully the declarations laid down in the constitution. Khatami can be seen as another stage in self-regulating clerical reform that had begun with the constitutional amendments undertaken by the previous administration in 1989. The problem thus arises of how to reconcile pluralistic notions such as democracy, freedom and civil society with the theocracy of a revolutionary state built on an undemocratic system of governance. The difficulty in attempting to solve this apparent contradiction can be clearly seen in Khatami's attempt to link the notion of velayat-e faqih with the democratic will of the people: "The pivot of the system which was created by the people is the supreme jurisconsult."[15] Khatami asserts that the people created the system and that the survival of that system lies in aligning it, including the faqih, with the declarations of the constitution. This refutes the very logic of the definition as laid down by Khomeini who declared that a jurisprudent "has the same authority that the Most Noble Messenger and the Imams had"[16] and which therefore establishes an undemocratic system of the subservience of the many to the infallible pronouncements of the few. In other words the faqih is above the constitution.

### The Question of Velayat-e Faqih

Khatami's comments betray how deeply entrenched and intractable the political system of the Islamic Republic really is. Velayat-e faqih

---

*The majority of the landslide seventy percent of the thirty million votes cast in the 1997 election for Khatami came from the most disenfranchised and reform-minded section of the electorate, women and students.

essentially means that any real power is located in the hands of the conservative elements within the ruling elite—the Supreme Leader, the Guardian Council and the Expediency Council, and their control of the judiciary. The reconstituted political system that emerged after the Second Republic allowed for the public voicing (within controlled parameters) of discordant elements of protest, which created the appearance of debate and democracy and offered the possibility (if not the reality) of change in a political system that had as its true objective the retention of power and the maintenance of clerical rule. That protests, demonstrations and discontent continued, and in fact increased throughout Khatami's presidency, may be attributed to a certain liberalization of the public intellectual climate, which created more opportunities for the voicing of discontent. But the lack of substantive reforms demonstrated the inability and unwillingness of the power structure to instigate meaningful and wholesale reforms within government and thus society.* The superficial changes that occurred merely led to demands for an increased pace of change and confirmed that the political structure of the Islamic Republic had to be radically altered or even removed if the full extent of these demands were to be met and meaningfully implemented.

This is the dilemma of the Islamic regime: how far it can introduce reform without ultimately annihilating itself. The ruling elite has attempted to surmount this problem by counterbalancing a limited form of political disenfranchisement with efforts to control and dictate the process of change. This control is facilitated by the conservative grip on the armed forces and the economy, which acted, in conjunction with Khatami's belief that political pluralism was the handmaiden of economic liberalization, as a means of preventing dissent from becoming action. "Conservatives run the judiciary, where they interpret the legislation any way they like, and hand out verdicts that promote their politics rather than implement the law. They control the army, police and *baseej*.... They run the mass media.... They control certain sectors of the economy. Thus we have two parallel, but unequal systems here."[17] The lack of progress on the economic front is another important factor in that control; by keeping the majority of the populace in a state of economic subsistence and by offering the possibility if not the reality of change. This illustrates Alexis de Tocqueville's famous observation that revolutions tend to happen not when things have been getting worse but when things have been getting better, or when an elite loses confidence in its authority.[18] The maintenance of the economic status quo benefits the ruling elite since it is they who possess the wealth, and the

*In an interview with students conducted in Tehran during the course of a research trip I made to Iran in September 2001, many expressed their frustrations with the slow pace of change. One student remarked, "All Khatami has done is change the psychology of the people."

means of acquiring and keeping it. Indeed, not a single significant economic bill, apart from the budget, was introduced to parliament during Khatami's first two years in office.[19]

The critical question governing any notions of change still focuses on the issue of velayat-e faqih. The comments of the conservative ideologue Ayatollah Mesbah Yazdi perfectly illustrate the precarious position of the reformers: "In a democracy, people can decide to change the rules of their lives through elections and parliament. In Iran no such change is possible because the rules are fixed for eternity. Those who expect the new parliament to change our system will soon be disappointed...the ultimate decision rests with the Leader."[20] However, the authoritarian nature of Islamic governance is derived from the system of velayat-e faqih and it is the institution itself rather than its actual manifestation that needs to be fundamentally altered. As Ali Mirsepassi has put it, "Religious tradition and the Revolution have entrapped many... because Ayatollah Khomeini has forced religious tradition into a situation where it does not belong. This offers an opportunity whereby our cultural traditions can be re-evaluated in their entirety.... It is my belief that in Iranian political thought monarchy has many bodies. We need to deal with it so that its present reincarnation in the 'rule of the jurist' does not last long."[21]

### The Intellectual and Cultural Debate

The question now becomes one of how to reformulate a new civil society given the fact that the clergy, through the theory and position of the velayat-e faqih, have conflated and eliminated the distinction that traditionally existed between politics, the state and religion. The attempt to democratize the fixture of the velayat-e faqih is the first step in separating the notions of religion and power. The most influential thinkers debating this issue at present are Abdolkarim Soroush* and Mohsen Kadivar.† But the key to appropriating and analyzing the terms of the debate lies in considering the historical background of the debates conducted in the immediate aftermath of the revolution, through the work of liberal ideologues such as Mehdi Bazargan and Ayatollah Motahari (see Chapter 2), and not least within the myriad and complex ideological legacy left by Ayatollah Khomeini himself.

---

*Born in 1945, Soroush was a lay religious thinker who had initially been appointed by Khomeini to the Committee of Cultural Revolution to Islamicize the school curriculum. An advocate of the revolution, by the late 1980s and early 1990s he had begun to voice his opposition to what he saw as the increased authoritarianism of the regime. Advocating a form of Islam compatible with democracy he drew large support from many sections of society but also drew the wrath of the ruling clerics who saw him as a threat to the system.

†A young cleric and seminary professor who offended the traditional clergy through a series of interviews and articles that called for the separation of politics and religion and criticized and questioned the practices of the ruling clerics. He was arrested and charged with undermining the velayat-e faqih and his court case attracted huge support and interest. Kadivar was found guilty and sentenced to eighteen months imprisonment.

## The New Intelligentsia

Soroush's religious revisionism implicitly attacks the religio-political manifestation of the Islamic Republic by calling for the separation of the influential body of religion from those who interpret it.* According to him the blurring of this division has lead to the present system of governance where the clergy have manipulated religious interpretation in order to reproduce the ideological positions that best serve to manipulate and justify their position of political power. In a similar vein Kadivar has argued against what he sees as the perversion of the notion of the velayat-e faqih, saying that its present interpretation has elevated it to the level of absolutism that has seen it become an instrument of arbitrary power devoid of legal restrictions and responsibilities, and as such has resulted in the institutionalization of divine ordinance for political purposes. Consequently, the people's rights have been treated as matters of secondary importance, and they and religion and the true ideals of the Islamic revolution have suffered and been corrupted as a result: "The central question that the clergy faces is whether it can preserve its independence"[20] and by extension the respect and support of the people. Such sentiments echo the thoughts of Ayatollah Montazeri—originally designated as Khomeini's successor—who stated that because "republic means a government of the people" the role of the velayat-e faqih should be purely supervisory, and that the religious leaders should "stop imitating the Imam because you are not he."[21] These arguments, and much of the reformist debate as a whole, are not new and derive much from the thought and ideological debates of the early years of the revolution. Ayatollah Motahari had repeatedly stated the need for a separation of religion and political power, highlighting the importance of social justice if Islam and the revolution were to survive and develop: "The future of our revolution will only be secure if we preserve justice and freedom, if we keep political, economic, cultural, intellectual and religious independence."[22] Others such as Ayatollah Shariatmadari went further in explicitly stating that the role of the ulama should be to advise rulers but not directly rule.

## The Religious and Historical Basis of Debate

These arguments did not endorse a total abandonment of the idea of velayat-e faqih but merely sought to reconsider its interpretation. The role of the faqih comprises a number of different meanings in Shia theology, and it denotes a guardianship that potentially extends to a number of areas of community life, quite distinct from Khomeini's controversial elevation of it to direct political authority. The faqih's gen-

---

*For more details on Soroush's work see Abdolkarim Soroush, "The Evolution and Devolution of Religious Knowledge," in *Liberal Islam*.

erally accepted and agreed-upon role of guardianship includes care for those who may be victimized, over the property and activities of the religious community and for the welfare of the Muslim community. This last point encompasses "the responsibility of serving as a social force aimed at carrying out the injunction to command the good and forbid the reprehensible."[23] In the Islamic Republic, though, the state talks of the virtues of the civil society but constantly subverts and undermines the notion by concentrating all political and cultural activities in its own hands. Their rule is being directed increasingly toward propaganda, maintaining public order and enforcing moral and cultural influence. This is the only way to protect the economic and political interests of the ruling elite—hardly a means of promoting a civil society in the interests of the public. The Italian theorist Antonio Gramsci describes a similar situation in his discussion of totalitarianism, where the state and party, "which claims moral, ethical leadership in the absence of a pluralism of the political and cultural forces remains on the terrain of coercion and economic-corporativism."[24]

The ruling apparatus, the velayat-e faqih, poses the greatest obstacle to change in Iran, because "the jurisprudent is positioned to guarantee institutional conformity to the agenda for restructuring consciousness and to articulate...the content of the genuine Islamic identity sought."[25] Therefore, only with the removal of the authority of office, or "until a new *faqih* emerges to totally redefine the very foundation of his authority"[26] will substantial and far-reaching social reforms begin to occur. Until that time power will remain linked to an office that stands in the way of reform. Khatami, well aware of this situation, declared, on 26 November 2000, that "after three and a half years as president I don't have sufficient powers to implement the constitution...the president is unable to stop the trend of violations or force implementations of the constitution."[27]

### Cinema and the Cultural Debate

Khatami's desire to introduce elements of a civil society seemed at first to hold much promise for those involved in the cultural field. The first signs indicating a new era of less restricted expression occurred in the press, as publications in circulation grew to 890 in 1998, nearly four times the number that appeared during the unprecedented but short-lived period of freedom that took place immediately after the fall of the shah. This figure is even more startling considering the fact that in 1996 fifteen daily newspapers accounted for most of the readership of two million and that two years later the corresponding figures were fifty newspapers and 3.5 million readers.[28] Khatami himself saw the important role of the press in society and encouraged this proliferation of publications: "The more independent and freer the press, the greater their representation of the public opinion."[29] These initiatives were strengthened by the appointment of the reformist, erudite and moderate candidate Dr. Ataollah Mohajerani to the crucial post of Minister of Culture and Islamic Guidance, who stated that, "We must value our artists, writers and filmmakers.... We must create a seedbed that allows these seeds of creativity to blossom. We must create an atmosphere of peace and tranquility in all centers of art and culture."[30]

For the cinema this meant a relaxation of the censorship laws, and number of previously banned films were given screening permits, including Ali Hatami's *Haji Washington* (1982), Dariush Mehrjui's *The Lady* (1992) and Mohsen Makhmalbaf's *A Moment of Innocence* (1996). Filmmakers also began to tackle more risqué and taboo subjects in their films, especially a number of women directors, who came to the fore during this period.* Tahmineh Milani's *Two Women* (1999) explored how a woman's destiny is controlled by outdated patriarchal laws, and Rakhshan Bani-Etemad's *The May Lady* (1998) dealt with a divorced woman's need for love and companionship.† The deputy for cinema affairs, Seifullah Daad, also announced the government's intention to redress the country's chronic shortage of cinemas by beginning a comprehensive theater construction program. The plan proposed to build cinemas in towns with a population over fifteen thousand people[31] and was one part of the government's plan to encourage the development of the industry. These policies were further enhanced by Daad's decision to leave cinema policies unchanged for five years (thus replacing the Ministry's fifteen-year-old policy of annual declarations) in order to create an atmosphere of stability that freed filmmakers from the uncertainty and capriciousness of official whims. Furthermore, the Khatami administration included in its Third Development Plan a number of proposals aimed at enhancing the Iranian film industry, which included regulations to improve productivity, encouraging private sector investment, inviting foreign investment in order to ameliorate the international image of the Iranian film industry, establishing an organization for the promotion of a national cinema, developing a visual media system throughout the country as well as a research and training program for all aspects of the cinema industry.[32] However, the cultural sphere in Iran is a volatile arena where reforms are hard fought and unstable because they must function within the ideological debates of competing political power blocs.

---

*In an interview at the London Film Festival in 1998, Samira Makhmalbaf stated that she felt that her film *The Apple* owed its existence to the new circumstances and changed atmosphere that prevailed in Iran as a result of the Khatami presidency. National Film Theatre, 12 November 1998.

†See Sheila Johnston and Hadani Ditmars, "Quietly Ruling the Roost," *Sight and Sound* 9, no. 1 (January 1999):18-20, for interviews with both directors.

## One Step Forward, Two Steps Back

The increasingly outspoken views of the press and the perceived liberalization of the cultural sphere caused alarm within the conservative ruling faction. And, like clockwork, on 7 July 1999 a new Press Law was introduced in order to counteract "those who were using the pretext of press freedom to plot against the system and to stem the tide of a new cultural invasion."[33] The new law was comprehensive in the scope of its control, requiring newspaper publishers to submit a list of their employees to the judiciary and for journalists to reveal their sources. Furthermore, it extended the powers of the Press Court, allowing it to overrule jury verdicts and conduct summary trials on those seen as endangering the security of the state. The closure of many publications soon followed, causing widespread demonstrations. However, the bill remained in force and further clauses were added to it a year later, which extended the responsibility for press violations to journalists and commentators and banned all publications from receiving foreign financial support or criticizing the constitution. The latter point was of particular significance because the implementation of the constitution formed the main plank of the reformist drive toward freedom and a new civil society. Not only the means but also the very terms of the debate were being arrogated by the government.

Having attempted to stifle the opposition press, and controlling television and radio, the conservatives moved to bring the cinema under tighter control. A new Cinema Law, similar to the Press Law, was drafted in 2000. The bill aimed to remove the permit requirement for screening a film and place the responsibility for the production and screening of their films onto the producer and director. Those within the industry voiced concern that this proposal rendered them defenseless against the judiciary and in fact increased the arbitrary power of the latter to intervene directly in screening decisions.[34] These fears were well founded, because for the first time ever, the Iranian judiciary intervened to ban the film *Party* (2001) by Saman Moghaddam.* The ambiguity of interpretation and the desire to present an image of moderation and reform encouraged the Ministry of Culture's removal of the need to submit detailed scripts for scrutiny before shooting

---

*This film depicted the plight of journalists and the incidence of censorship at the time. It tells the story of Amin Haghi, who is imprisoned for publishing the memoirs of his brother, a celebrated martyr of the war with Iraq, in a weekly newspaper. The memoirs question whether it was reasonable to continue the war after 1982, after all the land Iraq had invaded was recovered and the Iraqis were suing for peace. Amin is imprisoned by the authorities for "anti-Islamic propaganda" and defaming the memories of martyrs. His wife and brother try to raise the bail money for his release by renting out their house for nightly parties where guests dance and consume alcohol. Amir is eventually released from prison only to be shot dead by a vigilante (an echo of the recent high-profile killing of intellectuals in the country) while taking his pregnant wife to the hospital. The film, despite being banned, was shown abroad and Hediyeh Tehrani, who starred in the film won the award for best actress at the ninth Pyongyang Film Festival in North Korea in 2002.

commenced. However, rather than encouraging greater freedom of expression this measure in fact placed the burden of censorship onto the filmmakers themselves. A film company could now make a film based on a short scenario and, having invested its time, money and resources, the film could be rejected by the ministry in the final stages before screening if they didn't like it. The incidences of censorship and the persecution of artists and intellectuals continued unabated under the Khatami administration. The most shocking incident came with the brutal murders of three authors and the former nationalist politician Dariush Forouhar and his wife in November 1998 by members of the intelligence agency. The film director Tahmineh Milani was arrested in August 2001 on charges of abusing the arts and using it as a tool to support "counter-revolutionary groups…and those waging war against God."[35] Despite the fact that she was released on bail the charges were not rescinded.[36]

## The State of the Industry

There was also a feeling among many within the industry that the medium was beginning to suffer both financially and artistically. Poor box office receipts and a twenty-five percent increase in production costs, which had seen the average Iranian film budget jump from $80,000 in 1999 to around $100,000 by the start of 2001, made it very difficult for any film to earn a profit.* One of the reasons attributed for the drop in audiences was the lack of invention, with many films simply repeating the same old story lines. Though successful at international festivals[37] Iranian films had become a very recognizable and generic form in danger of being molded into a "European-based film culture" pandering to a "universalizing festival taste."[38] Iranian films were running the risk of becoming clichéd, culturally co-opted and lacking in artistic invention. It is against these charges and in a bid to reclaim the domestic cultural space that Makhmalbaf's *The Silence* (1998) must be considered.

### *The Silence*

*Sokut* (*The Silence*, 1998) is a continuation of the style and poetic preoccupations begun in *Gabbeh*. Makhmalbaf once again "returned to the roots of Iranian-Persian narrative and visual culture, combining the pictorial beauty of medieval illustration with the ornate structures of the national mythology."† The film continued to explore and celebrate the

---

*Film International, 9. These economic problems were symptomatic of those occurring throughout the economy as a whole. Inflation was officially running at twenty percent, unemployment was at fifteen percent and economic growth was registered at just two percent. See also The Economist, August 14, 1999: 49.

†Simon Louvish, "Gabbeh," Sight and Sound 6 no. 12 (December 1996): 47. The two films share another point of similarity: both were banned by the authorities. The "guardians of morality" cited the immoral scene of a young girl dancing as their reason for refusing The Silence a screening permit.

beauty, passion and spirituality of life, but where *Gabbeh* (1996) worked through the medium of color, *The Silence* revolves around an exploration of sound and in this sense can be seen as another meditation on the elemental forms involved in the process of artistic creation. However, *The Silence* is much more deeply and firmly rooted in a tangible Persian cultural tradition, in this instance emanating from the poetry of Omar Khayyam. Makhmalbaf has eliminated the multi-perspective narrative technique used in many of his third-period films and focused solely on the individual, which gives his protagonist more psychological and emotional depth.

This shift of perspective also moves from the purely individual to the person's position and identity within the social experiences of conflict and everyday dilemmas. In this respect *The Silence*, in its form and thematic preoccupations, embraces the complex cultural debate comprised of an oscillating engagement and disengagement with the real and a definition of the self through art. This is a notion that is complicated further by Makhmalbaf's developing relationship with God, which can now be seen to exhibit many attributes of Sufi mysticism. These factors create a work committed to a politics of the personal, one that engages with a specifically Persian-Islamic historical and cultural discourse. This attempt to define the self in the space between culture and society intimately ties the film to the present intellectual debates in Iran—those who seek to define and develop the notions of freedom and the individual's place within society as the prerequisite of a civil state.

Filmed in Tajikistan, *The Silence* tells the story of Khorshid ("sun" in Persian), a ten-year-old blind boy who works as a tuner of traditional musical instruments.* Khorshid's blindness has sensitized him to sound, and the simple sensations of everyday life intoxicate him. However, Khorshid's family, who rely on his salary, are being threatened with eviction. Khorshid's mother tells him to apply for an advance on his wages so that they can pay the landlord. But Khorshid becomes caught up and distracted by the minutiae of everyday life, forgets to ask for the advance and eventually loses his job. The film ends with Khorshid's family being evicted as he stands in the bazaar, having mentally incorporated all the sounds he has experienced during the day, conducting Beethoven's Fifth Symphony to the noise and rhythm of coppersmiths beating their pots.

---

*This is Makhmalbaf's second film shot exclusively outside of Iran (although parts of *The Cyclist* were shot in Pakistan). The first was *Time of Love*, which was shot in Turkey after being refused a shooting permit in Iran. Makhmalbaf states that his reason for shooting abroad was the increasing severity of the censorship laws, which meant that he would "have had to change things and make certain concessions." See Mamad Haghighat, "*The Silence*: Interview with Mohsen Makhmalbaf," http://www.filmlinc.com/archive/programs/11-99/makh/silint.htm

## Art and Life: A Changing Relationship

*The Silence* is Makhmalbaf's attempt to explore universal themes of compassion, humanity and spirituality, by placing the individual in a space between the harsh realities of life and the poetic possibilities of art, all expressed in the details of the everyday, through which he seeks to transcend the brevity and bitterness of life. This film confirms Makhmalbaf's movement from the concerns, preoccupations and doubts of the past toward an aspirational and inspirational poetics of the personal that turns toward life and seeks to emphasize the "astonishing brightness which lives on in the hearts of darkness."[39] Makhmalbaf breaks from the pattern of his previous output by examining the artistic and intellectual evolution of the central theme of blindness. In his earlier film *Two Sightless Eyes,* part of the miraculous tradition of Islamic cinema, blindness was seen as an ailment requiring the intervention of God, the supernatural result of which allowed access to the light. *The Silence* makes clear that there is no longer any need for divine intervention or the performance of a miracle because the notion of light and seeing has taken on a less literal and more complex set of meanings, far removed from religious dogma. In this instance if there is no light there exists no corresponding shadow and darkness, as light only comes into being or takes on meaning in the presence of darkness. Khorshid's blindness is a kind of darkness but he banishes it with sound, and the film itself is pervaded by light. Makhmalbaf infuses *The Silence* with light and color, which he uses to create a garden of beauty that functions as a type of dreamscape through which Khorshid wanders in creating his own picture of reality. This is a reality brought into being by his accumulation of sound as a means of understanding and creating a world that is for him knowable and poetic. Thus Makhmalbaf and Khorshid are collaborators in bringing into being a work of art molded by light, color and sound that they take from the world around them.

Khorshid becomes the source of light through his actions, as he revels in all aspects of the quotidian. Khorshid elevates the mundane by challenging the ways in which the world is perceived, and subsequently leads to a reappraisal of accepted meanings—in one scene Khorshid equates the sound of an apple to its probable taste. It is this emphasis on the self and the creative process within the present, shorn of the distresses of the past and the anxieties of the future, that most clearly illustrates the film's Khayyamic* influences and leads Makhmalbaf to assert that the film itself "is a kind of contemporary representation of the spirit of Khayyam."[40]

---

*Omar Khayyam was an eminent poet, astronomer, philosopher and mathematician who was born in Nishapur in the Khorasan region of eastern Iran in the latter half of the eleventh century. His most famous poetic work is the *Rubaiyat,* a series of quatrains, which celebrate the joys of the present, believing life to be fleeting and death a finality of nothingness.

## The Khayyamic Vision

Many of Khayyam's poetic preoccupations are prominent in *The Silence*. The Khayyamic vision posits a paradise of this world built on the simple pleasures of adequate sustenance, shelter, art and companionship. For Khayyam the brevity of life commands that one should live for the moment, embrace romantic love and revelry, which are the only source of solace from the harshness of life. This celebration of life is underpinned with a heavy skepticism that sees life on this earth as an end in itself, with human beings possessing only corporeal existence and lacking spiritual souls. This pessimism, though, is tempered by a humanity enthralled with life as it is:

> Ah, make the most of what we yet may spend,
> Before we too into the Dust Descend;
> Dust into Dust, and under Dust, to lie,
> Sans Wine, sans Song, sans Singer and—sans End![41]

This is a path that Makhmalbaf seeks to travel through Khorshid's collection of sounds in a bid to create an art-based "reality" that acts as an alternative to the harsher reality of life—in this instance music and sound as a bulwark against the pain of eviction and poverty. In a scene near the start of the film Khorshid, while riding on the bus, hears two young girls trying to learn a poem by heart. The poem is reminiscent of Khayyam and reflects the film's and Khorshid's approach to life:

> "Speak no more of what happened yesterday
> Don't worry about what happens tomorrow
> Do not rely on the future or the past
> Seize the moment and do not waste time."

However, Makhmalbaf differs from Khayyam because he does not share the poet's pessimism, and he is keenly aware that the vision of an alternative artistic reality can only be brought into being by a transformation of the materials existing within a certain social reality. This interaction of art and reality takes place in the scene with the girls on the bus. Khorshid repeats the verse to the girls and they ask how he could know it if he is blind. He replies by telling them that the eyes distract: "If you close your eyes you will learn better." They close their eyes and recite the verse only to realize on opening them that they have missed their stop. Until this point the scene is filmed in a simplistic but rhythmic series of shot-reverse-shots—the girls are framed together in a medium close-up while Khorshid is framed by himself. Initially, the section alternates between the girls trying to learn the poem by rote while Khorshid listens intently, consumed by the words and their meaning. This pattern is repeated when Khorshid, having learned the poem, begins to teach it to the girls, encouraging them to feel the words and to let themselves become lost in their meaning. The scene ends with a reverse long shot from the back of the bus as the girls realize in a panic that they have missed their stop. Here Makhmalbaf formally renders the world of the senses into separate entities existing beside one another; he shows their interdependence and interaction with one another and highlights that only through their interaction, interruption and intrusion of reality do they coalesce and form meaning. The visual sense of the girls and the aural sense of Khorshid cannot be separated from their position within reality and indeed are derivations of one another— the girls reciting the poem makes it known and Khorshid makes its artistry, essence and meaning felt. Thus Makhmalbaf has presented an alternative perception of art through the individual's ability to construe the world differently. This representation and interpretation, embodied through Khorshid's blindness, operates within the realm of the possibilities of the moment, one very much rooted in and engaged with the particular nuances and experiences of everyday reality.

This marks a fundamental difference with the work of Khayyam, whose vision of a paradise garden is an idealistic, pristine world untouched by man. For his part, Makhmalbaf views the garden as one that is created, and can only be created, by man through the tool of art, exemplified by the final scene of the film when all the sounds that Khorshid has collected are transformed into a Beethoven symphony by the banging of coppersmiths. The banal is removed from its natural function and transformed into the epic—the elements preexist but it is only through their artistic transformation by man that they acquire meaning and form and offer the possibility of an enhanced environment. Makhmalbaf is once again showing the cultural basis of life and the important functioning of art within it, which for him offers the possibility of bringing "about a revolution wherein all people would arrive at decisions that may or may not be related to the aspirations of this revolution but would naturally result from the event."

Nationalism has been a constant element of Persian literature since writing in Persian began. This cultural partisanship has manifested itself "through the depiction of social history, local color, regional customs, dialects...all of which imply the authors' deep attachment to the region."[43] As such it has been a social, political and personal search for an authentic national and historical identity. For Khayyam, and others such as Ferdowsi, as well as many modernist Iranian writers like Sadeq Hedayat and Mehdi Akhavan Sales, this search led to a deep-seated nostalgia and sadness at the loss of Iran's pre-Islamic grandeur. Makhmalbaf has approached this loss not through recourse to some essentialist pristine essence but by a critical engagement of the very notion and nature of Persian art itself, through which an understanding of the present might be achieved. In this sense Makhmalbaf once again visits the work of Forugh Farrokhzad in attempting to develop a socially attached, universally transformative voice through a poetics of the personal.

## The Search for the Self in a Poetics of the Personal

Forugh Farrokhzad's poems express a feminist sensitivity that counteracts the conventional moral order and the problems of patriarchy, encouraging her readers to paint the world anew. Her work was attached to the reality of the world she inhabited, but she attempted to articulate an alternative picture of an ideal but un-romanticized Persian garden in which individuals were engaged in a personal struggle to define their own identity. Her refusal to detach herself from the reality of the present sets her apart from Khayyam, despite the fact that both see the perfect image of life as represented in the idyllic Persian garden. Farrokhzad's garden is brought into being through poetry based on personal experience and firmly located in the images and language of everyday life;

> Those days are gone
> Those days like vegetation rotting in the sun
> > rotted in the sun.
> And those alleys high with the scent of acacia
> and lost in the noise
> of crowded avenues without return.
> And the girl who colored her cheeks
> with geranium petals, ah,
> Is now a lonely woman,
> Is now a lonely woman."[43]

*The Silence* is rife with elements of the everyday. Most striking and vivid, perhaps, is the scene in which the young girl, Nadereh, puts flower petals on her nails and cherries on her ears to imitate nail polish and earrings, a process whereby innocence, and the viewer's perception of it, are transformed by the displacement of the connotation of these accouterments. The girl, in transfiguring cherries and flower petals—the beauty and innocence of natural things—sheds her own innocence in a novel way, becoming "now a lonely woman." This image is enhanced in the following scene where Nadereh dances to the sound of Khorshid playing the *tar*, a Persian string instrument. Through a series of close-ups of her nails and ears the transformation is accentuated, before cutting to wide shots of her dancing, showing her final metamorphosis.

The works of Khayyam and Farrokhzad serve as complements and counterpoints to one another. They allow the oscillation between artistic engagement and detachment to take place. Makhmalbaf's uses a Persian literary and cultural milieu for his continuing development as an artist attempting to express the universal and emotive aspects of humanity—"the reality of life, its joys and pains"[44]—through an examination of the particularity of the local. Makhmalbaf examines Iran's cultural history, and its manifestation within current social and political developments, and appeals to universal themes beyond the local, as a way of challenging an Iranian nativism and a primordial, exclusionary essence that has historically blighted Iranian cultural development and debate. By contrast, Iranian modernists such as Jalal Al-e Ahmad and Ali Shariati "attempted to construct a 'local' image of Iranian culture in opposition to the 'universal' West,"[45] although this was in essence, and practice, an essentially insular and reactionary project. For Makhmalbaf the transformative power of art opens the possibility of a heterogeneous space for debate, which served as a timely intervention in the civil society debate of the Khatami era.

## The Nature of God

The search for the self through a Persian cultural discourse is but one half of the Persian-Islamic debate. Due attention must also be paid to the religious and spiritual aspects of the Iranian cultural tradition if cultural myopia and exclusion are to be avoided. In Makhmalbaf's developing relationship with God the moral didacticism of his early career has been replaced by an intimate and personal religious spirituality, enthralled by the beauty of the world and the joy of living. Makhmalbaf has remarked, "I accept God in my heart. But I would never try to persuade someone else to accept him. This is a personal matter. The details which attract us to the world are the details of living."[46]

The search for an individualistic relationship with God, combining elements of mysticism and personal spirituality, form the main elements of Sufi belief. In this sense an appeal to Sufism could be seen as another strand of the debate undertaken by Soroush and others who call for a separation of the authority of religious belief from those who interpret it. Therefore, a personal faith stands in contradistinction to the ideologues of the Islamic Republic who continuously emphasize religious practice and code over belief. In fact, historically the origins of Sufism lay in a form of social-political protest "against the ulama, the learned clerics of Islam, who, in Sufi perception, exhibited more interest in political power than religion."[47]

Sufism as a mystical and intuitive religious belief attempts to erase the void between man and God through the establishment of a personal faith that was felt to have been lost through the sober, didactic and legalistic traditions of official dogma. While the ulama see God in terms of omnipotence and order, Sufis perceive God in terms of love and they use a multitude of forms such as "music, song and dance to help in the search for God, to help the worshipper achieve mystical union with God."[48] As a mode in Persian poetry Sufism represented an approach to life's dilemmas that emphasized the spirit over the concerns of the material world, as evidenced in the poetry of Hafez:

> With tulip blood on rose-leaves, it is written
> That he who mellows quaffs the ruby wine.
> See fortune grasped when havoc swept the world,
> The Sufi with his cup did not repine.[49]

Makhmalbaf uses Sufism as a counterpoint to Khayyamic resignation and as a means of reclaiming an innocence that is lost in Farrokhzad. The narrative of the film, built on Khorshid following the sounds he hears, is structured and counterpointed by the actual songs that he hears, which in turn serve as a Sufistic commentary on his wanderings. The first song he hears asks, "You never ask me how I'm feeling." This is followed by one which warns the listener not to go astray, "The wise man and the fool are both me," and the last song he hears before conducting his symphony says to "go away from your loved ones and destroy your dwelling". Here, however, Makhmalbaf does not ignore the harsh reality of life, for at the end of the film we see that Khorshid's family has been evicted. Makhmalbaf has attempted to show that the spiritual and the mundane must always coexist, are in fact derived from one another and are not mutually exclusive. This method of intellectual and spiritual exploration is only made possible through a Persian-Islamic discourse, which historically has promoted the idea of individualism and the rejection of the blandishments of this life. Michael Hillmann has explained well the relationship of Hafez's poetry to the social realities of his time, as well as given a good reason for the continuing esteem in which Hafez is held in Iran: "Few Iranians could afford to live lives of love or survive on thoughts of love. Iranians have needed both art that transcended their realities and artists, like Hafez, who maintain the fiction of the ideal."[50] This continues to be the case in Iran today where a dialogue within Iran is more urgently needed than Khatami's much vaunted call for a dialogue between civilizations. And the first step in this direction is an examination of Iran's own cultural tradition and laying bare its competing and conflicting historiographies in an attempt to examine critically the endless array of the diverse and sometimes opposing aspects of the Iranian psyche.

It is at the level of the cultural that this examination can occur, as Makhmalbaf has explained, "Democracy before being a political issue is a cultural issue. We have no tradition of public discourse."[51] For Makhmalbaf, the making of new democratic discourses becomes the task of the artist, particularly given the present regime's attempt to stifle all debate and to stem the emergence of alternative ideologies. Hillmann highlights the importance of this cultural project by referring to the

Islamic Republic as a continuation of the Sohrab and Rostam narrative from Ferdowsi's *Shahnameh*.[52] In this sense the theocratic regime is not a revolutionary movement but a coup d'état in which "one patriarchal son-killing force was replaced by another" so that the historically dominant patriarchal order could continue, albeit in a superficially different guise. He goes on to state that a true cultural revolution can only happen in Iran with "a victory for the Sohrabs or a compromise by which their values would play a part." Makhmalbaf appropriates the fractured multiplicity of Iranian cultural narratives in the hopes of challenging the dogmatic and despotic interpretation of the past and its tyrannical manifestation in the present, while holding hope for the future.

### Safar-e Qandehar (Kandahar)

Filmed in the area along the border between Iran and Afghanistan, *Kandahar* (2004) is Makhmalbaf's ardent humanitarian plea "to tell the world something of the sadness and problems of people in Afghanistan."[53] The story concerns the plight of an exiled Afghan woman, Nafas, who has returned to Afghanistan to save her sister who has threatened to commit suicide at the next eclipse of the sun. In the race to get to Kandahar we are presented with a picaresque series of events as Nafas meets a number of different characters who accompany her on her journey. These include an Afghan refugee family returning from Iran, a twelve-year-old boy who has been expelled from a religious school because he cannot memorize texts from the Qur'an, a black American disguised as a village doctor who came to Afghanistan in a search for God, and workers at a Red Cross camp who are dispensing artificial limbs.* The film ends with Nafas joining a wedding party on their way to Kandahar before being discovered and led away by the Taliban at a militia checkpoint. The final image of the film is of a solar eclipse.

Made before Afghanistan emerged onto the world stage and became embedded in the universal consciousness following the terrorist attacks of 11 September 2001, the film attempts to tell "the story of a people's devastation and a country's destruction [and how] people's lives reflect the state of their war-shattered economy."[54] Traditionally the

---

*Controversy arose over the identity and murky past of the actor Hassan Tantai, who played the doctor in the film. Authorities in the US claimed that he was in fact David Belfield, the prime suspect in the murder of former Iranian diplomat Ali Akbar Tabatabai at his home near Washington, DC, in July 1980. Following the murder it is alleged that Belfield/Tantai, who has also been known as Daoud Salahuddin and Hassan Abdul Rahman, fled to and was given asylum in the Islamic Republic, where he worked for the state-run Tehran-based English-language newspaper *Iran Daily* before leaving to fight with the mojahedin against the Soviets in neighboring Afghanistan. Makhmalbaf's response to these allegations was that he was not aware of them before he made the film and that while categorically denouncing violence he was not prepared to condemn someone's "past actions, which were predicated on his past convictions, on the basis of other people's present beliefs." For Makhmalbaf's full response, see his article "The Trial of Che Guevara in Gandhi's Court," *The Guardian*, January 11, 2002.

view from Iran of Afghanistan has been one of a problem that needs to be solved, and also a means of gaining increased geopolitical influence in Central Asia. Indeed, Afghanistan is one of the key issues that must be resolved "if President Khatami is to push forward his reform agenda at home," given the drain on resources caused by funding Shia militia groups and in attempting to stop "the drugs, weapons and sectarian spillover" across the border.[55] Political and economic development within Iran is also dependent on a resolution of the problems in Afghanistan, because the Iranian economy now shoulders the burden of supporting some three million Afghan refugees living within its territory.* Finally, the two countries share a strong historical and cultural alliance, especially among the Hazara Shiites and the Persian-speaking Tajik tribes, as Afghanistan was once part of the Persian Empire.

## Limbs of the Same Body

In *Kandahar,* however, Makhmalbaf focuses instead on human suffering and hopelessness as themes with which to elicit a response, predicated on a belief in the universal compassion and connectedness of humankind, according to the Iranian poet Sa'di's famous dictum "All people are limbs of the same body."[56] This reference to Sa'di is instructive, as the poet, in his most famous work, *Golestan (The Rose Garden)*, offers the metaphor of the rose garden as an eternally blooming paradise that provides a place of solace from an unforgiving landscape and the harshness of life. Whereas in *The Silence* Makhmalbaf has attempted to articulate the notion of the garden as an artistic creation emanating from and giving respite from the harshness of life, in *Kandahar* the garden is gone, leaving only harshness and desolation, the life of a barren desert. He is attempting to use film as a way to highlight the bitterness of life and, in so doing, to make a desperate plea for something to be done. Despite Makhmalbaf's ardent commitment, the film is fraught with difficulty and this in a sense highlights the limitations of art in effecting tangible change in the face of complex social and political problems. Forsaking the conviction that film can engender positive change inevitably leads to a sense of frustration, despair and doubt, a fact with which Makhmalbaf himself seems familiar: "And even now that I have finished making *Kandahar,* I feel vain about my profession. I don't believe that the little flame of knowledge kindled by a report or a film can part the deep ocean of ignorance.... Why did I make that film?"[56] This uncertainty and confusion and the gulf between aims and execution ultimately and adversely effect the outcome of the finished film.

---

*President Khatami, in his first meeting with the interim Afghan leader Hamid Karzai, spoke about the need to establish a repatriation program that would initiate the return of refugees back to Afghanistan. Forty thousand refugees was cited as a starting figure. BBC *World Service News*, February 24, 2002.

### The Voice of Despair

The problems with *Kandahar* are manifold but perhaps its main flaw is its failure to deal effectively and in any real or substantive way with the plight of the Afghan people themselves. The film is packed with metaphors and striking images that serve as a checklist of the various problems besetting the country: land mines, lack of adequate healthcare, poverty and the oppression of women. However, none of these issues are fully addressed, with Makhmalbaf, according to one critic, preferring instead to indulge in "uncertainties of tone and brazenly rhetorical flourishes, which make one wonder how heartfelt it is."[57] The centering of foreign eyes and voices (a returning Afghan exile and a black American, as well as the time given to two female Red Cross workers) as the driving force of the narrative and its episodic nature relegates the Afghan people to background objects of curiosity, depriving them of independent action and voices, consequently stripping them of human dignity and emotional force.

This is perhaps best evidenced in the scene in which a group of Afghan amputees race across the desert to catch artificial limbs being dropped from a helicopter. Here human dignity, hopelessness and despair are somewhat caricatured and rendered impotent by an aestheticization that lacks subtlety, and amounts to a crude form of symbolic grandstanding as the outcome of the race and the incongruity of such a surreal event serves as an end in itself. Indeed this scene also serves to highlight the tension and uncertainty evident throughout the film between Makhmalbaf's desire to present the harsh realities of an annihilated society through a formal rendering that is at times lyrical and arresting and serves to distract and undermine his ardent calls for social reform and cultural education. This sense of displacement is exacerbated by the fact that those Afghans who are allowed to speak do so at a local and seemingly inconsequential level—the old man escorting Nafas across the border under the pretext that she is his wife tells her not to shame him; Nafas's twelve-year-old guide is seen constantly trying to sell her a ring; and a young man who agrees to take her to Kandahar is more concerned with selling a pair of artificial legs. It is left to the "foreigners" to comment on the "real" issues through a series of mini polemics: Nafas tells of her sister's oppression under the Taliban and the American tells of the inadequacy of healthcare and education. However, if Makhmalbaf's project is to move people to action "by the general shame of the collective human condition"[58] the means by which this is to be achieved also seem confused.

The film portrays the ineffectiveness of international agencies like the UN, as in the scene where the old man and his family who take Nafas across the border are given a UN flag with the words "This will protect you," only to be robbed of all their possessions shortly afterward by tribal militiamen. The same sense of hopelessness pervades the scene where the efforts of the Red Cross are revealed to be limited and inconsequential. Makhmalbaf has stated that he believes that international organizations can only "remedy the deep and extensive wounds of this nation in a limited way and nothing more" and that the only solution for Afghanistan lies in a "rigorous scientific identification of its problems and presentation of real images of a nation that has remained obscure and imageless."[59] However, even these limited efforts are shown to be ineffectual, with no alternatives offered and the supposed depiction of real images as a first step in identifying and making known the obscure lack depth and meaning beyond the level of simplistic polemics and sloganeering.

## The Importance of the Local

*Kandahar* is part of a body of recent Iranian cinema, including Hassan Yektapanah's *Djomeh* (2001) and Abolfazl Jalili's *Delbaran* (2001), that have attempted to focus on Afghan-related issues. But apart from *Kandahar*, the other films have tended to treat the topic of Afghanistan from within Iran. Jalili's film *Delbaran* deals with the plight of a young illegal Afghan refugee trying to make a living in Iran. *Delbaran*'s innate sense of the local culture and the understanding of the complex social and political situation of the local environment allows the film to demonstrate the struggle and hardship of the everyday from a position of knowledge that projects it to the level of the universal, which in this case speaks volumes on the suffering of Afghanistan's people, but which also allows for the exploration of larger themes such as human compassion and the connectedness of the human race. This *Kandahar* fails to do primarily because it is detached from an identifiable cultural source and therefore fails to engage with the complexities of its subject matter in a meaningful way. As the Iranian cinematographer Ali Reza Zarrindast has stated, "The essence of artists from our part of the world is created by our culture, by our environment and our society."[60]

However, while *Kandahar* may be somewhat less than successful in realizing Makhmalbaf's desire to make known the suffering of Afghan society, it does, with regard to his aims, stand as an ardent attempt to bring Afghanistan to the attention of the world. Hidden for so long from the consciousness of the rest of the world, at least before September 11, Makhmalbaf has taken the first step in what was to be a voyage of discovery for himself and a preoccupation that was to lead him and members of his family back to Afghanistan to continue to focus on the theme of human suffering, keep the country in the minds eye of the world and call for something to be done.* This zealous commitment to

---

*Makhmalbaf shot a short film on video, *Afghan Alphabet* (2001), focusing on the problems of women's education in Afghanistan. His daughter Samira made *At Five in the Afternoon* (2003) which dealt with the oppression of women and one Afghan woman's dream of becoming president of her country. Also, calling attention to suffering and injustice has been a hallmark of much of Makhmalbaf's work and it has continued with his work on Afghanistan, where he has sought to use the communicative power of film to reveal a hidden society. As one character in the film states, "Weapons are the only thing modern in Afghanistan," Makhmalbaf for his part has attempted to make a disenfranchised nation known through the modern cultural weapon of the cinema.

Indeed, throughout this period Makhmalbaf has attempted to define the relationship between art, the self and the state, and the way in which the former can be an active element in illuminating the possibilities of change in society. Despite his misgivings at times and a certain crisis of faith in the face of enormous human suffering fundamentally his work still holds the belief in cinema's ability to highlight the problems of a people—*Kandahar*—or reinvent the notion of the individual through a freedom of expression denied them under the harsh realities of a repressive environment, as in *The Silence*.

---

Makhmalbaf's wife, Marzieh Meshkini, made *Stray Dogs* (2003), which focuses on Afghanistan and tells the story of two children trying to survive in Kabul while their mother is in prison. Makhmalbaf, in an essay entitled "The Buddha Was Not Demolished in Afghanistan, It Collapsed out of Shame," makes a case for exposing the sad story of Afghanistan, a country disfigured and now neglected by the powerful nations of the world. Makhmalbaf Film House, http://makhmalbaf.com/articles.asp?a=a16

# CONCLUSION

Having not made a feature film since *Kandahar*, Makhmalbaf has, for the moment it seems, devoted himself to what he wryly calls making filmmakers. He established the Makhmalbaf Film House in 1996, and planned to accept around a hundred students through examination and train them for four years in all aspects of the cinematic arts. At first the project ran into problems and objections from the Ministry of Culture, who feared the emergence of a new generation of Makhmalbafs making politically engaged and socially critical cinema. Undaunted, Makhmalbaf persevered and established the school in his home with family and friends as his first students. Using a hands-on, collaborative approach, students study a wide range of subjects, with classes running for eight hours a day over a four-year period, and work in different capacities on each other's film projects. In this regard the school became a production house and the work that has emerged from it is remarkable, introducing the world to a new generation of talented Iranian filmmakers.

The most prominent among them is Makhmalbaf's eldest daughter, Samira, who has directed three films, *The Apple* (1998), *Blackboard* (2000) and *At Five in the Afternoon* (2003), which have received worldwide recognition and acclaim. Other members of the Makhmalbaf family have also contributed to the prolific output of the film house. His youngest daughter, Hana, has directed a short film entitled *The Day My Aunt was Ill* (1997) as well as a documentary on the making of Samira's *At Five in the Afternoon*, called *Joy of Madness* (2003). Makhmalbaf's wife, Marzieh Meshkini, directed *The Day I Became a Woman* (2000) an episodic and surreal examination of the different stages of maturity in the lives of women in Iran, as well as *Stray Dogs* (2003), which continued the efforts to highlight the plight and suffering of the Afghan people. Maysam, Makhmalbaf's son, while directing his own documentary, *How Samira Made The Blackboard* (2000) was also the photographer on her film *The Apple*, Mohsen Makhmalbaf's *The Silence* and Samira's *Blackboard*, as well as editing the first episode of *The Day I Became a Woman*.

This collaborative approach has built a unified and creative body of work that bears many of the hallmarks of Mohsen Makhmalbaf's own philosophy of cinema (he has collaborated on the scripts and editing of all of Samira's films) and as a result has suffered many of the same problems at the hands of the authorities. These films for the most part are socially committed works that reflect a personal politics grounded in moral, political and narrative ambiguities, exhibiting a poetic symbolism that is at turns preoccupied with the process of creativity. Similarly, the success of the Makhmalbaf Film House productions abroad has been mirrored by problems at home, where they are either banned, as was the case with *The Day My Aunt was Ill* and *How Samira Made the Blackboard,* or are subject to a kind of clandestine censorship—they are shown in a couple of movie theatres for a short while and disappear before anyone finds out about the screenings.

Makhmalbaf's own efforts to return to filmmaking have also been fraught with difficulty. His latest project, *Amnesia,* again reflects his desire to engage with difficult and controversial issues as a means of understanding the development of Iran socially, politically and culturally. *Amnesia* reflects two decades of pain and suffering of the Iranian people, and more particularly that of artists, under the Islamic regime. The script tells the story of a blind man who lost his sight in the war with Iraq and now works as a censor of poetry, film (in one self-reflexive scene he calls for Samira Makhmalbaf's *Blackboard* to be banned, echoing many critics' remarks, explaining, "The girl's father makes all her films. Iranian girls do not possess such merits"), books and newspaper articles. However, the blind man questions his ideals and zealous faith in the Islamic Republic when his son, who has been imprisoned for writing and reciting "infected" poetry, is executed.

In *Amnesia,* Makhmalbaf once again engages with cinema as a means of documenting and commenting on the social, cultural and political problems that continue to plague Iranian society. While this has been a constant theme in his work, *Amnesia* brings together the elements of all of Makhmalbaf's previous work. Again there is the theme of blindness (from *Two Sightless Eyes* and *The Silence*), which here connotes suffering the side-effects of fighting hard for a cause, and as a commentary on the arbitrariness of censorship. The blind man's almost unwilling disillusionment recalls Haji's (who was also damaged by the war with Iraq) eventual breakdown in *Marriage of the Blessed.* The hopelessness and despair of life in a repressive society, where a sense of madness (the blind man's wife's amnesia) pervades, recalls *Nights of the Zayandeh-Rud.* The weight of the past and personal memory—the wife has forgotten all, and the blind man cannot forget his service to the nation in war, and is trying to right his son's wrongs—invoke *A Moment of Innocence.* One scene, in which the blind man chooses to censor Yasujiro Ozu's masterpiece, *Tokyo Story,* not because the film is offensive but because Ozu was a "nihilist," directly addresses the absurdity of censorship and revisits issues raised in *Once Upon a Time, Cinema.* The film also highlights the centrality of art in Makhmalbaf's work, and *Amnesia* is in part inspired by the poetry and the figure of Farrokhzad—her poem "Gift" is included in the script. Finally, *Amnesia* revisits the Sufi themes first explored in *Time of Love* and *Gabbeh,* when the old blind man visits the countryside. Where *Gabbeh* looked at color as an organic, God-given tool of the artist, *Amnesia* shows it as an expression of pure human emotion, the sadness of the human heart. As in *Time of Love,* water and the sea are considered regenerative—the old man sits on the beach and explains that the "melody of the waves" have made him better, that "nature is heaven." *Amnesia* also reflects a strong autobiographical element, which serves as a commentary on Makhmalbaf's own journey as an artist, from the constant reappraisal of his own beliefs to his confrontations with the authorities, which in exposing hypocrisy, calling for moderation, inclusion, personal freedom and freedom of speech, echoes the words of Farrokhzad, who speaks out of the "deep darkness," to "bring a light / and a small hatch / through / which / I can look at the crowd in the fortunate street."*

On 4 May 2004 the Ministry of Culture and Islamic Guidance refused a shooting permit for *Amnesia,* causing Makmalbaf to remark that a new censorship strategy seems to be emerging, one that aims "to push Iranian artists to migrate from the country."[1]

The problems for filmmakers remain constant: censorship, the tension between an official state film industry and artists attempting to articulate their concerns on difficulties besetting the country; and the fact that these films are more popular and more widely seen abroad, used as a tool by the regime to promote the illusion of a culturally vibrant and liberal society that advocates free speech and freedom of expression. This pattern is clear in the development of Makhmalbaf's cinema, as he has been both insider and outsider. From his early promotion of the virtues of the Islamic regime, under the guise of an "Islamic cinema," through his disillusionment and critique of the failings of the revolution as articulated in his Mostazafin Trilogy, to the eventual castigation and censorship of his work by the authorities, his films have at all times been deeply engaged with and influenced by the historical development of the Iranian nation. Through a variety of cinematic formats he has examined pertinent issues such as the nature of God, in the dogmatic pedantry of *Nasuh's Repentance* and the Sufi-inspired contemplation of *The Silence,* or the failure of the revolution to deliver on

---

This has been transcribed by Makhmalbaf in the script of *Amnesia* from Farrokhzad's poem "Gift." See Forugh Farrokhzad, *Another Birth.*

its promises, in *The Peddler* or *Nights of the Zayandeh-Rud*, which are specifically relevant under the changed ideological circumstances. In this sense Makhmalbaf's films are characterized by an immediate engagement with the historical moment, and located in an understanding of the present. His films, in their articulation of social and political concerns, have been predicated on an increasingly esoteric search for the self and a meditation on the individual's place in a larger society. Over time, personal stories have gained precedence over the desire to present a collective history, or else the personal has begun to allow a way in to an understanding of a more expansive reality. *Time of Love* zooms in on the intense and passionate relationships between men and women, and draws a dichotomy between their freedom to make decisions for themselves and the codes imposed on them by civil society. The restorative autobiography *A Moment of Innocence* reassesses Iran's Islamic revolution and what it has meant for two people. *Once Upon a Time, Cinema, The Actor,* and *Salaam Cinema* are Makhmalbaf's own meditations on his relationship to film and the wider ramifications of the artist's role and social responsibilities. Though they lack the rhetorical issue-driven broadsiding of his early films, Makmalbaf's later work does not provide a model of detached or solipsistic cinema. Rather, the individual's story has become a means of gaining an intimate understanding of the vagaries of history (*Nights of the Zayandeh-Rud*), sociopolitical commentary (*Marriage of the Blessed*), and cultural specificity (*Gabbeh*) in an attempt to show these abstractions at a more immediate, human and naturally meaningful level. By bringing the history of individuals, regions and marginalized groups to the fore Makhmalbaf's work underlies hybrid identities countercultural currents. He presents individuals in conflict with a problematic environment not entirely of their own making, trying to understand, survive and actively make sense of it rather than be passively guided by fate or providence.

Makhmalbaf's cinema stands as a perfect reflection of the interactional and symbiotic development of an artist and the society from which he emerges. Makhmalbaf's is a political cinema, heavily entwined with the historical development of the Islamic Republic and its cultural representation, structured by the themes of search and belief. His initial work was religiously and politically dogmatic, with the individual subsumed in the pursuit of grand ideological claims. Makhmalbaf's unfaltering faith led to a search for justice and the questioning of belief in absolutes; his critique derived from the recognition of the failures of the revolution to deliver on its promises by someone who still believed in its ideals. This doubt was transformed into a desire to use art as a means of examining social reality through a dissection of the means of representation. His most recent films have seen him come full circle, but now the individual and a personal spiritual union with God have taken pride of place, with the ideological and the political becoming, if anything, obstacles to those goals. In this sense his films have been ardent attempts to document, through the life of the individual, the nation, its evolution, artistic development and tradition. This urgent social and humane agenda comes from a passionate commitment to art and its power to communicate and articulate the problems and frustrations of people, and to combine personal interests and aspirations with popular discontent. While Makhmalbaf's films at times lack subtlety, they nonetheless act as chronicles or indices of Iran's social and political fabric. Located firmly within the complexities of modern Iran they represent an artist's honest attempt to bear witness to his age by making films as an inspirational means of artistic expression.

# FILMOGRAPHY

## *Feature Films*

### Tobeh-Nasuh (Nasuh's Repentance)
1982; color; 35 mm; 100 mins.
Director: Mohsen Makhmalbaf
Scriptwriter: Mohsen Makhmalbaf
Director of Photography: Ebrahim Ghazizadeh
Editor: Iraj Emami
Music: Hesameddin Seraj
Sound: Eshagh Khanzadi
Still Photographer: Ahmad Talayi
Cast: Farajolah Salahshour, Mohammad Kasebi, Esmat Jampour,
   Behzad Behzadniya

### Do Chashme Bisou (Two Sightless Eyes)
1983; color; 35 mm; 102 mins.
Director: Mohsen Makhmalbaf
Scriptwriter: Mohsen Makhmalbaf
Director of Photography: Ebrahim Ghazizadeh
Editor: Iraj Golafshan
Music: Hesameddin Seraj
Makeup: Abdollah Eskandari
Dubbing: Iraj Nazeriyan
Cast: Mohammad Kasebi, Majid Majidi, Reza Cheraghi, Habib Valin-
   ezhad, Ghasem Kharrazani, Esmat Makhmalbaf, Fatemeh Meshkini,
   Hamid Derakshan, Behzad Behzadpour, Hossein Sabri, Ebrahim
   Majidi

### Este'azeh (Fleeing from Evil to God)
1984; color; Cinemascope; 89 mins.
Director: Mohsen Makhmalbaf

Scriptwriter: Mohsen Makhmalbaf
Director of Photography: Ebrahim Ghazizadeh
Editor: Iraj Golafshan
Makeup: Abdollah Eskandari

Dubbing: Iraj Nazeriyan
Cast: Mohammad Kasebi, Majid Majidi, Morteza Masaeli, Ali Derakh-
shi, Mohammad Takhtkeshiyan, Massoud Ghandi

## Baykot (Boycott)

1985; color; 35 mm; 85 mins.
Director: Mohsen Makhmalbaf
Scriptwriter: Mohsen Makhmalbaf
Directors of Photography: Faraj Haydari, Ebrahim Ghazizadeh
Editor: Roubik Mansouri
Production Design: Masoud Ghandi, Mohammad-Bagher Ashtiyani
Makeup: Abdollah Eskandari
Dubbing: Manoucher Esmaili
Special Effects: Ali Rastger, Morteza Rastgar, Hassan Saberi
Cast: Majid Majidi, Mohammad Kasebi, Zohreh Sarmadi, Ardalan
Shoja-Kaveh, Saeed Kashan-Fallah, Esmail Soltaniyan, Bahman Rouz-
behani, Ali-Akbar Yeganeh, Reza Cheraghi, Irandokht Dowlatshahi,
Ali Hesami, Naser Forough, Ali Tavakoli, Massoud Nabavi, Ali Shi-
razi, Esmat Makhmalbaf, Ebrahim Abadi

## Dastforush (The Peddler)

1987; color, 35 mm, 90 mins.
Director: Mohsen Makhmalbaf
Scriptwriter: Mohsen Makhmalbaf
Editor: Mohsen Makhmalbaf
Music: Majid Entezami
Dubbing: Manoucher Esmaili

First Episode—"Bachey-e Khoshbakht" ("The Happy Child")
Director of Photography: Homayoun Payvar
Makeup: Fatemeh Ardakani
Cast: Zohreh Sarmadi, Esmaeel Soltaniyan, Mohammad Talaie,
Somayyeh Ebrahimi, Maryam Schirazi, Esmat Makhmalbaf, Ali Tavak-
koli, Kamran Nowrouz, Azam Bahrami, Ali Schirazi

Second Episode—"Tavallod-e Yek Pirzan" ("Birth of an Old Woman")
Director of Photography: Mehrdad Fakhimi
Production Design: Hassan Farsi
Makeup: Abdollah Eskandari

Cast: Morteza Zarrabi, Mahmoud Basiri, Moharram Zeinalzadeh, Davoud Ghanbari, Naser Forough, Mohsen Derakhshani,
Mohammad-Reza Bagheri, Rasoul Ahadi

Third Episode—"Dastforush" ("The Peddler")
Director of Photography: Ali-Reza Zarrindest
Production Design: Hossein Khosrojerdi
Makeup: Abdolhamid Ghadirian
Special Effects: Reza Fatehi
Cast: Behzad Behzadpour, Jafar Delghan, Farid Kashan-Fallah,
Mohammad-Ali Mozhdehi, Davoud Rahmati, Hossein Gorouhi,
Kamal Abbasi, Ahmad Khayyatbashi, Mohammad Alaghband, Habib
Haddad

## Bicycleran (The Cyclist)

1989; color: 35 mm: 83 mins.
Director: Mohsen Makhmalbaf
Scriptwriter: Mohsen Makhmalbaf
Director of Photography: Ali-Reza Zarrindast
Editor: Mohsen Makhmalbaf
Production Design: Mohammad Makhmalbaf
Music: Majid Entezami
Makeup: Abdollah Eskandari
Dubbing: Manoucher Esmaili
Cast: Moharram Zeinalzadeh, Esmail Soltaniyan, Samira Makhmalbaf,
Mahsid Afsharzadeh, Hossein Hajjar, Firouz Kiyani, Mohammad-Reza
Maleki, Shahnaz Babaieyan, Mansour Farma, Mohammad Dowlatabadi

## Arusi-e Khuban (Marriage of the Blessed)

1989; color and b&w; 70 mins.
Director: Mohsen Makhmalbaf
Scriptwriter: Mohsen Makhmalbaf
Director of Photography: Ali-Reza Zarrindast
Editor: Mohsen Makhmalbaf
Production Design: Mohsen Makhmalbaf
Music: Babak Bayat
Makeup: Abdollah Eskandari
Dubbing: Manoucher Esmaili
Special Effects: Reza Shrafoddin
Cast: Mahmoud Bigham, Roya Nownahali, Mohsen Zehtab, Hossein
Moslemi, Ebrahim Abadi, Iraj Saghiri, Esmat Makhmalbaf, Hosssein
Hosseinkhani, Ameneh Kholdebarin, Karim Zargar

### Nobat-e Asheghi (Time of Love)

1991; color; 35 mm; 70 mins.
Director: Mohsen Makhmalbaf
Scriptwriter: Mohsen Makhmalbaf
Director of Photography: Mahmoud Kalari
Editor: Mohsen Makhmalbaf
Production Design: Mohammad Nasrollahi
Sound: Jahangir Mirshekari
Cast: Shiva Gerede, Abdolrahman Palay, Manderes Samanjihar, Aken
    Tunj, Jalal Khosrowshahi

### Shabha-ye Zayandeh-Rud (Nights of the Zayandeh-Rud)

1991; color; 35 mm; 75 mins.
Director: Mohsen Makhmalbaf
Scriptwriter: Mohsen Makhmalbaf
Director of Photography: Ali-Reza Zarrindast
Editor: Mohsen Makhmalbaf
Production Design: Mohammed Jamalpour
Music: Iraj Saeed Eftekhari
Sound: Jahangir Mirshekari, Sassan Bagherpour
Makeup: Majid Eskandari, Afteh Razavi
Cast: Manoucher Esmaili, Mozhgan Naderi, Parvaneh Gouharani,
    Zeinab Rahdari, Mehrdad Farid, Mohsen Ghasemi, Afsaneh Heidari-
    yan, Nahid Rashidi, Maryam Naghib

### Nasseredin Shah, Actor-e Cinema (Once Upon a Time, Cinema)

1992; color and b&w; 35 mm; 92 mins.
Director: Mohsen Makhmalbaf
Scriptwriter: Mohsen Makhmalbaf
Director of Photography: Faraj Haydari
Editor: Davud Yusafian
Production Design: Hassan Farsi
Music: Majid Entezami
Sound: Ahmad Askari
Makeup: Abdollah Eskandari
Cast: Ezatollah Entezami, Mehdi Hashemi, Mohammad-Ali Keshavarz,
    Akbar Abdi, Fatemeh Motamed-Arya, Dariush Arjomand, Mahaya
    Petrsiyan, Jahangir Forouhar, Morteza Ahmadi, Saeed Amirsolei-
    mani, Moharram Zeinalzadeh, Parvaneh Massouri

### Honarpisheh (The Actor)

1993; color; 35 mm; 86 mins.
Director: Mohsen Makhmalbaf
Scriptwriter: Mohsen Makhmalbaf
Director of Photography: Aziz Sa'ati

Editor: Mohsen Makhmalbaf
Production Design: Reza Alagheband
Music: Ahmad Pezhman
Sound: Jahangir Mirshekari, Sassan Bagherpour
Makeup: Abdollah Eskandari
Cast: Akbar Abdi, Fatemeh Motamed-Arya, Mahaya Petrosiyan, Hamideh Kheirabadi, Parvin Soleimani, Hossein Panali, Mohammad-Reza Sharifinia, Hossein Shamlou

## Salaam Cinema

1995; color, 35 mm, 89 mins.
Director: Mohsen Makhmalbaf
Scriptwriter: Mohsen Makhmalbaf
Director of Photography: Mahmoud Kalari
Editor: Mohsen Makhmalbaf
Music: Shahdad Rohani
Sound: Nezameddin Kiaee
Cast: Azadeh Zangeneh, Maryam Keyhan, Feizollah Gheshlaghi, Hamid Gheshlaghi, Hamid Gheshlaghi, Hamed Gheshlaghi, Shaghayegh Jowdat, Mohammad-Hadi Mokhtariyan, Nader Fazhi, Maziyar Alipour, Arezou Ghanbari

## Nun va Goldun (A Moment of Innocence)

1996; color; 35 mm; 78 mins.
Director: Mohsen Makhmalbaf
Scriptwriter: Mohsen Makhmalbaf
Director of Photography: Mahmoud Kalari
Editor: Mohsen Makhmalbaf
Production Design: Reza Alagheband
Sound: Nezameddin Kiaee
Music: Majid Entezami
Cast: Mirhadi Tayyebi, Ali Bakhshi, Ammar Tafti, Maryam Mohammad-Amini, Moharram Zeinalzadeh, Fariba Faghiri, Lotfollah Gheshtagi, Mohsen Makhmalbaf, Hana Makhmalbaf

## Gabbeh

1996; color; 35 mm; 72 mins.
Director: Mohsen Makhmalbaf
Scriptwriter: Mohsen Makhmalbaf
Director of Photography: Mahmoud Kalari
Editor: Mohsen Makhmalbaf
Production Design: Mohsen Makhmalbaf
Music: Hossein Alizadeh
Sound: Mojtaba Mirtahmasb
Still Photographer: Mohammad Ahmadi

Cast: Abbas Sayyahi, Shaghayegh Djodat, Hossein Moharrami,
Roghayyeh Moharrami, Parvaneh Ghalandari

### Sokut (The Silence)

1998; color; 35 mm; 76 mins.
Director: Mohsen Makhmalbaf
Scriptwriter: Mohsen Makhmalbaf
Director of Photography: Ebrahim Ghafouri
Editor: Mohsen Makhmalbaf
Production Design: Mohsen Makhmalbaf
Sound: Behrouz Shahamat
Cast: Tahmineh Normat Ova, Nadereh Abdollah Yeva

### Safar-e Qandehar (Kandahar)

2001; color; 35mm; 85 mins.
Director: Mohsen Makhmalbaf
Scriptwriter: Mohsen Makhmalbaf
Director of Photography: Ebrahim Ghafouri
Editor: Mohsen Makhmalbaf
Production Design: Akbar Meshkini
Music: Mohammad Reza Darvishi
Sound: Behrouz Shahamat, Faroukh Fadai
Still Photographer: M. R. Sharifiniya
Cast: Niloufar Pazira, Hassan Tantai, Sadou Teymouri, Hayatalah Hakimi,

## *Short Films*

### Images from the Qajar Dynasty

1993; color and b&w; 18 mins.
Director: Mohsen Makhmalbaf
Scriptwriter: Mohsen Makhmalbaf
Director of Photography: Aziz Salati
Editor: Mohsen Makhmalbaf
Music: Ahmad Pezhman
Sound: Ahmad Kalantari

### Sang va shisheh (Stone and Glass)

1993; color; video; 20 mins.
Director: Mohsen Makhmalbaf
Scriptwriter: Mohsen Makhmalbaf
Director of Photography: Aziz Salati
Editor: Mohsen Makhmalbaf
Narrator: Parviz Bahram

### Madreseh-ye keh bad bord (The School Blown Away by the Wind)
1997; color; 35 mm; 8 mins.
Director: Mohsen Makhmalbaf
Scriptwriter: Mohsen Makhmalbaf
Director of Photography: Mahmoud Kalari
Editor: Mohsen Makhmalbaf
Music: Hossein Alizadeh
Sound: Mojtaba Mirtahmasb
Still Photographer: Mohammad Ahmadi
Cast: Abbas Sayyahi, Mohammad-Hassan Karami, Abdollah Jahanpour, Tahmineh Jahanpour, Maryam Jahanpour, Marziyeh Jahanpour, Zahra Jahanpour, Afrasiab Jahanpour

### Dar (The Door)
1999; (Part of *Kish Tales*); color, 35 mm.
Director: Mohsen Makhmalbaf
Scriptwriter: Mohsen Makhmalbaf
Director of Photography: Mohammad Ahmadi
Editor: Maysam Makhmalbaf
Sound: Neyam Kiaee
Cast: Mohammad Nabhan, Nourieh Mahigiran

### Test-e Demokrasi (Testing Democracy)
2000; (Part of *Tales of an Island*); color; video; 40 mins.
Directors: Mohsen Makhmalbaf, Shahabeddin Farokhyar
Assistant Director: Najmeddin Farokhyar
Scriptwriter: Mohsen Makhmalbaf
Sound: Behrouz Shahamat, Hassan Serajiyau
Still Photographer: Mohsen Rastani

### Alefbay-e Afghan (Afghan Alphabet)
2001; color; digital video; 46 mins.
Director: Mohsen Makhmalbaf
Scriptwriter: Mohsen Makhmalbaf
Director of Photography: Marzieh Meshkini
Music: Mohammad Reza Darvishi
Sound: Mojtaba Mirtahmasb
Still Photography: Marziyeh Meshkini
Cast: Maryam Ozbak, Ghafour Barahouyi and refugees in Iran and Afghanistan

# NOTES

### Notes to Introduction

1. Ghanoonparvar, *Prophets of Doom: Literature as Socio-Political Phenomenon in Iran,* 1.
2. Cheshire, "The Figure in the Carpet," 63.
3. Rizaee, *Persian Meditations,* 1993.
4. Wood, "Toronto Film Festival 1998: *The Apple,*" 58.
5. Golmakani, "Beyond the Shadow of a Doubt," 55.
6. King, *Magical Reels: A History of Cinema in Latin America,* 66.
7. Karimi-Hakkak, "Of Hail and Hounds: the Image of the Iranian Revolution in Recent Persian Literature," 152.
8. Abrahamian, *Khomeinism: Essays on the Islamic Republic,* 38.
9. Tabatabai, "Iran: Islamic Visions and Grand Illusions," 130.
10. Makhmalbaf, "Mirror Images," 19.
11. Khomeini, *Islam and Revolution: Writings and Declarations of Imam Khomeini,* 285.
12. Tabatabai, "Iran: Islamic Visions and Grand Illusions."
13. Wayne, *Political Film: The Dialectics of Third Cinema,* 149.
14. Wright, *In the Name of God: The Khomeini Decade.*
15. Tabatabai, "Iran: Islamic Visions and Grand Illusions."
16. Karimi-Hakkak, "Of Hail and Hounds," 155.
17. Makhmalbaf, "Mirror Images."
18. Beig-Agha, "Iranian Cinema in the Marketplace," 110.

### Notes to Chapter 1

1. Herodotus, *The Histories,* 1.135.
2. Maghsoudlou, *Iranian Cinema.*
3. Amiri, "Interview with Dariush Mehrjui."
4. Mohammadi and Srebreny-Mohammadi, *Small Media, Big Revolution: Communication, Culture and the Iranian Revolution,* 54.
5. Golmakani, "Pre-Revolution Years of Iranian Cinema," 17.
6. Omid, "The Iranian Cinema."
7. Jameson, *The Geopolitical Aesthetic: Cinema and Space in the World System.*
8. Burton, "Marginal Cinema and Mainstream Critical Theory," 12.
9. Dissanayake, *Colonialism and Nationalism in Asian Cinema,* xvi.
10. Samini, "A Survey of Literary Adaptation in Iranian Cinema: A New Birth of Post-Revolution Cinema," 99.
11. Ghosh, "Shooting Image Weapons: The Place of Manthan as Third Cinema in India."
12. Akrami, "The Blighted Spring: Iranian Political Cinema in the 1970s."
13. Issari, *Cinema in Iran 1900-1979,* 240.

14. Chanan, *Twenty-five Years of the New Latin American Cinema*, 12.
15. Salmane, *Algerian Cinema*, 41.
16. Pearson, "Le cinèma iranien," 11.
17. Issari, *Cinema in Iran 1900-1979.*
18. Akrami, "The Blighted Spring," 138.
19. Naficy, "Cinematic Exchange Relations: Iran and the West."
20. Talebinead, "The New Wave in Iranian Cinema, from Past to Present," 10.
21. Puchala, "Third World Thinking and Contemporary International Relations," 147.

## Notes to Chapter 2

1. Lerner, *The Passing of Traditional Society: Modernizing the Middle East*, 377.
2. Halliday, "The Iranian Revolution: Uneven Development and Religious Populism."
3. Jalal Al-e-Ahmad, *Gharbzadegi: Plagued by the West*, 33.
4. Khomeini, *A Clarification of Questions: An Unabridged Translation of Resaleh Towzih al-masael* 21.
5. Foucault, "Iran: The Spirit of a World without Spirit."
6. Keddie, *Religion and Politics in Iran: Shi'ism from Quietism to Revolution*; Bakhash, *The Reign of the Ayatollahs: Iran and the Islamic Revolution*; Arjomand, *The Turban for the Crown*; Rahnema and Nomani, *The Secular Miracle Religion: Politics and Economic Policy in Iran*; John Foran, *A Century of Revolution: Social Movements in Iran.*
7. Rahnema, "Iranian Intellectuals in the Twentieth Century."
8. Moaddel, *Class, Politics and Ideology in the Iranian Revolution.*
9. *The Koran Interpreted: A Translation*, by A. J. Arberry Macmillan, 1955. Sura 5: 56.
10. Motahari, *Piramun-e Enghelab-e Islami* 145.
11. Mackey, *The Iranians: Persia, Islam and the Soul of a Nation*, 54
12. Ashraf and Banuazizi, "The State, Classes and Modes of Mobilization in the Iranian Revolution."
13. Fischer *Iran: From Religious Dispute to Revolution*, 197.
14. Issari, *Cinema in Iran, 1900-1979.* 246.
15. Khomeini, *Islam and Revolution.*
16. Abrahamian, *Khomeinism: Essays on the Islamic Republic.*
17. Ashraf and Banuanzizi, "The State, Classes and Modes of Mobilization."
18. Rahnema, *An Islamic Utopia: A Political Biography of Ali Shariati*, 315.
19. Dorraj, *From Zarathustra to Khomeini: Populism and Dissent in Iran*, 66.
20. Khomeini, *Islam and Revolution*, 244.
21. Khomeini, *Khat Imam, Kalam Imam*, 102.
22. Rahnema and Nomani, *The Secular Miracle.*

23. *Kayhan*, April 3, 1979.
24. Halliday, "The Iranian Revolution: Uneven Development and Religious Populism," 35
25. Geertz, *The Interpretation of Cultures.*
26. Mirsepassi, *Intellectual Discourses and the Politics of Modernization: Negotiating Modernity in Iran,* 13
27. Mohammadi and Sreberney-Mohammadi, *Small Media, Big Revolution.*
28. Khomeini, *Islam and Revolution.*
29. Mehdi Bazargan, *Bazyabi-e Arzeshha.*
30. Abrahamian, "The Guerrilla Movement in Iran, 1963-1977," 9
31. Abrahamian, *Khomeinism.*
32. Rahnema and Behdad, *Iran after the Revolution: Crisis of an Islamic State,* 10
33. *Kayhan,* June 19, 1979.
34. Algar, trans., *Constitution of the Islamic Republic of Iran.*
35. Schirazi, *The Constitution of Iran:* 35
36. *The Constitution of the Islamic Republic of Iran,* 18.Tehran: Department of Translation and Publication Islamic Culture and Relations Organisation, 1997, p.18.
37. Ibid., 37.
38. Bahar, "Guardians of Thought: Limits on Freedom of Expression in Iran."
39. Schirazi, *The Constitution of Iran.*
40. Maghsoudlou, *Iranian Cinema.*
41. Daryoush, *International Film Guide 1982.*
42. Golmakani, "The Tide Turns," 2
43. Karmimi-Hakkak, "Of Hail and Hounds."
44. McDonnell, "Iranian Revival."
45. Khomeini, *Islam and Revolution,* 30
46. Naficy, "Iranian Cinema," 676
47. Rajaee, "Iranian Ideology and Worldview: The Cultural Export of Revolution," 75
48. Kazemi, "State and Society in the Devotees of Islam."
49. Schirazi, *The Constitution of Iran,* 136-138
50. Abdo, "Iranian Film Comes Through the Big Chill of the Hardline Years," 20.
51. Hassan, "Iran's Islamic Revolutionaries: Before and After the Revolution."
52. Rejaee, *Gozideh Sokhanan Pardehe Tazvir,* 31
53. Khomeini, "The Deprived Will Dominate the Arrogant."
54. Khomeini, *Ettela'at,* June 26, 1980.
55. Khomeini, "Imam Khomeini Commends Services of Islamic Revolutionary Corps."

56. Abrahamian, *Khomeinism,* 4
57. Simpson and Shubart, *Lifting the Veil: Life in Revolutionary Iran,* 87
58. Haghayeghi, "Politics and Ideology in the Islamic Republic of Iran."
59. Khomeini, "Payam-e Hazrat-e Emam."

**Notes to Chapter 3**

1. Mottahedeh, *The Mantle of the Prophet: Religion and Politics in Iran,* 144.
2. Siavoshi, "Regime Legitimacy and High-School Textbooks," 210.
3. Robert Graham, *Iran: The Illusion of Power,* 199-200.
4. Wilber, *Iran, Past and Present,* 38
5. Burckhardt *Art of Islam: Language and Meaning.*
6. Khazaie, *The Arabesque Motif in Early Islamic Persian.*
7. Shafik, *Arab Cinema: History and Cultural Identity,* 48.
8. Burckhardt, *Art of Islam: Language and Meaning,* 29
9. Beg, *Fine Arts in Islamic Civilization,* 47
10. Grabar, *The Formation of Islamic Art,* 82-83
11. Ettinghausen, "Introduction: The Immanent Features of Persian Art," xiv.
12. Blondel Saad, *The Image of Arabs in Modern Persian Literature.*
13. Ferdowsi, *Shahnahmeh,* 829-30.
14. Samini, "A Survey of Literary Adaptation in Iranian Cinema."
15. Shafik, *Arab Cinema: History and Cultural Identity,* 49
16. Khomeini, *A Clarification of Questions.*
17. Abrahamian, *Khomeinism,* 92
18. Haghayeghi, "Politics and Ideology in the Islamic Republic of Iran," 42
19. Mohsenpour, "Philosophy of Education in Post-revolutionary Iran," 85-86
20. Siavoshi, "Regime Legitimacy and High-School Textbooks."
21. Haghayeghi, "Politics and Ideology in the Islamic Republic of Iran," 43
22. *Iran Times,* page 5, February 22, 1991.
23. IRIB Television First Program Network, December 10, 1992, as reported in FBIS, December 11, 1992.
24. *The Constitution of the Islamic Republic,* 130.
25. Chelkowski and Dabashi, *Staging a Revolution: The Art of Persuasion in the Islamic Republic of Iran,* 266
26. Aufderheide, "Real Life is More Important than Cinema: Interview with Abbas Kiarostami," 31
27. Issa and Whitaker, 199: 29
28. Bahar, *Life and Art: The New Iranian Cinema,* 98
29. Rizaee, *Persian Meditations,* 37.
30. Motavalli, "Exiles."

31. Halliday, "Iranian Foreign Policy Since 1979," 92.

32. Hosseini, "From Homo Economicus to Homo Islamicus: The Universality of Economic Science Reconsidered," 103-121.

33. Parvin and Vaziri, "Islamic Man and Society," 120.

34. Zahedi, "Mohsen Makhmalbaf: In Search of the Lost Horizon," 36.

35. Dabashi, *Close Up: Iranian Cinema Past, Present and Future*, 182-184.

36. Khomeini, *Pithy Aphorisms*, 53-54.

37. Sura 5: 39.

38. Martin, *Creating an Islamic State: Khomeini and the Making of a New Iran*, 31.

39. Dabashi, *Close Up*, 132.

40. *The Constitution of the Islamic Republic of Iran*, Article 7, page 22.

41. Ibid., Article 6a, page 22.

42. Martin, *Creating an Islamic State*, 42-43.

43. Sura 7: 166.

44. Moin, : *Life of the Ayatollah*, 175-180.

45. Behrooz, *Rebels With A Cause: The Failure of the Left in Iran*, 95.

46. *Ettela'at*, July 5, 1980.

47. Abrahamian, *Radical Islam: The Iranian Mojahedin*.

48. Behrooz, *Rebels With A Cause*, 160-161.

49. Martin, *Creating an Islamic State*, 95.

50. Dabashi, *Close Up*, 184-188.

51. Golmakani, "A History of the Post-Revolutionary Cinema."

52. Kalhor, *Post-Revolution Iranian Cinema*, 11.

**Notes to Chapter 4**

1. Menashri *Iran: A Decade of War and Revolution*, 354.

2. Hiro, *The Longest War: The Iran-Iraq Military Conflict*, 255.

3. *New York Times*, October 19, 1980.

4. Ramazani, "Khomeini's Islam in Iran's Foreign Policy," 9.

5. Trab Zemzemi, *The Iran-Iraq War: Islam and Nationalisms*.

6. Halliday, "Iranian Foreign Policy Since 1979," 92.

7. Golmakani, "The Tide Turns," 5.

8. Makhmalbaf, *Film* (Tehran), 125.

9. Rahnema and Behdad, *Iran after the Revolution*, 88.

10. Hiro, *The Longest War*, 250-251.

11. *Kayhan*, February 26, 1991.

12. *Mahnameh-ye Baressiha-ye Bazaargani* [Monthly trade reports] 3, Summer 1991.

13. *Kayhan*, April 26, 1990.

14. Omid, *Islam and the Post-Revolutionary State in Iran*, 177.

15. Hunter, *Iran After Khomeini*, 44.

16. Menashri, *Iran: A Decade of War and Revolution*, 277-280.

17. Abrahamian, *Khomeinism*, 51-52.

18. *Ettela'at,* February 9, 1982.
19. Omid, *Islam and the Post-Revolutionary State in Iran,* 156.
20. *Kayhan,* February 14, 1983.
21. *Jomhouri Islami,* September 3, 1984.
22. *Jomhouri Islami,* September 8, 1984.
23. Golmakani, "New Times, New Perceptions," 28
24. Hunter, *Iran After Khomeini,* 123.
25. Farsoun and Mashayekhi, *Iran: Political Culture in the Islamic Republic,* 23.
26. *Film Monthly,* volume 13, May 1984.
27. Golmakani, "New Times, New Perceptions," 26.
28. Naficy, "Islamizing Film Culture in Iran," 200.
29. Ibid., 200-201.
30. *Film International,* Autumn 1994, pp.54-55.
31. Cordesman, *Iran and Iraq: The Threat from the Northern Gulf,* 78.
32. Omid, *Islam and the Post-Revolutionary State in Iran,* 175.
33. Bahar, "Guardians of Thought," 107.
34. Golmakani, 1999: 5.
35. Rizaee, *Persian Meditations,*18.
36. Goudet, "Entretien avec Mohsen Makhmalbaf," 25.
37. Rosenbaum, "Makhmalbaf and Dostoevsky: A Limited Comparison."
38. Thoraval, "In the Eyes of a Foreign Addict," 62-63.
39. Makhmalbaf, "Mirror Images," 19
40. Johnson, "*The Peddler.*".
41. Makhmalbaf, 1995: 9.
42. Talebinezhad, "The New Wave in Iranian Cinema, from Past to Present," 9.
43. Solanas and Getino, "Towards a Third Cinema," 6.
44. Armes, *Third World Filmmaking and the West,* 80-85.
45. Makhmalbaf, "Reality is a Prison: Interview with Ahmad Talebinezhad and Houshang Golmakani."
46. Goudet, "Entretien avec Mohsen Makhmalbaf," 23.
47. 1991 Makhmalbaf
48. Sura 2: 210.
49. Rizaee, *Persian Meditations,* 18.
50. "*Der Radfahrer (The Cyclist),*" *Variety.*
51. See Pearson, "Le cinèma iranien," *Cinemarabe* 9 (June/July 1978).
52. Menashri, *Iran: A Decade of War and Revolution,* 287.
53. Abrahamian, *Khomeinism,* 51.
54. Dissanayake, *Colonialism and Nationalism in Asian Cinema,* xxi.
55. "*Arusi-ye Khuban (Marriage of the Blessed),*" *Variety.*
56. Nayeri, "Iranian Cinema: What Happened in Between?"
57. Cheshire, "Where is Iranian Cinema Now?"
58. Dabashi, "Mohsen Makhmalbaf's *A Moment of Innocence,*" 117.

59. Smith, "*Salaam Cinema,*" 44.

60. Ditmars, "From the Top of the Hill," 13.

61. Goudet, "Entretien avec Mohsen Makhmalbaf," 25.

62. Haneef, *Islam and Muslims,* 114.

63. Hosseini, "From Homo Economicus to Homo Islamicus," 103-121.

64. Sura 64: 9.

65. Nayeri, "Iranian Cinema: What Happened in Between?" 28.

## Notes to Chapter 5

1. "After Khomeini," *The Economist,* June 10-16, 1989:18.

2. Wright, *The Last Great Revolution: Turmoil and Transformation in Iran,* 24.

3. Naficy, "Iranian Cinema" (1999), 24.

4. Simpson and Shubart, *Lifting the Veil,* 216.

5. Haghayeghi, "Politics and Ideology in the Islamic Republic of Iran," 48.

6. Abrahamian, "Khomeini: Fundamentalist or Populist?" 116.

7. Schirazi, *The Constitution of Iran,* 132.

8. Ehteshami, *After Khomeini: The Iranian Second Republic,* 76.

9. Ansari, *Iran, Islam and Democracy: The Politics of Managing Change,* 22.

10. Lenin, *Marx, Engels, Marxism,* 53.

11. Sefy, "Despotism and Disintegration of the Iranian Economy, 1500–1800, 7.

12. Farzin, "The Political Economy of Foreign Exchange Reform," 184-9.

13. Brumberg, *Reinventing Khomeini The Struggle for Reform in Iran,* 153.

14. Khomeini, "Iranian New Year Speech," *Foriegn Broadcast Information Service,* March 24, 1980.

15. *FBIS–NES,* September 21, 1988.

16. Golmakani, "Beyond the Shadow of a Doubt," 54.

17. Duagoo, "Government Policies," 65.

18. Tahami, "Making Ends Meet," 4.

19. Rizaee, *Persian Meditations,* 22.

20. *Ettela'at,* January 4, 1995.

21. Sayyad, "The Cinema of the Islamic Republic of Iran."

22. Naficy, "Veiled Vision/Powerful Presence: Women in Post-revolutionary Iranian Cinema," 148.

23. "Salaam Cinema: The Films of Mohsen Makhmalbaf," Pacific Cinematheque, http://www.cinematheque.bc.ca/archives/makh.html.

24. Beig-Agha, "Iranian Cinema in the Marketplace."

25. Makhmalbaf, *Film,* March/April 1991:125.

26. Ansari, *Iran, Islam and Democracy,* 80.

27. Wright, *The Last Great Revolution,* 89.

28. Naficy, "Islamizing Film Culture in Iran," 205

29. Taken from a speech given in the Iranian Majles on 11 August 1992, as quoted in Mehdi Moslem's *Factional Politics in Post Khomeini Iran.*

30. *Ettela'at,* August 17, 1994.
31. *Reuters,* "Iran Filmmakers Want Less State Control," March 10, 1994.
32. Alami, "Twenty Years of Iranian Cinema," 66
33. Ditmars, "From the Top of the Hill," 13
34. Khazaie, *The Arabesque Motif in Early Islamic Persian.*
35. *Zan-e Ruz,* September 22, 1992. See also Haideh Moghissi, "Public Life and Women's Resistance."
36. Golmakani, "New Times, Same Problems," 21
37. Interview by the author with film producer S. A. Moussazadeh, March 25, 2002.
38. Deborah Young, *"Ruzi, Ruzagari, Cinema (Once Upon A Time The Movies),"* 110.
39. Zahedi, "Mohsen Makhmalbaf: In Search of the Lost Horizon," 39.
40. Tahami, "Making Ends Meet, 61.
41. Dabashi, *Close Up,* 199.
42. Ibid., 188.
43. Makhmalbaf, "The Unbearable Lightness of Determinism," 39.
44. Dabashi, "Mohsen Makhmalbaf's *A Moment of Innocence,*" 96.
45. Smith, *"Salaam Cinema,"* 44.
46. Ibid.
47. Golmakani, "Once and for All: Behind the Scene Report on *Salaam Cinema,*" 58
48. Rava, "L'Individu, L'Art et L'Avenir Démocratique: Un Entretien avec le Cinéaste Mohsen Makhmalbaf," 219.
49. Golmakani, "Once and for All," 59
50. Clarens "Vers un quatrième cinema," 21
51. Macnab, *"A Moment of Innocence,"* 51
52. Rosenbaum, "Packaged Fables."
53. Walsh, *"Gabbeh* and *A Moment of Innocence:* Two Films Directed by Mohsen Makhmalbaf."
54. Ridgeon, *Makhmalbaf's Broken Mirror: The Socio-Political Significance of Modern Iranian Cinema,* 26
55. Ali Behdad, "Sevrugin—Orientalist or Orienteur?"
56. Ahmadi and Makhmalbaf, *Gabbeh,* 5.
57. Yarshater, "The Modern Literary Idiom," 303.
58. Sura, 31: 10.
59. Papadopoulo, *Islam and Muslim Art,* 57
60. Shaked, *From Zoroastrian Iran to Islam,* 41
61. Khazaie, *The Arabesque Motif in Early Islamic Persian,* 269
62. Sura 4: 100
63. Chanan, "The Changing Geography of Third Cinema," 377
64. Asha "The Evolution and Development of Iranian Cinema," 277

**Notes to Chapter 6**

1. Ehteshami, *After Khomeini*, 116-119
2. Wright, *The Last Great Revolution*, 24
3. Frye, *The Golden Age of Persia: The Arabs in the East*, 2
4. Judah, *The Guardian*, 90-96
5. Ansari, *Iran, Islam and Democracy*, 96
6. Hiro, *Neighbors Not Friends*, 225
7. Boroujerdi, *Iranian Intellectuals and the West*, 22
8. Bohrer, *Sevruguin and the Persian Image: Photographs of Iran 1870–1930*, 85
9. Dupont, "Film Takes Iranians Back to a Dark Time."
10. Morgan, *Medieval Persia, 1040–1797*, 7
11. Ajami, "Iran: The Impossible Revolution," 144
12. Wright, *The Last Great Revolution*, 29
13. Lyden, "Freedom Beyond the Veil."
14. Brumberg, *Reinventing Khomeini: The Struggle for Reform in Iran*, 220.
15. Ibid., 221.
16. Rose, "Velayat-e Faqih and the Recovery of Islamic Identity in the Thought of Ayatollah Khomeini," 177
17. Hiro, "Iran Puts Government Assassins in the Dock," *The Observer*, December 17, 2000.
18. See Alexis de Tocqueville, *Democracy in America* and *The Old Regime and the Revolution.*
19. de Roquefeuil, "Iran's Reformist President Dogged by Economic Failure."
20. Eric Rouleau, "La Républic Islamique d'Iran Confrontée à la Société Civile."
21. Speech, reprinted in *Kayhan*, December 4, 1997.
22. Motahari, "The Nature of the Islamic Revolution," 218
23. Rose, "Velayat-e Faqih and the Recovery of Islamic Identity," 169
24. Sassoon, *Gramsci's Politics*, 224
25. Rose, "Velayat-e Faqih and the Recovery of Islamic Identity," 187
26. Brumberg, *Reinventing Khomeini*, 248
27. *The Observer*, December 17, 2000.
28. Hiro *Neighbors Not Friends.*
29. BBC Summary World Broadcast ME/2999 MED/13, August 16, 1997, as quoted in Ansari, *Iran, Islam and Democracy*, 126.
30. BBC Summary World Broadcast ME/3005 MED/12, August 23, 1997, as quoted in Ansari, *Iran, Islam and Democracy*, 125.
31. "Through a Persian Looking Glass."
32. Mohammadi, "The Impact of Globalisation on Iranian Cinema."
33. Wright, *The Last Great Revolution*, 261-263
34. "If Iranian Cinema Needs a Law?"
35. Associated Press, "BC-Iran-Director Arrested," August 31, 2001.

36. See "Solidarity: a letter from Milos Stehlík and Ray Privett, Facets Multimedia, and Hanif Kureishi on behalf of the filmmakers who have signed a letter of solidarity with the plight of the Iranian filmmaker Tahmineh Milani," *Sight and Sound* 11, no. 12 (December 2001): 68.

37. Mulvey, "Kiarostami's Uncertainty Principle," 24

38. Ibid.

39. Saffarian, "A Dream and a Fantasy, A Lure and a Flash," 116

40. Mamad Haghighat, "*The Silence:* Interview with Mohsen Makhmalbaf."

41. Khayyam, *Rubaiyat.*

42. Dabashi, *Close Up*, 206

43. Karimi-Hakkak, *An Anthology of Modern Persian Poetry*, 140.

44. Dabashi *Close Up*, 211

45. Mirsepassi, *Intellectual Discourses and the Politics of Modernization*, 13

46. Dabashi *Close Up*, 211

47. Mackey, *The Iranians: Persia, Islam and the Soul of a Nation*, 74

48. Lewis, *The Middle East: A Brief History of the Last 2,000 Years*, 239

49. *Hafez in English*, 55-56.

50. Hillmann, *Iranian Culture: A Persianist View*, 88

51. Dabashi, *Close Up*, 205

52. Hillmann, *Iranian Culture: A Persianist View.*

53. Mohsen Makhmalbaf, interview for "Meridian on Screen," *BBC Radio 4*, May 30, 2001. See also "The Buddha Did Not Collapse."

54. Pazira, "Refuge in the Dust," 13

55. Rashid, *Taliban: Militant Islam, Oil and the New Great Game in Central Asia*, 205-206

56. Makhmalbaf, "Limbs of No Body: The World's Indifference to the Afghan Tragedy," 3

57. Andrew, "*Kandahar*," 18

58. Nouraei, "A Disguised Black American in Search of God," 21

59. Makhmalbaf, "Limbs of No Body," 23-26.

60. "Meridian on Screen," *BBC Radio 4*, May 30, 2001.

**Notes to Conclusion.**

1. Dan de Luce, "They Want Us to Emigrate."

# BIBLIOGRAPHY

Abdo, Geneive. "Iranian Film Comes Through the Big Chill of the Hardline Years." *The Guardian,* November 13, 1998.

Abrahamian, Ervand. "The Crowd in Iranian Politics, 1905-53." In *Iran: A Revolution in Turmoil.* Edited by Haleh Afshar. Albany: State University of New York Press, 1985.

————. "The Guerrilla Movement in Iran, 1963-1977." *MERIP Reports* 86 (March-April, 1980).

————. *Iran Between Two Revolutions.* Princeton: Princeton University Press, 1982.

————. "Khomeini: Fundamentalist or Populist?" *New Left Review* 186 (March-April 1991).

————. *Khomeinism: Essays on the Islamic Republic.* Berkeley: University of California Press, 1993.

————. *Radical Islam: The Iranian Mojahedin.* London: I.B. Tauris, 1989.

"After Khomeini," *The Economist,* June 10-16, 1989:18.

Ahmadi, Mohammed, and Mohsen Makhmalbaf. *Gabbeh*: Film Script and Photographs. Tehran: Ney Publishing House, 1997.

Ajami, Fouad. "Iran: The Impossible Revolution." *Foreign Affairs* 67, no. 2 (Winter 1988/89).

Akrami, Jamsheed. "The Blighted Spring: Iranian Political Cinema in the 1970s." In *Film and Politics in the Third World.* Edited by John D. H. Downing. New York: Praeger, 1987.

Alami, Akbar. "Twenty Years of Iranian Cinema." *Donyaa-ye Sokhan: Scientific, Social & Cultural Monthly* 83 and 84 (November 1998–March 1999).

Al-e-Ahmad, Jalal. *Gharbzadegi: Plagued by the West.* Translated by Paul Sprachman. New York: Columbia University Press, 1982.

Algar, Hamid, trans. *Constitution of the Islamic Republic of Iran.* Berkeley: Mizan Press, 1980.

Amiri, Noushabeh. "Interview with Dariush Mehrjui." *Cinemaya,* Winter/Spring 1998.

Anderson, Benedict. *Imagined Communities: Reflections on the Origins and Spread of Nationalism.* New York: Verso, 1991.

Andrew, Geoff. "*Kandahar.*" *Sight and Sound* 11, no. 7 (July 2001).

Ansari, Ali. *Iran, Islam and Democracy: The Politics of Managing Change.* London: The Royal Institute of International Affairs, 2000.

Arberry , A. J., trans. *The Koran Interpreted: A Translation.* New York: Macmillan, 1955.

Arjomand, Said Amir. *The Turban for the Crown: The Islamic Revolution in Iran.* New York: Oxford University Press, 1988.

Armes, Roy. *Third World Filmmaking and the West.* Berkeley: University of California Press, 1987.

"*Arusi-ye khuban (Marriage of the Blessed).*" *Variety,* August 16, 1989.

Ash, Timothy Garton, *The Polish Revolution: Solidarity.* New Haven: Yale University Press, 2002.

Asha, Sadek. "The Evolution and Development of Iranian Cinema: from Film-Farsi to the Post-Revolutionary Cinema, with Particular Reference to Islam and Popular Entertainment Culture." PhD diss., University of Sussex, 1999.

Ashraf, Ahmad and Ali Banuazizi. "The State, Classes and Modes of Mobilization in the Iranian Revolution." *State, Culture and Society* 1, no. 3 (Spring 1985).

Aufderheide, Pat. "Real Life is More Important than Cinema: Interview with Abbas Kiarostami." *Cineaste* 21, no. 3 (February 1993).

Avery, Peter, Gavin Hambly and Charles Melville. *The Cambridge History of Iran.* Vol. 6. "From Nadir Shah to the Islamic Republic." Cambridge: Cambridge University Press, 1991.

Ayoob, Mohammad. "Subaltern Realism: International Relations Theory Meets the Third World." In *International Relations Theory and the Third World.* Edited by Stephanie G. Neuman. New York: St. Martins Press, 1998.

Bahar, Sarveraz. "Guardians of Thought: Limits on Freedom of Expression in Iran." *Middle East Watch,* August 1993.

Bakhash, Shaul. *The Reign of the Ayatollahs: Iran and the Islamic Revolution.* New York: Basic Books, 1984.

Barnard, Tim. *Argentine Cinema.* Toronto: Nightwood Editions, 1986.

Baxandall, Lee. "Fidel Castro Words to the Intellectuals." In *Radical Perspectives in the Arts.* Edited by Lee Baxandall. Harmondsworth: Penguin, 1972.

Bazargan, Abdol Ali. *Moshkelat va Masael Avalin Enqelab.* Tehran: 1984.

Bazargan, Mehdi. *Bazyabi-e Arzeshha.* Vol.1. Tehran, 1984.

Beg, Muhammad Abdul Jabar, ed. *Fine Arts in Islamic Civilization.* Kuala Lampur: University of Malay Press, 1981.

Behdad, Ali. "Sevrugin—Orientalist or Orienteur?" In *Sevruguin and the Persian Image: Photographs of Iran 1870–1930.* Edited by Frederick N. Bohrer. Seattle: University of Washington Press, 1999.

Behrooz, Maziar. *Rebels With A Cause: The Failure of the Left in Iran.* London: I.B. Tauris, 1999.

Beig-Agha, Mohsen. "Iranian Cinema in the Marketplace." *Film International,* Winter-Spring 1996.

Blondel Saad, Joya. *The Image of Arabs in Modern Persian Literature.* Lanham, MD: University Press of America, 1996.

Bohrer, Frederick N., ed. *Sevruguin and the Persian Image: Photographs of Iran 1870–1930.* Seattle: University of Washington Press, 1999.

Boroujerdi, Merhad. *Iranian Intellectuals and the West: the Tormented Triumph of Nativism.* Syracuse: Syracuse University Press, 1996.

Brumberg, Daniel. *Reinventing Khomeini The Struggle for Reform in Iran.* Chicago: University of Chicago Press, 2001.

Burckhardt, Titus. *Art of Islam: Language and Meaning.* Translated by Roland Michaud. London: World of Islam Festival, 1976.

Burton, Julianne. "Marginal Cinema and Mainstream Critical Theory." *Screen* 26, nos. 3-4 (1985).

Chanan, Michael. "The Changing Geography of Third Cinema." *Screen* 38, no. 4 (Winter 1997).

Chanan, Michael. *Twenty-five Years of the New Latin American Cinema.* London: Channel Four/BFI, 1983.

Chelkowski, Peter and Hamid Dabashi. *Staging a Revolution: The Art of Persuasion in the Islamic Republic of Iran.* London: Booth-Clibborn Editions, 2000.

Cheshire, Godfrey. "Reflections/Observations on Current Iranian Film: Kiarostami and Makhmalbaf." *Film Comment* 29 (March/April 1993).

———. "The Figure in the Carpet." *Film Comment* 33 (July-August 1997).

———. "Where is Iranian Cinema Now?" *Film Comment* 29 (March-April 1993).

Clarens, Bernard. "Vers un quatrième cinema." *Cinemarabe* 7-8 (April/May 1978).

*The Constitution of the Islamic Republic of Iran.* Tehran: Department of Translation and Publication Islamic Culture and Relations Organization, 1997.

Cordesman, Anthony H. *Iran and Iraq: The Threat from the Northern Gulf.* Boulder, CO: Westview Press, 1994.

Cowie, Peter. "Tehran." *Sight and Sound* 44 (Spring 1975).

Culhane, Hind Rassan. *East/West, An Ambiguous State of Being: the Construction and Representation of Egyptian Cultural Identity in Egyptian Film.* New York: Peter Lang Publishing, 1994.

Dabashi, Hamid. *Close Up: Iranian Cinema Past, Present and Future.* New York: Verso, 2001.

———. "Re-reading Reality: Kiarostami's *Through the Olive Trees* and the Cultural Politics of a Post-revolutionary Aesthetics." *Critique: Journal for Critical Studies of Iran and the Middle East* 7 (Autumn 1995).

———. "Mohsen Makhmalbaf's *A Moment of Innocence.*" In *Life and Art: The New Iranian Cinema.* Edited by Rose Issa and Sheila Whitaker. London: The British Film Institute, 1999.

Daryoush, Hazhir. "Iran." *International Film Guide 1982.* London: Tantivy Press, 1982.

de Luce, Dan. "They Want Us to Emigrate." *The Guardian,* June 10, 2004.

de Roquefeuil, Christophe. "Iran's Reformist President Dogged by Economic Failure." *Agence France Press,* May 22, 1999.

*"Der Radfahrer (The Cyclist)." Variety,* April 1, 1991

Dissanayake, Wimal, ed. *Colonialism and Nationalism in Asian Cinema.* Bloomington: Indiana University Press, 1994.

Ditmars, Hadani. "From the Top of the Hill." *Sight and Sound* 3, no. 12 (December, 1996).

Dorraj, Manochehr. *From Zarathustra to Khomeini: Populism and Dissent in Iran.* Boulder, CO: Lynne Rienner Publishers, 1990.

Duagoo, Mohammad-Mehdi. "Government Policies." *Cinemaya: The Asian Film Quarterly* 22 (Winter 1993–1994).

Dupont, John. "Film Takes Iranians Back to a Dark Time." *International Herald Tribune,* February 16, 2001.

Ehteshami, Anoushiravan. *After Khomeini: The Iranian Second Republic.* New York: Routledge 1995.

Espinosa, Jorge Garcia. "For an Imperfect Cinema." In *New Latin America Cinema: Theory, Practices and Transcontinental Articulations.* Edited by Michael T. Martin. Vol. 1. Detroit: Wayne State University Press, 1997.

Ettinghausen, Richard. "Introduction: The Immanent Features of Persian Art." In *Highlights of Persian Art.* Edited by Richard Ettinghausen and Ehsan Yarshater. Boulder, CO: Westview Press, 1979.

Fanon, Frantz. *The Wretched of the Earth.* Translated by Constance Farrington. New York: Grove Press, 1963. .

Farrokhzad, Forough. *Another Birth: Let Us Believe in the Beginning of the Cold Season.* Translated by Ismail Salami. Tehran: Zabankadeh Publications, 2000.

Farsoun, Samih K., and Mehrdad Mashayekhi, eds. *Iran: Political Culture in the Islamic Republic.* New York: Routledge, 1992.

Farzin, Hossein. "The Political Economy of Foreign Exchange Reform." In *Iran After the Revolution: Crisis of an Islamic State.* Edited by Saeed Rahnema and Sohrab Behdad. London: I.B. Tauris, 1995.

Featherstone, Mike, ed. *Global Culture: Nationalism, Globalization and Modernity*. Newbury Park, CA: Sage, 1990.

Ferdowsi, Abolqasem. *Shahnameh*. Translated by Dick Davis. Washington, DC: Mage Publishers, 2005.

*Film Monthly* 13 (May 1984).

*Film Monthly* 14 (June 1984).

Fischer, Michael M. J. *Iran: From Religious Dispute to Revolution*. Cambridge: Harvard University Press, 1980.

Foran, John, ed. *A Century of Revolution: Social Movements in Iran*. Minneapolis : University of Minnesota Press, 1994.

Foucault, Michel. "Iran: The Spirit of a World Without Spirit." In *Politics, Philosophy, Culture: Culture, Interviews, and Other Writings, 1977–1984* by Michel Foucault. Translated by Alan Sheridan. Edited by Lawrence D. Kritzman. New York: Routledge, 1988.

Frye, Richard Nelson. *The Golden Age of Persia: The Arabs in the East*. London: Weidenfeld & Nicholson, 1975.

Gabriel, Teshome. "Colonialism and 'Law and Order' Criticism." *Screen* 27, nos. 3-4 (1986).

———. *Third Cinema in the Third World: The Aesthetics of Liberation*. Ann Arbor, MI: UMI Research Press, 1982.

Gamble, Andrew, David Marsh, and Tony Tant. *Marxism and Social Science*. Urbana: University of Illinois Press, 1999.

Geertz, Clifford. *The Interpretation of Cultures*. New York: Basic Books, 1973.

Ghanoonparvar, M. R. *Prophets of Doom: Literature as Socio-Political Phenomenon in Iran*. Lanham, MD: University Press of America, 1984.

Ghosh, Nandita. "Shooting Image Weapons: The Place of Manthan as Third Cinema in India." *Deep Focus* 6 (1996).

Golmakani, Houshang. "Beyond the Shadow of a Doubt." *Cinemaya* 22 (Winter 1993-94).

———. "A History of the Post-Revolutionary Cinema." From Chicago Film Center's Tenth Annual Festival of Films from Iran, October 24, 1999.

———. "New Times, New Perceptions." *Cinemaya* 4 (Summer 1989).

———. "New Times, Same Problems." *Index on Censorship* 22 (1992).

———. "Once and for All: Behind the Scene Report on *Salaam Cinema*." *Film International,* Autumn 1994.

———. "The Sweet Smell of Success: Iranian Cinema Since 1979." *Film International* 1, no. 1 (Winter 1993).

———. "The Tide Turns." *Cinemaya* 45 (Autumn 1999).

Grabar, Oleg. *The Formation of Islamic Art.* New Haven: Yale University Press, 1987.

Graham, Robert. *Iran: The Illusion of Power.* New York: St. Martin's Press, 1978.

Guevara, Che. "Notes on Man and Socialism in Cuba." In *Che Guevara Speaks: Selected Speeches and Writings.* Edited by George Lavan. New York: Merit Publishers, 1967.

Gupta, Udayan. "New Visions in Indian Cinema." In *Film and Politics in the Third World.* Edited by John D. H. Downing. New York: Praeger, 1987.

Hafez , Khajeh Shams al-Din Mohammad, *Hafez in English.* Tehran: Parsa, 1998.

Haghayeghi, Mehrad. "Politics and Ideology in the Islamic Republic of Iran." *Middle Eastern Studies* 29, no. 1 (January 1993).

Haghighat, Mamad. "*The Silence*: Interview with Mohsen Makhmalbaf." Film Society of Lincoln Center, http://www.filmlinc.com/archive/programs/11-99/makh/silint.htm

Halliday, Fred. *Iran: Dictatorship and Development.* New York: Penguin, 1979.

———. "Iranian Foreign Policy Since 1979." In *Shi'ism and Social Protest.* Edited by Juan R. I. Cole & Nikki Keddie. New Haven: Yale University Press, 1986.

———. "The Iranian Revolution: Uneven Development and Religious Populism." In *State and Ideology in the Middle East.* Edited by Fred Halliday and Hamza Alavi. New York: Monthly Review Press, 1988.

Haneef, Suzanne. *Islam and Muslims.* Lahore: Kazi Publications, 1979.

Hassan, Riaz. "Iran's Islamic Revolutionaries: Before and After the Revolution." *Third World Quarterly* 6, no. 3 (July 1984).

Herodotus. *The Histories.* Translated by Aubrey de Sèlincourt. New York, Penguin, 1996.

Hillmann, Michael C. *Iranian Culture: A Persianist View.* Lanham, MD: University Press of America, 1990.

———. *A Lonely Woman: Forugh Farrokhzad and Her Poetry.* Washington, DC: Mage Publishers, 1987.

———. *The Longest War: The Iran-Iraq Military Conflict.* New York: Routledge, 1991.

Hiro, Dilip. "Iran Puts Government Assassins in the Dock." *The Observer,* December 17, 2000

———. *Neighbors Not Friends: Iraq and Iran After the Gulf Wars.* New York: Routledge, 2001.

Hirst, David. "Iranian Voters Set for Power Showdown." *The Guardian,* June, 7 2001.

Hosseini, Hamid. "From Homo Economicus to Homo Islamicus: The Universality of Economic Science Reconsidered." In *Modern Capitalism and Islamic Ideology in Iran. Edited* by Cyrus Bina and Hamid Zangeneh. New York: St. Martin's Press, 1992.

Hunter, Shireen T. *Iran After Khomeini.* New York: Praeger, 1992.

"If Iranian Cinema Needs a Law?" *Film International* 8, no. 4 (Spring/Summer 2001).

"Iran Filmmakers Want Less State Control." *Reuters,* March 10, 1994.

Issa, Rose, and Sheila Whitaker, eds. *Life and Art: The New Iranian Cinema.* London: BFI, 1999.

Issari, Mohammad Ali. *Cinema in Iran, 1900-1979.* Metuchen, NJ: The Scarecrow Press, 1989.

Jameson, Fredric. *The Geopolitical Aesthetic: Cinema and Space in the World System.* Bloomington: Indiana University Press: 1992.

Johnson, William. "*The Peddler.*" *Film Quarterly* 43, no. 3 (1990).

Johnston, Sheila and Hadani Ditmars. "Quietly Ruling the Roost." *Sight and Sound* 9, no. 1 (January 1999).

Judah, Tim. "A Revolution Crumbles." *The Guardian,* October 15, 2002.

Kalhor, Mehdi. *Post-Revolution Iranian Cinema.* Tehran: Ministry of Ershad-e Eslami, 1982.

Kamali, Masoud. *Revolutionary Iran: Civil Society and State in the Modernization Process.* Brookfield, VT: Ashgate, 1998.

Karimi-Hakkak, Ahmad, ed. *An Anthology of Modern Persian Poetry.* Selected and translated with an introduction by Ahmad Karimi-Hakkak. Boulder, CO: Westview Press, 1978

Karimi-Hakkak, Ahmad. "Of Hail and Hounds: the Image of the Iranian Revolution in Recent Persian Literature." *State, Culture and Society* 1, no. 3 (Spring 1985).

Kazemi, Farhad. "State and Society in the Devotees of Islam." *State, Culture and Society* 1, no. 3 (Spring 1985).

Keddie, Nikki, and Eric Hooglund. *The Iranian Revolution and the Islamic Republic.* Syracuse: Syracuse University Press, 1986.

Keddie, Nikki, and Mark Gasiorowski. *Neither East Nor West: Iran, The Soviet Union and the United States.* New Haven: Yale University Press, 1990.

Khazaie, Mohammad. *The Arabesque Motif in Early Islamic Persian.* London: Institute of Islamic Studies, 1999.

Khomeini, Ayatollah Ruhollah, *A Clarification of Questions: An Unabridged Translation of Resaleh Towzih al-masael.* Translated by J. Boroujerdi. Boulder, CO: Westview Press, 1984.

———. "The Deprived Will Dominate the Arrogant." Speech on Iranian Radio and Television, April 3, 1979.

———. "Imam Khomeini Commends Services of Islamic Revolutionary Corps." Press Release, Government of the Islamic Republic of Iran, August 1983.

———. *Islam and Revolution: Writings and Declarations of Imam Khomeini.* Translated and annotated by Hamid Algar. Berkeley: Mizan Press, 1981.

———. "Iranian New Year Speech." *FBIS*, March 24, 1980.

———. *Khat Imam, Kalam Imam.* Tehran: Entesharat Noor, 1982.

———. "Payam-e Hazrat-e Emam." *Pasdar-e Eslam* 84, November/December 1988.

———. *Payam-e Enghelab* 93, 1983.

———. *Pithy Aphorisms.* Tehran, 1994

———. "[Speech]." *Ettela'at,* June 26, 1980.

————. "[Speech]." *Kayhan,* December 4, 1997.

————. *Velayat-e Faqih: Hokumat-e Islami.* Tehran, 1978.

King, John. *Magical Reels: A History of Cinema in Latin America.* New York: Verso, 1990.

Lenin, V. I. *Marx, Engels, Marxism.* Moscow: Progress Publishers, 1968.

Lerner, Daniel. *The Passing of Traditional Society: Modernizing the Middle East.* Glencoe, IL: Free Press, 1958.

Lewis, Bernard. *The Middle East: A Brief History of the Last 2,000 Years.* New York: Scribners, 1995.

Louvish, Simon. "*Gabbeh.*" *Sight and Sound* 6, no. 12 (December 1996).

Lyden, Jacki. "Freedom Beyond the Veil." *The Guardian,* July 17, 1999.

Mackey, Sandra. *The Iranians: Persia, Islam and the Soul of a Nation.* New York: Dutton, 1996.

Macnab, Geoffrey. "*A Moment of Innocence.*" *Sight and Sound* 8, no. 2 (December 1998).

Maghsoudlou, Bahman. *Iranian Cinema.* New York: New York University Press, 1987.

Makhmalbaf, Mohsen. "The Bhudda Was Not Demolished in Afghanistan; It Collapsed out of Shame." Makhmalbaf Film House. www.makhmalbaf.com

————. "Limbs of No Body: The World's Indifference to the Afghan Tragedy." *The Iranian,* June 20, 2001.

————. *Film* (Tehran), March/April 1991.

————. "Mirror Images." *Cinemaya: The Asian Film Quarterly* 13, no. 3 (Autumn 1991).

————. "Reality is a Prison: Interview with Ahmad Talebinezhad and Houshang Golmakani." *Film International,* Autumn 1995.

————. "The Unbearable Lightness of Determinism." *Film International,* Summer 1993.

Malkmus, Lizbeth and Roy Armes. *Arab and African Film Making.* Atlantic Highlands, NJ: Zed Books, 1991.

Martin, Vanessa. *Creating an Islamic State: Khomeini and the Making of a New Iran.* London: I.B. Tauris, 2000.

Mazuri, Ali. "Ideological Encounters of the Third World." *Third World Book Review* 7, no. 6 (1986).

McDonnell, Stephen. "Iranian Revival." *Sight and Sound* 50 (Winter 1980-1981).

McLachlan, Keith, ed. *The Boundaries of Modern Iran.* New York: St. Martin's Press, 1994.

Mehrabi, Massoud. "Iran's Cinema History." *Cinema '96,* July 1996.

Menashri, David. *Iran: A Decade of War and Revolution.* New York: Holmes and Meier Publishers, 1990.

Mirsepassi, Ali. *Intellectual Discourses and the Politics of Modernization: Negotiating Modernity in Iran.* Cambridge: Cambridge University Press, 2000.

Moaddel, Mansoor. *Class, Politics and Ideology in the Iranian Revolution.* New York: Columbia University Press, 1993.

Moghissi, Haideh. "Public Life and Women's Resistance." in *Iran After the Revolution: Crisis of an Islamic State.* Edited by Saeed Rahnema and Sohrab Behdad. London: I.B. Tauris, 1996.

Mohammadi, Ali and Annabelle Mohammadi-Sreberny. *Small Media, Big Revolution: Communication, Culture and the Iranian Revolution.* Minneapolis: Minnesota University Press, 1994.

Mohammadi, Ali. "The Impact of Globalisation on Iranian Cinema." *Asian Cinema* 13, no. 1 (Spring/Summer 2002).

Mohsenpour, B. "Philosophy of Education in Post-revolutionary Iran." *Comparative Education Review* 32, no.1 (February 1988).

Moin, Baqer. *Khomeini: Life of the Ayatollah.* London: I.B. Tauris, 1999

Montaigne, Fen. "Iran: Testing the Waters of Reform." *National Geographic* 196, 1 (July 1999).

Morgan, David. *Medieval Persia, 1040–1797.* New York: Longman, 1988.

Moslem, Mehdi. *Factional Politics in Post-Khomeini Iran.* Syracuse: Syracuse University Press, 2002.

Motahari, Ayatollah Morteza. "The Nature of the Islamic Revolution." In *Iran: A Revolution in Turmoil.* Edited by Haleh Afshar. Albany: State University of New York Press, 1985.

———. *Piramun-e Enghelab-e Islami.* Tehran: Entesharat Sadra.

Motavalli, John. "Exiles." *Film Comment* 19 (July/August 1983).

Mottahedeh, Roy. *The Mantle of the Prophet: Religion and Politics in Iran.* New York: Simon and Schuster, 1985.

Mulvey, Laura. "Kiarostami's Uncertainty Principle." *Sight and Sound* 8, no. 5 (June 1998).

Naficy, Hamid. "Cinematic Exchange Relations: Iran and the West." In *Iran and the Surrounding World: Interactions in Culture and Cultural Politics.* Edited by Nikki R. Keddie and Rudi Matthee. Seattle: University of Washington Press, 2002.

———. "Iranian Cinema." In *Life and Art the New Iranian Cinema.* Edited by Rose Issa and Sheila Whitaker. London: BFI, 1999.

———. "Iranian Cinema." In *The Oxford History of World Cinema.* Edited by Geoffrey Nowell-Smith. Oxford: Oxford University Press, 1996.

———. "Islamizing Film Culture in Iran." In *Iran: Political Culture in the Islamic Republic.* Edited by Samih K. Farsoun and Mehrdad Mashayekhi. New York: Routledge, 1992.

———. "Veiled Vision/Powerful Presence: Women in Post-revolutionary Iranian Cinema." In *The Eye of the Storm: Women in Post-revolutionary Iran.* Edited by Mahnaz Afkhami and Erika Friedl. London: I.B. Taurus 1994.

Nayeri, Sarah. "Iranian Cinema: What Happened in Between?" *Sight and Sound* 3, no. 12 (December 1993).

Newman, Kathleen. *Mediating Two Worlds: Cinematic Encounters in the Americas.* London: BFI, 1993.

Nichols, Bill. "Discovering Form Inferring Meaning." *Film Quarterly* 47, no. 3 (Spring 1994).

Nouraei, Jahanbaksh. "A Disguised Black American in Search of God." *Film International* 8, no. 4 (Spring/Summer 2001).

Omid, Homa. *Islam and the Post-Revolutionary State in Iran.* New York: St. Martin's Press, 1994.

Omid, Jamal. "The Iranian Cinema." *American Cinematographer,* February 1974.

Papadopoulo, Alexandre. *Islam and Muslim Art.* Translated from the French by Robert Erich Wolf. New York: H. N. Abrams, 1979.

Parvin, Manoucher, and Mostafa Vaziri. "Islamic Man and Society in the Islamic Republic of Iran." In *Iran: Political Culture in the Islamic Republic.* Edited by Samih K. Farsoun and Mehrdad Mashayekhi. New York: Routledge, 1992.

Pazira, Nelofer. "Refuge in the Dust." *Sight and Sound* 11, no. 7 (July 2001).

Pearson, Lyle. "Le cinèma iranien." *Cinemarabe* 9 (June/July 1978).

Pickthall, M. M. trans. *The Koran.* Reading: Star Books, 1989.

Pines, Jim and Paul Willemen, eds. *Questions of Third Cinema.* London: BFI, 1989.

Puchala, D. J. "Third World Thinking and Contemporary International Relations." *International Relations Theory and the Third World.* Edited by Stephanie G. Neuman. New York: St. Martin's Press, 1998.

Rahnema, Ali, and Farhad Nomani. *The Secular Miracle: Religion, Politics and Economic Policy in Iran.* London: Zed Books, 1990.

Rahnema, Ali. "Iranian Intellectuals in the Twentieth Century." *Critique: Journal for Critical Studies of Iran and the Middle East* 15 (Fall 1999).

Rahnema, Ali. *An Islamic Utopia: A Political Biography of Ali Shariati.* London: I.B. Tauris, 1998.

Rahnema, Saeed, and Sohrab Behdad, eds. *Iran after the Revolution: Crisis of an Islamic State.* London: I.B. Tauris, 1996.

Rajaee, Farhang, ed. *The Iran-Iraq War: The Politics of Aggression.* Gainesville: University Press of Florida, 1993.

———. "Iranian Ideology and Worldview: The Cultural Export of Revolution." In *The Iranian Revolution: Its Global Impact.* Edited by John L. Esposito. Miami: Florida International University Press, 1990.

———. *Revolutionary Iran: Challenge and Response in the Middle East.* Baltimore: The John Hopkins University Press, 1988.

Ramazani, R. K. "Khomeini's Islam in Iran's Foreign Policy." *Islam in Foreign Policy.* Edited by Adeed Davisha. Cambridge: Cambridge University Press, 1983.

Rashid, Ahmed. *Taliban: Militant Islam, Oil and the New Great Game in Central Asia.* New York, I.B. Tauris, 2000.

Rava, F. "L'Individu, L'Art et L'Avenir Dèmocratique: un Entrieten avec le Cinèaste Mohsen Makhmalbaf." *Europe Revue Litteraire Mensuelle* 76 (1998).

Rejaee, Mohammed Ali. *Gozideh Sokhanan Pardehe Tazvir.* Tehran: Nashr-e Saberin, 1981.

Ridgeon, Lloyd. *Makhmalbaf's Broken Mirror: The Socio-Political Significance of Modern Iranian Cinema.* Durham: University of Durham, 2000.

Rizaee, Behjat. *Persian Meditations.* London: Bra Books, 1993.

Robertson, Roland. "Social Theory, Cultural Relativity and the Problems of Globality." In *Culture, Globalism and the World System: Contemporary Conditions for the Representation of Identity.* Edited by Anthony D. King. Binghamton: State University of New York, 1991.

Rocha, Glauber. "An Esthetic of Hunger." In *New Latin America Cinema: Theory, Practices and Transcontinental Articulations.* Edited by Michael T. Martin. Vol. 1. Detroit: Wayne State University Press, 1997.

Rose, Gregory. "Velayat-e Faqih and the Recovery of Islamic Identity in the Thought of Ayatollah Khomeini." *Religion and Politics in Iran: Shi'ism from Quietism to Revolution.* Edited by Nikki R. Keddie. New Haven: Yale University Press, 1983.

Rosenbaum, Jonathan. "Packaged Parables." *Chicago Reader.* http://www.chireader.com/movies/archives/0897/08297.html

———. "Makhmalbaf and Dostoevsky: A Limited Comparison." *Bulletin of the 10th Festival of Film from Iran.* Film Centre of Chicago, October 24, 1999.

———. "Tortured Genius: Films by Mohsen Makhmalbaf." *Chicago Reader.* http://www.chireader.com/movies/archives/0497/04117.html

Rouleau, Eric. "La Republic Islamique d'Iran Confrontèe à la Sociètè Civile." *Le Monde Diplomatique,* June 1995, http://wwww.monde-diplomatique.fr/1995/Rouleau/1542.html

Saffarian, Nasser. "A Dream and a Fantasy, A Lure and a Flash." *Film International* 7, nos. 2 & 3 (Autumn 1999-Winter 2000).

Said, Edward W. *Orientalism,* London: Peregrine Books, 1985.

Salmane, Hala. *Algerian Cinema.* London: BFI, 1976.

Samini, Naghmeh. "A Survey of Literary Adaptation in Iranian Cinema: A New Birth of Post-Revolution Cinema." *Film International* 7, nos. 2 & 3 (Autumn/Winter, 1999/2000).

Sanadjian, Manucheher. "The World Cup and Iranians' 'Home-Coming': A Global Game in a Local Islamicized Context." In *Islam Encountering Globalization.* Edited by Ali Mohammadi. New York: RoutledgeCurzon, 2002.

Sassoon, Anne Showstack. *Gramsci's Politics,* Minneapolis: University of Minnesota Press, 1987.

Sayyad, Parviz. "The Cinema of the Islamic Republic of Iran." *Iran Nameh* 4, no. 3 (Spring 1996).

Schirazi, Asghar. *The Constitution of Iran: Politics and State in the Islamic Republic.* Translated by John O'Kane. London: I.B. Tauris, 1998.

Sefy, Ahmad. "Despotism and Disintegration of the Iranian Economy, 1500–1800." In *Essays on the Economic History of the Middle East.* Edited by Elie Kedourie and Sylvia Haim. London: Frank Cass & Co., 1988.

Shafik, Viola. *Arab Cinema: History and Cultural Identity,* Cairo: American University in Cairo Press, 1998.

Shaul, Shaked. *From Zoroastrian Iran to Islam.* Brookfield, VT: Variorum, 1995.

Shohat, Ella and Robert Stam. *Unthinking Eurocentrism: Multiculturalism and the Media.* New York: Routledge, 1994.

Siavoshi, Susan. "Regime Legitimacy and High-School Textbooks." In *Iran after the Revolution: Crisis of an Islamic State.* Edited by Saeed Rahnema and Sohrab Behdad. London: I.B. Tauris, 1995.

Simpson, John and Tira Shubart. *Lifting the Veil: Life in Revolutionary Iran.* London: Hodder and Stoughton, 1995.

Smith, Colin "Twenty Years On, Iran's Veils Fall." *The Observer,* January 13, 1999.

Smith, Gavin. "*Salaam Cinema.*" *Film Comment,* July/August 1996.

Solanas, Fernando, and Octavio Getino. "Towards a Third Cinema." *Cineaste* 4, no. 3 (Winter 1970-71).

Solhjoo, Tahmasb. "Political Films in Iranian Cinema, Past and Present." *Film International* 7, nos. 2-3 (Autumn/Winter 1999/2000).

"Solidarity: a letter from Milos Stehlík and Ray Privett, Facets Multi-media, and Hanif Kureishi on behalf of the filmmakers who have signed a letter of solidarity with the plight of the Iranian filmmaker Tahmineh Milani." *Sight and Sound* 11, no. 12 (December 2001)

Soroush, Abdolkarim. "The Evolution and Devolution of Religious Knowledge." In *Liberal Islam*. Edited by Charles Kurzman. Oxford: Oxford University Press, 1998.

Tabatabai, Mohsen. "Iran: Islamic Visions and Grand Illusions." *Film and Censorship: the Index Reader*. Edited by Ruth Petrie. London: BFI, 1997.

Tahami, Massoud. "Making Ends Meet." *Film International* 1, Summer 1993.

———. "February Blossoms." *Film International* 2, no. 4 (Winter 1994).

Talebinezhad, Ahmad. "The New Wave in Iranian Cinema, from Past to Present." *Hamshahri* 3, no. 639 (March 7, 1995).

———. "Fiction, Yet Documentary." *Film International* 6, no. 4 (Spring 1999).

Tapper, Richard, ed. *The New Iranian Cinema: Politics, Representation and Identity* London: I.B. Tauris, 2002.

Thompson, Kirstin, and David Bordwell. *Film History: An Introduction.* New York: McGraw-Hill, 1994.

Thoraval, Yves. "In the Eyes of a Foreign Addict." *Cinemaya: The Asian Film Quarterly* 22 (Winter 1993-1994).

"Through a Persian Looking Glass." *Film International* 6, no. 4 (Spring 1999).

Tocqueville, Alexis de. *Democracy in America*. Translated, edited, and with an introduction by Harvey C. Mansfield and Delba Winthrop. Chicago: University of Chicago Press, 2000.

———. *The Old Regime and the French Revolution*. Edited with an introduction and critical apparatus by François Furet and Françoise Mèlonio; translated by Alan S. Kahan. Chicago : University of Chicago Press, 1998.

Trab Zemzemi, Abdel-Majid. *The Iran-Iraq War: Islam and Nationalisms*, San Clemente: United States Publishing Company, 1986.

Walsh, David. "*Gabbeh* and *A Moment of Innocence*: Two Films Directed by Mohsen Makhmalbaf." World Socialst Website, September 23, 1996, http://www.wsws.org/arts/1996/sep1996/iran-s96.shtml

Wayne, Mike. *Political Film: The Dialectics of Third Cinema*. London: Pluto Press, 2001.

Wiesehöfer, Josef. *Ancient Persia*. London: I.B. Tauris, 2001.

Wilber, Donald N. *Iran, Past and Present*, Princeton: Princeton University Press, 1976.

Wood, Robin. "Toronto Film Festival 1998: *The Apple*." *Cineaction* 48 (1998).

Wright, Robin. *In the Name of God: The Khomeini Decade*. New York: Simon and Schuster, 1989.

————. *The Last Great Revolution: Turmoil and Transformation in Iran*. New York: Vintage Books, 2001.

Yarshater, Ehsan. "The Modern Literary Idiom" In *Iran Faces the Seventies*. Edited by Ehsan Yarshater. New York: Praeger, 1971.

Deborah Young. "*Ruzi, Ruzagari, Cinema (Once Upon A Time The Movies)*." *Variety*, March 23, 1992.

Zahedi, Hassan S. "Mohsen Makhmalbaf: In Search of the Lost Horizon." *Film International* 1, no. 3 (Summer 1993).

## ABOUT THE AUTHOR

Eric Egan studied communications at Trinity College, Dublin, and earned an MA in Cinema Studies and a PhD in Iranian Cinema at Nottingham Trent University in England. He has published articles on the cinema of Iran, Pakistan, India, and Egypt, as well as on cultural policy and media in developing countries. He lives in Dublin, Ireland, where he teaches film studies at University College, Dublin.